Praise for **CHALLENGING THE MYTHS OF AUTISM**

"An insightful and respectfully crafted unshackling of anxiety-provoking and inaccurately perpetuated myths of autism that will ultimately change the way we think, work and accept the 'differences' of those with ASD."

—JANINE FLANAGAN, MD, FRCPC
Developmental Paediatrician, Assistant Professor,
Department of Paediatrics, University of Toronto

"Autism remains one of the most perplexing and least understood human conditions, with a half-century history of controversy and divisiveness regarding issues ranging from how it is defined, to its causes and treatments. Outdated "truths," even when disproven, die hard, and strongly stated opinions too often are accepted as fact. In this important book, Jonathan Alderson says "Enough already!" to seven of the most blatant myths about autism. He does so by providing research evidence and years of clinical experience to support his arguments, always with the noble intention of putting an end to the damage that these myths cause for persons with ASD and their families. This book is a must read for professionals and family members and an important necessary step to allow our understanding of autism to progress."

—BARRY M. PRIZANT, Ph.D., CCC-SLP
Director, Childhood Communication Services, Adjunct Professor,
Center for the Study of Human Development, Brown University

"My son has reached amazing heights thanks in part to Jonathan and the knowledge he shared with my family and me. *Challenging the Myths of Autism* should be required reading for every parent, doctor, teacher and therapist who ever interacts with a person with autism. This book clearly dispels many of the myths about autism that continue to live today. As a doctor who treats many children with this condition, I am disheartened to hear parents repeat these myths as fact. Every parent needs to know that what they think is fact about autism may be just fiction. Jonathan's book, supported by excellent research and studies, is a big positive to helping persons with autism reach their full potentials. Read this book and rejoice in the knowledge that your child with autism has so much to offer."

—WENDY EDWARDS, MD, Paediatrician and autism specialist

"As the father of a teenage girl with autism, I've seen first-hand Jonathan's remarkable work with families around the world. Researchers, educators and parents alike should read Jonathan's forward-thinking book, filled with unique insight and compassion, to see the incredible possibility as our understanding of autism is changing."

—DAVID PATCHELL-EVANS, CEO of GoodLife Fitness and founder of the Kilee Patchell-Evans Autism Research Group

"Informed by sound research and years of hands-on experience, Jonathan Alderson explodes several misconceptions that have prevented persons on the autism spectrum from achieving their potential. Ranging from affection and socialization, to repetitive behaviors, imagination, and intelligence, Alderson offers a wealth of practical advice and a myriad of illuminating new perspectives. Sure to become an essential resource for parents, caregivers and professionals, this eye-opening book encourages readers to appreciate the potential of autistic people and to engage them as full participants in the human drama."

—MARK OSTEEN, PhD, author of *One of Us: A Family's Life with Autism* and editor of *Autism and Representation*

CHALLENGING THE MYTHS OF AUTISM

CHALLENGING THE MYTHS OF AUTISM

UNLOCK NEW POSSIBLITIES AND HOPE

JONATHAN ALDERSON, ED.M.

C Collins

Challenging the Myths of Autism
Copyright © 2011 by Jonathan Alderson. All rights reserved.

Published by Collins, an imprint of HarperCollins Publishers Ltd.

First edition

HarperCollins books may be purchased for educational, business, or sales promotional use through our Special Markets Department.

HarperCollins Publishers Ltd
2 Bloor Street East, 20th Floor
Toronto, Ontario, Canada
M4W 1A8

www.harpercollins.ca

Library and Archives Canada Cataloguing in Publication
Alderson, Jonathan, 1968–
Challenging the myths of autism: unlock new possibilities and hope / Jonathan Alderson.

ISBN 978-1-55468-870-8

1. Parents of autistic children. 2. Autism in children.
I. Title.
RJ506.A9A54 2011   618.92'85882   C2011-900481-X

Printed and bound in the United States
RRD 9 8 7 6 5 4 3 2

To Hilary, my mother and most magnificent teacher.
Your love and joy for life led the way.
Thank you for your strength.

CONTENTS

A psychiatrist has just one hour, squeezed in among a dozen other appointments, to observe a three-year-old's range of behaviours. The boy is already falling well behind his peers. He can speak but doesn't have conversations, and he doesn't play with toys normally. He lines up any objects he finds in rows and if someone moves them he tantrums as if his world has been destroyed. The psychiatrist is looking for a variety of clues that may add up to the necessary group of symptoms for a diagnosis. It's a complex process. After asking the parents a list of standard questions, the doctor is fairly certain their son has autism, but he's uncertain as to what degree.

At the end of the hour, the psychiatrist writes down autism spectrum disorder (ASD) on a form, followed by "moderate" in parentheses. The parents are devastated. He says he can't predict how far the boy will develop and hands them a list of phone numbers they can call to get their son on waiting lists for services as soon as possible. As they leave, a thousand unanswered questions flood their minds.

Autism is an enigma affecting as many as 1 child in 100. It is estimated that there are almost 200,000 children with the disorder in Canada alone. We can't measure autism in blood or in urine; it is isn't associated with a person's temperature or blood pressure. Instead, autism is characterized by a group of behavioural symptoms that the doctor observes and then, using a rating scale like the ADOS, determines if the child looks "autistic enough." Autism is typically first detected in early childhood but sometimes not until later. Children with autism have a range of complex neurodevelopmental impairments that affect communication and language, socialization and relationships, and they may display stereotyped behaviour of repetitious and ritualized routines.

Autism is a spectrum disorder, which means the symptoms range from mild to moderate to severe. Classic autism is considered fairly severe, while Asperger's syndrome is considered a milder form of autism. However, the criteria for diagnosing autism have changed over time and are still being debated to this day. In other words, there still isn't consensus about what autism even is. It's not uncommon for parents to get two or more different opinions about the severity of their child's autism, or even confirmation that it's autism at all.

Yet more children will be diagnosed this year with autism than with AIDS, cancer, and diabetes combined. Rates of diagnosis have gone up dramatically over the past ten years especially. This fact alone leads to a widely debated issue: Some say the increase is due to the definition of autism being broadened to include more kids with milder forms of the disorder who, in the past, would have been labelled as "delayed learners" or "socially awkward." Others believe rates have increased because of vaccines, or because the environment is getting more toxic. There is so little consensus, entire books have been written for and against each of these theories, packed with science and real-life anecdotes to support either compelling side of the argument.

Even though researchers have been looking at autism in children for about 70 years, since it was first identified in the early 1940s, we still don't know much about what causes it. The autism-vaccine link is hands-down *the* most debated and contentious issue. The arguments aren't explained well in the media and so "Vaccines Cause Autism" headlines have triggered more fear than understanding. Some researchers, like Dr. Andrew Wakefield, have proposed that the measles virus in the measles, mumps, and rubella (MMR) vaccine finds its way into the intestines and causes an inflamed bowel condition similar to Crohn's disease. According to the theory, the inflammation causes leaks of proteins back into the blood, affecting the brain and causing autism. But, as chronicled by Paul Offit in *Autism's False Prophets,* Wakefield's research has been harshly criticized and discredited, most importantly, by his own medical community. Offit and others call Wakefield's MMR theory a myth. However, in a situation as enigmatic as autism itself, there are two, three, and even more sides to most theories concerning the condition. In *Evidence of Harm, New York Times* reporter David Kirby presents compelling reports and data that vilify drug companies and support Dr. Wakefield's vaccine-autism link. (Recently, Wakefield authored his comprehensive self-defence, *Callous Disregard.*) Meanwhile, parents are left to sort through mountains of conflicting information while their children's health is at stake. The number of children getting the MMR vaccine has decreased and, as a direct result, the number of children infected with the measles virus has gone up. Outbreaks of measles have resurfaced in underimmunized communities (putting children at risk for brain inflammation and even death), demonstrating the high stakes of sorting myth from truth.

Recently, there has been a flurry of genetic studies, and a few genes have been identified that might make a child more susceptible to developing symptoms. However, most researchers agree that autism is not dependent on genetics alone but is likely a matter of epigenetics, in which genes interact with triggers in the environment. There still is no evidence of a simple "autism gene."

While experts cannot agree on what causes autism, there's also no consensus on exactly how to treat it. By far, the most widely promoted and researched approach is behaviour therapy. In Canada this is the treatment of choice of provincial governments and school boards. Research has shown behaviour therapy can help to educate and improve the functional behaviour of up to 50 percent of children with autism. But what about the other 50 percent? Since children diagnosed with autism have multiple learning and behaviour challenges, there is no one treatment or therapy that can deal with all of their needs. As a result, there has been a wide-open market for almost any type of service or product for treating autism. Treatments on offer range from swimming with dolphins to infrared saunas, cod liver oil, intensive desk-work drills, skin-brushing regimes, hyperbaric oxygen therapy (HBOT), dance classes, video games, and specially trained dogs. The number of options that parents have to choose from is overwhelming. Some of these treatments are based on scientific evidence. Others seem more fiction than fact.

I had just finished four years of child development and educational psychology studies at university with plans for a career improving the curriculum in public schools. No one in my family had autism. I didn't have any neighbours or friends that I knew of with autism, and the disorder wasn't covered in the media like it is today. I had no previous experience with autism beyond a few pages in a psychology textbook. In these pages, I had learned that children with autism also have mental retardation, except for a few savants who are super-intelligent in one specific area. I learned that people with autism are aloof and sadly can't share affection with others. The textbook also explained that children with autism can't form attachments to their parents, and can't learn how to play like other kids do.

The summer after my graduation, I had an experience that would shape the direction of my career and my life's interest since. I was invited to observe a play-therapy session at the Autism Treatment Center of America, nestled in the Berkshires of Massachusetts.

Settling into one of the centre's small observation rooms, I peered into a simply furnished therapy room through a large two-way mirror. An impish four-year-old boy wearing a tiny black yarmulke ran in circles around a small table. He had been diagnosed with autism and his family had travelled from Israel for intensive training in the centre's Son-Rise Program. The young boy was being chased playfully by an enthusiastic therapist, her arms out-stretched with animated fingers ready for the tickle finale. And the child was laughing. I was mesmerized: his behaviour didn't look anything like what my textbook described autism to be. How was it possible that he was playing an interactive game and enjoying the affection? Was my textbook wrong?

Then, suddenly the fun stopped. The boy seemingly shut down. Standing still, he looked up at a shelf of toys. The therapist leapt to the toys, eager to start another game. But the boy just turned away. He was no longer engaged. He looked lost and began to walk slowly away from her. He crawled under the little table and stared off into the space in front of him. I was intrigued. How could he so easily tune out his cartoonish-ly animated adult playmate? Why did the tickle-chase end so suddenly? Then, in the same seemingly random way, a smirk emerged on the boy's face. A flash of his eyes toward the therapist signalled "more chase." He was re-engaged.

Over the next 20 years, I dedicated myself to reading as much as I could about the disorder. I attended conferences on behavioural interventions and biomedical treatments. I worked with hundreds of families and spent hours upon hours in therapy sessions with children diagnosed across the autism spectrum. The more children I met, the more diversity I saw. The autism described in books, on TV, and in the media was an averaged caricature that didn't match what I witnessed in reality, and I was most disturbed by the negative impact of some of the more stereotypical characterizations of people with autism. Through the din of debates about genes and vaccines I think we sometimes forget that we are talking about real people, a population with a very wide range of strengths and challenges and personalities. How we talk about people with autism and how we characterize them impacts how we treat them. For example:

- The belief that autistic children can't share affection with others has led therapists to use hug or holding therapies where children are held tightly, often against their will, for hours at a time. Screaming and trying to escape, some children have been held down by several adults who believe these therapies can force a healthier bond to form.

- The belief that the majority of autistic children are mentally retarded led to thousands being placed in mental institutions and pushed aside in special-education classrooms. Low expectations and condescending attitudes resulted in less opportunity for children with autism to learn, participate, and be included fully with others.

- The belief that people diagnosed with autism don't have imagination blinds us from seeing their different kinds of creativity and unique thinking capacities. Unusual interests, play, and behaviour are judged as inappropriate instead of as creative and valued, and are shut down.

These perennially inaccurate descriptions, and many more, are what I call the myths of autism. Each one of the seven examined in this book is rooted in *some* observable evidence in *some* individuals with autism. However, there are many different and equally plausible interpretations. In the same way that bogus treatments can mislead parents and give false hope, these caricatures of people with autism mislead parents, therapists, and the general public to underestimate the potential of children with autism. These persistent myths dehumanize and limit the ways in which we look at people with autism. They influence research, policy, treatment, and our personal relations with people with autism, and they need to be challenged.

Calling these stereotypical characterizations "myths" is one way of debunking them and encourages us to reconsider and re-examine our assumptions about people with autism. Barry Neil Kaufman, author of *Happiness Is a Choice*, writes with clarity about beliefs we hold and their powerful impact on our feelings and behaviour. What we believe about a person with autism is the lens through which we greet and interact with them.

The "mythologies" of autism shackle our awareness. They inhibit us from recognizing the *unlimited* possibilities for interaction with each *unique* person with autism. In our education and interactions with these special people, could we put aside definitions and celebrate uniqueness? Choosing to see possibility can lead to hope and can reinvigorate patience and acceptance. A young mother loses hope when she is told that if her autistic child doesn't learn to speak before the age of five he will likely never talk. Fear and anxiety become her focus. Impatience and judgment manifest. By the time the child reaches the age of five, if he is not yet talking, the mother is now less likely to hear her child's speechlike sounds, and even less likely to interpret any she does hear as attempts to communicate. The myth has become fact. However, there is hope. Much hope. Examples of children who learned to speak after the five-year barrier break the myth. Examples of children who have learned alternate modes of communication equally challenge the hopelessness.

During the past five years in particular, researchers around the world have uncovered new understandings of the biology of autism. Most often spurred on by determined parents ("Dr. Moms"), pioneering medical researchers are leading the way in redefining autism from what was previously a psychological disorder to a neurobiological one. Now, we also need to update how we talk about the symptoms and the prognosis.

In the pages that follow, I invite you to put aside any preconceived notions of autism. It is my intention, with the help of these real-life stories, history, and research, that this book will stimulate discussion and respectfully provoke examination of the current beliefs, and ultimately help us see more possibilities in people with autism.

CHAPTER ONE

THE MYTH OF AFFECTION

"Children with Autism Avoid and Can't Share Affection"

Many, but not all, children with autism reject social
interactions and dislike hugs and affection.
Anne O'Connor, *Sunday Business Post*

Usually, signs of autism are evident soon after birth to a parent
who is willing and able to grasp that a child is oblivious to love and affection.
For inexplicable reasons, the autistic child bridles at forming
attachments to mother, family and the human race.
Douglas Martin, *The New York Times*

The voice on the other end of the phone was distressed. Aidan had hit another child on the nose in the playground that morning and he was only in kindergarten, the mother explained. Aidan's parents asked me to observe him at school and assess how I might help. He had recently been diagnosed with pervasive developmental disorder (PDD) and fit the profile of moderate autism. Aidan's teachers also were concerned about his social development.

I sat in a kid-sized chair out of the way and watched him wander around the classroom, often holding a toy action figure, and mostly on his own. He was not communicating—his words were jumbled and unclear as he talked to himself. He was extremely hyperactive and had almost no attention span. He couldn't sit still for a hug or to sit in his mother's lap.

Working closely with his parents and the teachers, we pulled him out of the school temporarily and set up a home-based supportive environment where he could learn more easily. I directed a team of therapists to focus on communication and social cooperation skills. During one of the training sessions in the family home, I watched and took notes as one of the therapists helped Aidan read a book. She sat across from him at a small table. They were both intensely focused on the words in the book. But it was under the table that the real interaction was taking place. Perhaps feeling comfortable with his therapist, Aidan casually stretched his leg out and gently rested his foot on his mentor's knee. I scribbled on my notepad, "He's showing affection!! He *initiated* physical . . . *gentle* . . . !" In my notes I underlined the words that were most remarkable, given Aidan's history. He was being affectionate, close, and seeking physical touch. The therapist didn't flinch or seem to notice this landmark moment, however. It didn't occur to her, since she didn't hold the belief that these kids aren't affectionate.

> In all of my work with children on the autism spectrum, I've witnessed example after example of their affectionate behaviour.

In all of my work with children on the autism spectrum, I've witnessed example after example of their affectionate behaviour. So, from the beginning of my career in this field, I questioned the characterization I had read in books and newspapers. Despite what they said, I knew that not *all* people with autism were devoid of affection. At the same time, I haven't been blind to the rejections—some autistic children move away from affectionate actions like hugs and kisses.

I wondered why some were affectionate while others weren't. Is this because they actually don't want affection, or are there physiological reasons like hypersensitivities or differences in thinking that explain why a person wouldn't want to be hugged or to hold hands? Since many children with autism can't communicate well enough to explain why they do what they do, we are left to assume and to judge. Unfortunately, we don't give them the benefit of the doubt.

Of all the characterizations about people with autism, this one in particular is potentially the most damaging. *New York Times* journalist

Douglas Martin's sweeping characterizations of a child who is "oblivious to love and affection," who can't form attachments to the human race, depict the autistic child as almost unhuman. Even though the statement is grossly exaggerated and unqualified, this sad portrait is now unfortunately painted in the minds of thousands of readers. How would one of these readers approach an autistic child? Differently than a relative who knew the child loved hugs, more than likely.

Most damaging is the divide that the myth wedges between parent and child.

Most damaging is the divide that the myth wedges between parent and child. Reinforced by countless websites, newspaper articles, and professionals, sadly some parents who accept this sentence are less likely to notice their special child's signs of affection. Their own affectionate behaviour toward the child may diminish too. After all, they've been told their autistic child doesn't want it anyway.

One reason why debunking this myth is so important is because of its implication that if a child rejects affection it's because his parents are not affectionate enough. Many parents, especially mothers, try to identify what they may have done or not done to cause their child's autism, torturing themselves with self-judgment.

Working in England many years ago, I learned this first-hand as I sat on a bench outside in a family's yard listening to one mother's story. She sat beside me weeping as she described the self-mutilation behaviour of her three-and-a-half-year-old son. Christopher was severely autistic, had no language, and seemed in constant distress. He would sit cross-legged on the floor and bang his forehead, smacking it down hard onto the stone floor. The boy had bruises and had even cut himself on several occasions. With blood gushing down her son's face, his mother had raced him to the local emergency ward. There, she faced a battery of questions as the hospital staff tried to understand how she could have "let" him do this to himself.

Sitting on the bench with me that day, the tears rolled down her cheeks. She talked rapidly, firing off all the possible ways she thought she might have caused her son's autism: "I wonder sometimes how he would have been if I'd listened to my mom and taken more vitamins during my pregnancy. And I can't help but think about that big argument I had with Rick [her husband] one night . . . I yelled and I was crying . . . and I wonder if that just scared Christopher so much that . . ." She couldn't finish the sentence. When her breathing calmed a bit, she didn't say anything more for a while. Then I asked, "What are you thinking?" "I love Chris so, so much—I would never want to hurt him. He's my little guy . . . and I can't bear the thought that I was the one who hurt him," she said. She stared down at the ground with tears falling onto her lap, intensely focused. "I just hate myself. . . . I knew I shouldn't have had that wine. . . . It was only a glass, or two . . . but I had this strong feeling it was wrong . . . but now I can't undo the past. I just want to do everything I can to help him be happy and stop hurting himself."

This mother's expression of deep love for her son was the opposite of uncaring. If only the hospital staff could know this too, and the neighbours who watched from their windows, judging Chris's parents when he threw tantrums in the driveway, and all those who are quick to assume that an out-of-control child in public must be the result of bad parenting. This is the legacy that parents of autistic children live with.

Without exception, every parent I've had the honour to work with has expressed mountains of love for their special-needs child. Yes, they have rough days, and like it does for every parent, patience runs thin sometimes. Life with a child with autism can be incredibly trying and tiring, but underlying the frustrations and the many adjustments required is love. Yet their feelings of rejection and guilt can prevent both the parent and the child from sharing and recognizing the very affection that forms a fundamental bond. The myth of affection is *the* most important myth to discuss and dispel.

WHERE DID THE MYTH COME FROM?

It's a fact: some children do reject affection. I've seen children with autism go limp like rag dolls when they're picked up. They're hugged but some don't hug back. Parents have told me about the rejection they feel when their child won't cuddle in their laps for storytime. Children with autism as young as two and three years old have held out their arms to block me from sitting too close, or they've simply stood up and walked away without a care for my playful overtures. The unsolved question is why.

Although we experience affectionate behaviour through touch, sight, sound, and smell, until fairly recently scientists haven't understood much about the biology and physiology of affection. The possibility that people with autism might experience these senses differently has not been widely promoted nor well understood. What feels like a soft, gentle, loving caress to you might feel like a painful swipe to a child with autism.

What feels like a soft, gentle, loving caress to you might feel like a painful swipe to a child with autism.

Without these insights, parents and doctors have interpreted autistic children's turning away from affectionate behaviour as a psychological or antisocial problem.

The myth that people with autism avoid and can't share affection was born out of the assumptions and judgments of guessing the psychology behind autistic behaviour. One of the most persistent and nefarious psychological explanations is that these children must have had unloving parents. This idea found its basis in the history of autism over two hundred years ago and lingers to this day. Remarkably, in 1798 a mute child was found wandering alone in the woods in southern France near Aveyron. Legend has it he was abandoned and raised by wolves. Most importantly, the French physician Dr. Jean-Marc Gaspard Itard* described how wild and unhuman the feral child he called Victor was when he first examined him, "expressing no kind of affection . . . and in short, indifferent to every body."[1] Itard also implied that the boy had not developed human affection because he had been alone in the wild without human contact or parental affection.

Fast forward over one hundred years and we find Itard's conclusion about lack of parental affection echoed by the man most agree discovered autism, Leo Kanner. He too blamed parents at first. In Kanner's now famous 11 case studies, he summarized that the group of children were "from the start anxiously and tensely impervious to people, with whom for a long time they do not have any kind of direct affective contact." He went on to pin the reason on parents, writing about the 11 families studied, "There are very few really warmhearted fathers and mothers."[2]

The belief that some parents aren't affectionate enough continued unchallenged for another two decades and was hyped during the 1960s when a man named Bruno Bettelheim promoted the emotionally cold parent theory, infamously using the term "refrigerator mothers."[†] In his book *The Empty Fortress,* supposedly based on real case studies conducted during his work as director of the orthogenic school at the University of Chicago, Bettelheim wrote, "The precipitating factor in infantile autism is the parent's wish that his child should not exist."[3]

In 1964, the tides of thought began to change against the refrigerator mother theory when Dr. Bernard Rimland released his seminal book *Infantile Autism: The Syndrome and Its Implication for a*

---

* Many celebrate Itard as the father of modern-day special education.

† The damning "refrigerator" label isolated mothers with autistic children, causing them to suffer guilt. Because of this, Bettelheim's work was discredited. Some of Bettelheim's former staff and students later exposed his temper and alleged abuses. Bettelheim ultimately committed suicide in 1990.

Neural Theory of Behavior. Writing as a medical doctor and father of an autistic son, Dr. Rimland rejected autism as a social-emotional illness caused by unloving parents (nurture) and argued strongly that it was a neurodevelopmental disorder with underlying biological causes (nature). Thus began the nature versus nurture debate. In the same year that Bettelheim published *The Empty Fortress,* Rimland founded the Autism Research Institute, which brought together and galvanized a large group of parents, researchers, and medical professionals who took up the neurobiological mantle. Impassioned and extraordinarily dedicated to helping families, Dr. Rimland challenged the status quo in a respectful way, basing his arguments on sound research and endless determination. Even Leo Kanner converted in the end, publishing a paper in 1971 suggesting a likely genetic (biological) basis for autism.[4]

That blaming parents has come into and out of fashion is evidence that researchers and theorists can sometimes get it wrong; they can change their minds. In a recent interview with author Adam Feinstein, the highly esteemed autism researcher Dr. Michael Rutter humbly offered the example of changing his own previously held position that autism did not likely have an underlying genetic cause. Having now switched his view in favour of a genetic basis, he admitted, "I think you need to be open when you make mistakes—we all make mistakes!"[5]

Rimland's group tipped the refrigerator-mother trend toward the field's current biomedical model, burying for good Bruno Bettelheim's false conclusions that unaffectionate parents were the problem. Unfortunately, the myth that autistic children themselves are unaffectionate was not buried. Genetic studies have barely scratched the surface and still can't explain the affection avoidance that seems to come with autism. Biologists don't have an answer either. So the void is filled with contemporary cognitive psychology theories that continue to perpetuate the myth that autistic people are indeed affectionless.

Today, psychologists explain differences in children's affection mostly through what they call attachment theory. According to the theory, the extent to which a child forms an "attachment" or bonds to his father and mother, in particular, determines how much the child shows affection back and accepts affection from others. In some cases, a child rejects the mother's affection, which, say the psychologists, may lead to her feeling dejected and being less affectionate toward her child. The child then feels rejected and in turn begins to shut down. A vicious cycle escalates. But how did the cycle begin in the first place? Attachment theorists are divided between nurture and nature: Do children reject parental affection because of genetics or because of something they have learned from the parents or others in their environment? Today, research tells us it is likely because of genetics and certainly not because of parents.

NEGATIVE IMPACTS OF THE MYTH

> I've spoken with parents who questioned their child's diagnosis of autism simply because the child was "too affectionate" to be autistic.

I've spoken with parents who questioned their child's diagnosis of autism simply because the child was "too affectionate" to be autistic. More concerning is that parents might not even seek a diagnosis in the first place. This could prevent a child from getting treatment and services he or she might need. As soon as parents notice developmental challenges, family members typically surf the internet for hundreds of hours trying to learn all they can. But the myths are embedded everywhere on the Web, and only confuse the situation.

One mother looking for answers posted a question on an internet parent-support site: *Anyone with an affectionate autistic child?* In her posting, she explained that her three-year-old autistic son has "always wanted to hug and kiss," which made her question if he really is autistic or not. In reply, another parent posted reassurances that her autistic son was extremely affectionate too. "He hugs and kisses all the time. So you're not alone with having an affectionate autistic child." The parents in this chat group were sharing stories and support, and trading answers about why their children might be affectionate despite their autism diagnosis. Clearly, as a profession, we are giving these parents the wrong messages if they are trying to figure out why their children are affectionate instead of being encouraged to enjoy it and to reciprocate in a typical and natural mother-and-child way.

A second reply by a different parent further illustrates the confusion: "I was also relieved to find that my son couldn't be autistic, since he was so affectionate. I was then shocked when we got a PDD-NOS* diagnosis." It's common that parents feel confused and angry about the discrepancies and contradictions in what they read and hear. These feelings can foster mistrust in professionals and "the system." Many families feel they can't trust the educators and therapists who would otherwise be able to help them.

The myth can mislead professionals too. Some physicians won't diagnose children as having autism if they display any affection. Instead, doctors often choose a different diagnosis or a less severe disorder. The negative implication is that children don't get access to services they may need and the parents don't really understand the treatment direction they should pursue.

An equally distressing result of some autism therapists' and doctors' belief in this myth is that they deny any affection that an autistic child does display. If you believe a child doesn't feel affection, then you might see his version of a hug as aggression, for example. Sadly, a loving moment between a parent and child is reinterpreted and downgraded as inappropriate behaviour.

---

* PDD-NOS stands for pervasive developmental disorder—not otherwise specified. This is the least severe of the autism spectrum disorders.

Jill Escher has a son diagnosed with autism whose affectionate behaviour had been discounted. I enjoyed the articles on her blog, *Autism Tomorrows: A Journal about the New Era of Autism Treatment* (www.autismtomorrows.blogspot.com); Jill's a critical thinker and open to a new narrative of autism. Coincidentally, although I've never met Jill, it turns out she had taken her family for training to the Son-Rise Program, where I spent many happy years working early on in my career. So I wrote to her and asked if she considered her son affectionate or not, and what she thought of the myth of affection. Through several emails, Jill described her son Jonny, now 11 years old, as having a "highly developed emotional radar rarely found in typical children," and "a deep reservoir of affection for his family. He is so snuggly and 'huggy,'" she wrote. "His family nickname is the love monster."

Jonny gives hugs and kisses freely now. But he didn't always. His mother explained that for a number of years Jonny was more distant. He was absorbed in his repetitive rituals, and didn't give much eye contact or pay attention to his family. He would wander for long periods of time and flick at things, shutting out people around him. He also went through periods of terrible tantrums.

Like most parents searching for answers in mountains of books and articles, Jill came across the idea that children with autism lack affection. This was reinforced by Jonny's psychologist, one of the most prominent clinicians in Silicon Valley. During an appointment Jill mentioned that Jonny, then about four years old, had developed a habit of kissing her a lot. The psychologist dismissively explained, "Oh, he's not kissing you; he's just seeking pressure." They had spent thousands of dollars for advice that parroted and perpetuated these sorts of myths.

And those tantrums, as it turned out, had nothing to do with "negative behaviours," as the psychologist and Jonny's behaviour therapists had continually asserted. Rather, Jonny's tantrums had been caused by undiagnosed gastrointestinal problems including parasites, esophagitis, and severe constipation. Once the underlying medical problems were addressed, Jonny's so-called behaviours resolved themselves quickly.

Some research has correlated gastrointestinal (stomach, gut, and digestion) problems with autism. More than half of the children I've worked with have had clinically diagnosed GI imbalances. In many cases this means the children are dealing with daily symptoms like stomach bloating, indigestion, acid reflux, constipation, diarrhea, and cramps. For Jonny, once his mother helped to manage these symptoms, he was better able to benefit from the education and loving relationships his parents provided for him.

All that kissing and hugging did in fact turn out to be affection. It would have been a tragedy had Jill and her family believed the popular characterization that her son, because of his autism, couldn't be affectionate. Nothing could have been further from the truth.

Some children on the spectrum are so affectionate that their loving behaviour is ironically judged as inappropriate. I've worked with children who don't understand yet the difference between family and a stranger. They will hug anyone they meet in public. Some of the kids don't understand or pay attention to personal space either. They can be interested in other people, stand too close, and are not afraid to reach out and touch. One little girl I worked with for several years, starting when she was just three years old, is now eight and entering middle school. She is fully mainstreamed without assistance and no longer meets her former autism diagnosis. As she matures, she continues to learn about socializing. Once an introverted, nonverbal child, she now makes friends with everyone she meets. If she meets someone for the first time, she will likely run up to them the next day and give them a big hug as if they have been best friends forever, a behaviour that is unusual and somewhat inappropriate in our North American culture. Treatment programs are implemented to reduce behaviours that don't work socially for a child, but unfortunately, these programs do not encourage or teach affectionate behaviours in ways that work. The child's affection is rejected and punished instead of nurtured into methods that work for the child.

The most damaging effect of the myth of affection is that caregivers stop being affectionate: "He doesn't want it anyway, so why bother?" Surprisingly, when training parents and therapists, I often have to include explicit instructions for them to express affection—to reach out and cuddle, hug, kiss, embrace, smile, and say loving things to the autistic person they are helping. "Really? I'm allowed to do that?" is a typical response. It's not because parents are unloving, of course, but many parents and therapists are trained to behave too clinically. The myth literally stops parents from sharing as much affection as they probably feel.

I'm particularly concerned about how this characterization negatively portrays autistic children and adults as less than human.

> I'm particularly concerned about how this characterization negatively portrays autistic children and adults as less than human.

Taken to an extreme, the belief morphs from "They push away from affection" to "They don't want affection," and ultimately to "They don't need affection." Journalist Lloyd Grove, for example, included the following quote in his *Washington Post* article about a family's journey to find treatment for their son with autism: "These children are not aware of self," says Jean Simmons, founder of the pioneering Linwood Children's Center in Ellicott City, Maryland. "They don't seem to need the affection of the human touch. They don't know what it is to be cold or hot. To be hungry or not. They are like beautiful little vegetables."

Despite quoting a "pioneering" educator, Mr. Grove doesn't include any other context for this distorted and degrading characterization of people with autism as "little vegetables" who don't need human touch. He doesn't provide explanation or offer a counterbalancing point of view. Instead, he employs this choice quote to sensationalize the story. What is the negative impact of promoting this characterization to hundreds of thousands of readers?

In their attempts to fix the perceived lack-of-affection problem, psychologists and researchers have developed some truly questionable treatments. From the profession that gave birth to the refrigerator-mother theory, Freudian psychotherapy (which is still widely practised as a treatment of choice for autism in France), comes forced holding. Contemporary psychiatrists like Foster Cline and Dr. Martha Welch have promoted holding therapies to the fore of autism treatments. Based on attachment theory, holding therapies teach parents and therapists that the reason some children have emotional and behavioural challenges is because they haven't bonded well enough with their parents. To foster this missing bond, parents and therapists are taught to "hug" their son or daughter so that they can assert authority over the child and establish eye contact. Videotaped holding therapy sessions I've seen show autistic children held against their will, squirming to get free, and screaming for release while being held by a parent who seems to be in distress as a supervising therapist coaches them to "hold on" no matter what.

Columbia University graduate and psychiatrist Dr. Welch promoted her version of this type of treatment in the early 1970s, in her book *Holding Time*. Her technique has evolved and is currently called prolonged parent-child embrace (PPCE) therapy. Without question, it's a positive step that showing affection toward children with autism and that including parents in the learning and therapeutic process is being promoted in the treatment field. However, holding a child against his or her will is not a technique I endorse in any way. Along with other holding therapy centres and trainers, Dr. Welch's PPCE therapy has met with a significant amount of criticism and opposition. It seems counterintuitive to hold a child against his will and force eye contact in order to promote more affection.

If you hold the belief that autistic children don't have the capacity for human affection then you might also believe that the only way to teach them something is to force them. The field of autism treatment has a history of forcing its largely unproven methods onto these special children. The late Dr. Ivar Lovaas is revered as the grandfather of applying behavioural analysis to the treatment of autism. His methods and advocacy for better treatments for autism have helped thousands of children around the world, and his legacy is mostly positive. However, as a pioneer researcher who began to practise in an era when there was less ethical scrutiny, he also has a history of not-so-humane treatment of some of the children he tried to help. For example, writing explicitly in his seminal behavioural programming manual, *Teaching Developmentally Disabled Children: The ME Book,* Lovaas directs parents to "Let him [your child] know you are displeased (yell at him and perhaps spank him if you have to) when he performs poorly."[6] Dr. Lovaas, like so many others, believed that his autistic subjects needed to be taught in a step-by-step manner the behaviours of affection. In 1965 he reported an experiment called "building social behaviour in autistic children by use of electric shock." Two five-year-old twin boys with severe autism and no language to communicate were administered "painful electric shock"[7] to train them to hug and kiss an adult researcher. (To be clear, Lovaas's use of electric shock happened only early in his career; however, shock is still used to control the behaviour of autistic people to this day.) In some cases of forced learning, a child will indeed learn to give the hug-behaviour or do the kiss-behaviour, but forced affectionate-behaviour is not truly affectionate, and it's not the kind of affection parents want from their kids.

Holding therapy and electric shock are just two of many inhumane, controlling approaches used to teach affection to children with autism. How can a child learn about affection from dominating adults forcing discomfort and pain on them?

WHAT DO RESEARCHERS TELL US ABOUT AUTISM AND AFFECTION?

Theories about why people with autism lack affection abound. The bulk of the research is based on two notions: people with autism don't have the cognitive capacity to understand affection or they don't actually feel affection. These days, most researchers shy away from the nurture side of development; no one wants to be lumped in with Bruno Bettelheim as a parent blamer. The majority of research therefore looks for biological differences. So far, most biological research has focused on genetics and brain development. Currently, the leading theories implicate various genes or genetic deletions, concluding that this population is simply built differently and is thus "naturally" affectionless. MRI and PET scans of autistic brains provide some evidence of structural differences that psychologists have tried to interpret as evidence that people with autism actually think differently than most of us.

Dr. Simon Baron-Cohen, a leading autism theorist, proposes that people with autism don't have the cognitive capacity to recognize and understand affection. The University of Cambridge professor has approached the autistic mind from various angles. Drawing on cognitive-psychological notions from his Theory of Mind and "mindblindness" to his extreme male brain (EMB) theory and the amygdala theory, among others, he is a model of curiosity and creative thinking supported by research. While not everyone agrees with his views, he challenges us to rethink autism disorders.

In his book *The Essential Difference,* Baron-Cohen hypothesizes that autism is an extreme form of maleness. His idea starts with the observation that men in general lack empathy compared to women. Therefore, he supposes, the lack of empathy (and affection) observed in autism may be the result of extreme or hypermaleness. He gathered evidence to support his extreme male brain theory by measuring testosterone levels in fetuses. His theory is anecdotally supported by the generally accepted rate that autism occurs four times more in males than females. He also points out that people with autism have an affinity for systems and putting things in order (a male trait) rather than an affinity for human relationships (a female trait). But the fact remains, there are thousands of young girls diagnosed with autism every year. One would expect that higher levels of testosterone would not only lead to a more male brain in these girls but would also impact their physical development. This has not been reported, however, and therefore challenges the hypothesis. There are others who are critical of contemporary psychiatric explanations of autism. For example, Timimi, Gardner, and McCabe examine what they believe are essentially judgments of boys' behaviour in *The Myth of Autism: Medicalising Men's and Boys' Social and Emotional Competence*.

Sociobiology is the study of the interaction between our social environment, our genes, and our behavioural learning and shaping that results in how we become social beings. Early social experiences with parents, siblings, caregivers, and other children may influence which genes are switched on or off, brain development, and hormonal patterns. Early social experiences help to shape an individual child's social attachments, communication, and social motivations in ways research is only just starting to investigate. In other words, your biology determines how you socialize and, at the same time, your early social experiences can influence aspects of your biology such as brain development and behaviour.

Some researchers suggest that people with autism have different brain development that leads them to focus more on objects than on people, for example. Imagine an infant whose brain is hard-wired to focus on objects instead of on his parents. The baby doesn't dislike affection, but because he isn't following his mother's loving gaze, he doesn't see her moving to pick him up. He might be looking at the light on the ceiling instead. As a consequence, he can't predict his mother's behaviour. So instead of raising his arms in anticipation of being lifted up, he's startled and starts to cry. The mother in turn feels bad that she's upset her baby, when she was just trying to cuddle him. Over time, the more she seems to upset him and the more he seems to reject her affection, the less confident she feels in handling her baby. Early associations between physical touch and defensiveness are reinforced. The child is not lacking affection or avoiding being loved, and neither is the mother. The original cause was a genetic predisposition for the child's brain to focus his attention on objects versus people.

Another example of a sociobiological difference that may occur in the autistic population was investigated by Simon Baron-Cohen and his colleagues. The researchers showed a group of adults with Asperger's syndrome picture cards of faces expressing different human emotions. The researchers measured how well the group could name the emotions. In the second phase of the test, the group was shown the same pictures but with only the eyes of the faces showing. In both cases, the autistic adults scored significantly lower than the "normal" control group. Baron-Cohen concluded that the autistic brain has a deficit in reading emotions. If this is true, it could also explain how autistic children would respond differently to affection, since affection also involves reading facial affect and nonverbal gestures.

Similar investigations into the autistic brain suggest that emotions are processed differently. A person on the autistic spectrum may clearly see the affection being offered, but their brain may interpret and understand the affection differently. Researchers at the University of Iowa looked at a part of the brain called the amygdala, where they found evidence of dysfunction in the autistic subjects. It's possible, they concluded, that there's a disconnect between seeing the affection and their stored understanding of what it means.

Other research has focused on nonverbal body language. People with autism often lack the typical behaviours that signal attention, interest, and affection. Without these, they can appear more emotionless and distant than they might actually be. Limited eye contact, not turning to face others, and not sharing toys are common descriptions of the behaviour of children diagnosed with autism. Even though any one of these traits might be caused by genetics or sensory disorders, it's easy to understand how these kids are often seen as "aloof" and "unfriendly." Again, we need to consider all the reasons why someone might not be able to maintain eye contact or respond to your affectionate "hello."

> While we can see a child pull away from affection, we can't know for certain that this means he doesn't want affection.

It seems that the default interpretation of children who pull away from offered affection is that they must not want affection or aren't affectionate. While we can see a child pull away from affection, we can't know for certain that this means he doesn't want affection. He moved away from the actual physical hug, but not necessarily from the loving and kind intention of the affection. This is a game-changing distinction.

Before concluding that a person with autism doesn't want or feel affection, consider that he or she might experience it differently. Humans are not all built the same. Even among the "neurotypical" (i.e., average) population there's a wide range of how people perceive their environments. Some people love loud rock concerts, while others can't bear sounds louder than talking; some people enjoy wool sweaters, but others can't stand the itch on their skin. We have to consider that some people with autism experience signals of affection differently. It might be more accurate for us to say, simply, they are *different* in affection rather than they're *lacking* in it.

REFRAMING THE DISCUSSION

During my training years as a young play therapist, I read books on autism, subscribed to parent–support group newsletters, and attended as many conferences as I could. It was a steep learning curve about an enigma that wasn't yet recognized as a spectrum disorder. I was warned early on that the kids I worked with were not going to be affectionate. "Don't be disappointed when they don't smile back at you," one lecturer cautioned. So when child after child was cuddly or smiled or played a tickle game with me I thought to myself, either I had a "natural talent" with autistic children or the early warning I had been given was a myth.

The more talks and conferences I went to, the more I noticed a common pattern in all of the presentations given by parents. They would begin with a similar intro: "I know they [the experts] say these kids aren't affectionate, and even though my son has a lot of the classic autistic behaviours, he is the cuddliest and most affectionate little love bird ever." It was as if the parents were trying to assure the audience that their children really were autistic despite their affectionate behaviours. Along with my own personal experiences through work as a play-therapist, the parents' descriptions countered the myth of affection. I wondered then why the characterization was still being written in so many places. I remember even trying to find an official source of the characterization and through my research learning that affectionate behaviour or lack of it isn't even in the criteria for diagnosis. The lack of affection characterization, really is a myth that has grown outside of the diagnosis.

In June 2010, the Vista Del Mar Child and Family Services in Los Angeles hosted a conference on autism. One of the panellists, Dr. Laurie Stephens, director of clinical services at Education Spectrum in California, described how she too came to question the myth:

> *At school in my abnormal psych class I was taught that they [autistic children] don't have emotions, and they don't understand what other people think and feel, and they have no empathy. . . . and then I started working with children and young adults [with autism] and I thought, well this is nothing*

like what was described in my textbook. These are people with amazing amounts of passion and interests and a desire to get along. They might just show it in a different way but it was clearly there.

After about three years of home-based intensive education and therapy, a family I was working with in the United States was ready to transition their five-year-old daughter, Maria, into public school. When I'd first met her she was almost mute and could not communicate. She ignored her younger sister and any other children. Her parents were distressed that she didn't seem to even notice the people around her. Now, after hundreds of hours of intensive therapy, Maria was a chatty and socially curious wondergirl. The week she started school, I was on hand during the first few days to facilitate her transition from home-therapy to school and to train the teacher. The mainstream senior kindergarten classroom was busy with noise and the movements of students grouped at activity centres. I sat quietly to the side, proudly watching my little buddy Maria. She sat enthusiastically with four other peers at a table with crayons and paper for colouring. At one point, a blue crayon that the student next to her had been using began to slowly roll toward the edge of the table. Maria saw the crayon, looked up at her peer, then back at the crayon as it fell onto the floor. Then, to my surprise, Maria gently tapped her new friend on the arm and said, "Um . . . excuse me . . . your crayon fell. . . . " She then bent down, picked up the crayon and handed it to the student. I was thrilled to see her demonstrate empathy and affection. Maria wasn't yet giving hugs to her friends, but she demonstrated caring for another person by help-ing them in a tangible way. In the literature and research on affection, this is called *social support*.

From social support, to cooperating, paying attention, and even just listening, there is a wider range of ways that humans express affection beyond physical closeness than we may typically recognize. Instead of putting so much research into explaining how and why the autistic population isn't affectionate, I propose that we ask more progressive questions: In what ways do people with autism express their sense of affection differently? And in what ways can we learn to express affection beyond our own limited repertoires so that those with autism can recognize and enjoy it too?

WHY MIGHT PEOPLE WITH AUTISM EXPERIENCE AFFECTION DIFFERENTLY?

Humans experience affection primarily through the senses. Our hearing identifies a friendly voice, our sight recognizes a loving smile, and our skin (tactile sense) distinguishes a kind touch. Accurately feeling through our senses is dependent on a healthy nervous system.

One explanation for why people with autism sometimes push away from being picked up, kissed, hugged, or having their hands held is that they may experience their senses differently than most of us. Some in the field suggest this is a processing disorder. Different sensory processing can change the way you react to sensory stimulation. For example, some people feel a light touch on their skin as painful. This would trigger a natural reflex to pull away quickly from the pain. Others won't even register a light touch and may ignore it altogether. In either case, it makes sense to assume the child doesn't want to be touched in that way, but it would be a false conclusion that he doesn't want affection.

So why would some people's senses react oddly like this? A modern term being used to describe these unusual sensory experiences is sensory integration dysfunction. The disorder is described clearly in *The Out-of-Sync Child,* a book by Carol Stock Kranowitz. Each of the senses can be experienced differently (some say dysfunctionally) as either hyper- or hyposensitive. For example, a person with a hypersensitive vestibular (balance) system interprets any vestibular input in an overreactive way. The system is overloaded and not able to filter out irrelevant sensory information. The result, as Kranowitz explains, is that "the hypersensitive child may misinterpret a casual touch as a life-threatening blow, [and] may feel he will fall off the face of the earth if he is nudged."[8] In contrast, a person with hyposensitivity is underresponsive and, compared to most people, underreacts to sensory stimulation. The hyposensitive person will often seek out the sensory stimulation they aren't getting enough of. For example, a child might jump around a lot to create vestibular sensation, or hum and screech to create auditory sensation. Kranowitz and many others are part of a well-established, although not yet medically recognized* field of specialists who help children improve their "sensory integration" through exercises in occupational therapy, speech and language therapy, vision therapy, and auditory integration therapy, among others.

Neurobiologist and author Oliver Sacks has turned his attention toward autism often. He too has described the different sensory issues of some adults with autism. Sacks's interview with Temple Grandin, an autistic adult and well-known professor of animal science at Colorado State University, is described in his book *An Anthropologist on Mars*, whose title came from Grandin's description about what it felt like to interact with neurotypical people. During his visit with Grandin at her home, Sacks was intrigued when she showed him an odd machinelike contraption she had in the apartment. As a younger child, Grandin craved deep pressure on her body. Even though she couldn't bear the touch of her aunt's embrace around her shoulders, she was constantly seeking full-body pressure by squeezing herself in between mattresses and furniture. In her teens, during a summer vacation visit to a farm, Grandin discovered a cattle squeeze chute. Cows are herded individually into the chute, where the side panels apply gentle pressure on the sides of the animal to calm and relax

---

* The medical academy is considering officially recognizing several sensory-based disorders, including sensory integration dysfunction, for entry in the *Diagnostic and Statistical Manual of Mental Disorders* 5th ed., *(DSM-V)*, due for publication in 2013.

the cows for veterinary work like vaccinations and branding. True to her autistic character, Temple climbed into the cattle squeeze chute herself to see if it would satisfy her quest for deep pressure. Sure enough, it did. In her autobiography, *Labeled Autistic,* she writes, "The effect was both stimulating and relaxing at the same time. But most importantly for an autistic person, I was in control—unlike being swallowed by an overaffectionate relative. . . . The squeeze chute provided relief from my nerve attacks."[9] For the rest of that year, Grandin set about designing her own customized human version of the squeeze chute that, now manufactured and available for purchase, she calls the squeeze or hug machine. She uses her personal machine at home daily to give herself deep-pressured, full-body hugs. This helps to desensitize her nervous system.

We can use sensory integration dysfunction to help deconstruct the myth of lack of affection. Some people with autism have described how a stroke of friendly affection on their arm feels like a painful scratch. Others report that they simply don't get much physical feeling from hugs. But don't conclude that this means they don't want you to be affectionate toward them. For some people with autism, their sensory nervous system registers and interprets stimulation of the senses in unique ways, ways that interrupt and inhibit the typical "dialogue of affection" between parent and child, for example. It's a fascinating idea to explore.

One of my Canadian colleagues, Paula Aquilla, is an insightful occupational therapist who specializes in sensory integration. She outlines some creative and fun therapeutic activities in her coauthored book *Building Bridges through Sensory Integration.* Speaking to me about her experience with autistic children and the myth of affection, Aquilla said we have to remember that "children who have autism are children first. They have the same emotional needs and the need to form relationships as any other child." In her work with families, she stresses to parents that "knowledge about how their child processes sensation can enable them to accurately interpret their child's responses and behaviours so they can provide sensations through cuddles, coos, smiles, and songs, etc., in a way that will be easier for their child to receive and interpret. They have more positive and successful relationships with their kids."

I attended one of Aquilla's seminars and found her examples revealing. She illustrated the many ways children with autism can experience social interactions differently due to sensory integration problems. A child with vestibular or balance hypersensitivity who is suddenly picked up in fun by an affectionate parent may recoil and scramble to get away, feeling out of control and disoriented. A child with hyposensitive vision may not fully perceive a loving caregiver's hand reaching out as an invitation to hold hands, so it shocks the child. Instead of taking her parent's hand, the child might pull back and turn away in defence. Still, I believe all of these children want affection and can share it in their own ways.

Differences in biochemistry, genetics, and neurology certainly must play a role. Nerves communicate different sensations to the brain via vitamins, minerals, and other basic nutrients. Some doctors propose that basic components of a healthy system may not be balanced in the autistic population, which in turn could affect the senses. A more commonplace sensory physiological experience that at least half of the world's population can relate to is the changes in feelings women may have before or during their menstrual cycle. The change in hormone levels can affect hunger, mood, and tactile sensitivity, among many other senses. The intricate shifts in biochemistry may make some women not want to be held too tightly, while others may crave more affection and touch during this time. This reaction is sensory-physiological because a change in the body's physiology affects changes in the senses. My point here is to illustrate how changes in the body's chemistry can affect social behaviour, including affection.

Besides biochemical differences, there is a long list of physical health problems that are commonly associated with autism.

In other words, children and adults with autism often suffer from chronic conditions that may be exacerbating their autistic tendencies. Seizure disorder, dyslexia, apraxia, vision problems, and eating disorders are common among the autistic population. Any one of these challenges could interfere with social development, and any one of them could cause a child to behave differently than expected and to react differently than expected to a parent's affection. As discussed earlier, there are reports of strong correlations between autism and gastrointestinal disorders. Chronic bloating, diarrhea, constipation, and acid reflux can make a child moody, frustrated, irritable, and sap her energy. When we don't feel well, we don't feel social.

A little boy with stomach cramps may not want to be picked up or tickled. This makes perfect sense and is acceptable behaviour, but the catch is that most children with autism can't tell their parents they feel ill. They don't have the language. Most often, the chronic illnesses go undetected. Without knowing the little boy has cramps, an affectionate sibling interprets her brother's rejection of tickles as rejecting affection.

> A little boy with stomach cramps may not want to be picked up or tickled.

Another common example in the field is picky eating. Many children with autism self-restrict themselves to a very limited diet. Obviously, this can lead to low nutrition levels of important vitamins, minerals, proteins, and healthy fats. Severely limited diets can lead to physiological disorders, toxin buildup, mood swings, and cognitive-behavioural implications. Any of these biological imbalances could lead to low motivation to be affectionate with others.

• *What People with Autism Themselves Have to Say*
A good way to better understand those with autism is to listen to people who actually are autistic. More than ever before, books,

magazines, online blogs and support groups are being created by youth, teens, and adults with varying degrees of autism. They talk about issues relevant to their experience of the world. They discuss the challenges they face trying to interact and fit into the "mainstream" world. Many talk about feelings and emotions.

Temple Grandin describes her ambivalence to affection in her autobiography. She explains how her nervous system didn't allow her to enjoy affection from one of her favourite aunts: "I liked her. Still, when she hugged me, I was totally engulfed and I panicked. It was like being suffocated by a mountain of marshmallows. I withdrew because her abundant affection overwhelmed my nervous system."[10] Grandin didn't reject her aunt's affection so much as the physical expression of it, the hugs themselves. With this subtle yet important shift we open up the possibility that autistic people do in fact want to receive affection but that we need to explore how to show it in ways that they want and like.

One evening I sat in an auditorium in London, Ontario, for a talk by Temple Grandin about her experience as a person with autism. She believes that her brain is wired differently, in such a way that socializing with others is challenging on many levels. Often oblivious to social norms, her communication style is direct and brutally honest. As a result, she often says things aloud that many of us only think privately to ourselves. The audience laughed at statements that sounded like jokes, but probably weren't. That evening, Temple Grandin spoke at length about meeting people and having friendships. "I don't get the big fuss," she stated matter-of-factly. "Why does everyone want lots of friends? They're a lot of work . . . and you gotta make sure not to hurt their feelings, and do all sorts of things like thank them for coming over to your house." At this point, the audience laughed even though Grandin was not joking. She continued, "And then after they come to your house for a meal or something, they're supposed to invite you to their house, and you have to say yes because otherwise you hurt their feelings, and then you have to get them something like a gift or some flowers. I think it'd just be a whole lot less fuss if we didn't have to do all that." There was something so refreshing about her authenticity and clarity on the subject of navigating friendships.

Most of us can probably relate to feeling, at some point in our lives, that relationships take a lot of work. Sharing and receiving affection is part of this complexity. It's okay to give a hug to your parents and siblings but not to the new neighbours. You should accept the affection your aunt shows you, but it wouldn't be affectionate to tell her she hugs you too hard for too long. For some people with autism, like Temple Grandin, it's the complexity and unpredictable nature of human affection and relationships they avoid. While people with autism may want to avoid confusing social norms, they don't, however, say that they don't want affection.

The advent of the internet has allowed people with Asperger's syndrome and high-functioning autistics to connect and share their ideas and experiences. There are hundreds of blogs by and for "Aspies" and "Auties" (monikers they themselves use). One writer posted her views about the myth of affection: "I am, without any doubt, affectionate," she asserted. "If I like someone, I pet them, snuggle into them, stand very close to them, sit practically in (or actually in) their lap. I find it very difficult to be near anyone I like without touching them" (www.autism-rocks.blogspot.com).

In her illuminating book *The Fabric of Autism,* the late Judith Bluestone offered important perspectives on how sensory processing differences affect many people with autism. Drawing from her own experiences as a person with autism, she supported her observations with science of the nervous system and brain function. Bluestone incorporated concepts from neuroscience and other fields to develop a therapeutic paradigm called the Holistic Approach to Neuro-Development and Learning Efficiency (HANDLE). By gently enhancing stressed sensory-motor systems, the therapy program aims to reduce a child's physical and emotional distress so that the child can pay attention to forming relationships, communicating, and learning: what some HANDLE practitioners call "neurodevelopmental readiness." The practitioners are keen, non-judgmental observers who watch for clues as to why the client is behaving the way he or she is.

During a HANDLE training course I attended, the therapists explained that hypersensitive olfaction (sense of smell) might lead to avoiding interaction with others who have strong breath or body odour, overpowering perfumes, and even hair sprays. The instructor, Valerie MacLean, director of the Phoenix Centre for Neurodevelopment in Peterborough, Ontario, also discussed a range of developmental delays and problems that can occur at birth and during the early years of growth.

At the training, MacLean shared an insightful example about tactile hypersensitivity and affection. A five-year-old mostly non-verbal boy seemed to reject affection from anyone, including his parents. He pushed away from hugs, and would fall to the floor and hide under the table. When someone approached him to give a kiss, he would hold his hand up and say, "No kisses!" When MacLean commented on the boy's unusually long hair, his parents explained he wouldn't let them cut it, and they could only trim his fingernails at night when he slept. Brushing his teeth was also a struggle. MacLean explained that his head and face were so hypersensitive that he was in a "defensive" mode, stopping any physical contact that might feel too intense or even painful. With several months of individualized HANDLE activities, MacLean helped her little student to be less "self-protective" and less defensive. He began to allow touch on his face and to accept affection from his parents. Eventually, he became very affectionate, giving hugs and kisses to his family. Without the caring therapy he received, this little boy might have continued to reject affection. Some might have concluded he wasn't affectionate. But instead, like in so many cases, he was indeed affectionate yet needed support to help manage some physical challenges he was experiencing. As I have proposed in this chapter, Judith Bluestone asked, "Why can't we simply conclude that people have different ways of relating, based on their neurophysiological and experiential make-up?"[11]

About six years ago, I worked with a wonderfully loving family in Ontario. Their son Michael was a tall three-year-old with thick curly black hair. In the beginning, his language wasn't developing and he avoided eye contact. He flapped his hands and flipped through books over and over. He had just been diagnosed with mild autism by the local expert psychiatrist at the time his parents contacted me. This same doctor tried to sell Michael's parents the myth explaining that "these kids can't distinguish between the way they love a chair and their own mother." Thankfully, they quickly decided not to buy into the ignorance.

In order to assess how to best customize the strategies I teach parents, I unobtrusively observe them while they play and interact with their child. Many of the children are hyperactive and have a low attention span so they move around a lot. To help guide them into activities and keep their attention, I see a lot of parents holding their child's hand or wrist, or pulling them into their laps. But usually the child isn't cooperating and a struggle ensues. When the child escapes he will then work even harder to avoid the adult so he isn't manipulated into another physical struggle. For Michael and his parents, they had been practising this cycle for more than a year and a half.

One of the recommendations I make to break this kind of cycle is to find ways to respect the child's autonomy, especially concerning his own body. Parents of nonverbal children often assume they can't hear or understand. But I encourage the parents to tell their children verbally when they're about to hold or grab or touch them anyway: "Hey Michael, I'm going to lift you out of the bath now." This kind of communication invites mutual communication and cooperation. It gives the child an opportunity to participate. Anticipating being lifted out of the bathtub, he may begin to raise his arms up or even stand up on his own. I've seen autistic children as young as two years old show signs of understanding by lifting their head to allow their face to be wiped clean after just a few days of parents communicating and giving verbal warning. I then suggest that the parents take a further step by paying more attention to when their child indicates, even subtly, when they want to move away from being held or touched. We discuss how to respect any nonverbal body language: Moving away means "no." Not forever, just for now. In safe settings, parents practise letting go of a child's hand who is pulling away and letting her go freely from their lap. This builds more trust and better experiences of shared affection.

Michael's mother had such a huge amount of love and affection for her son that she couldn't help but reach out to hug him and squeeze him and give him kisses all over his face, even if he resisted. Each time I watched this cat-and-mouse game, I smiled at this mother's relentless affection despite her son's rejections. She was smothering him with love and he spent much of his time trying to scramble away.

I observed some important clues that suggested Michael had his own reasons for avoiding his mother's affection. I noted that around the house, whenever there was a loud or high-pitched noise, he covered his ears. His parents told me he would run away when they turned on the vacuum cleaner or the blender in the kitchen, and he ran to his bedroom when the dishwasher was turned on. He was very likely hearing (hyper-) sensitive. With this information, I went back and observed the hug-escape cycle even more closely. I noticed each time his mother gave him a hug she would also speak all sorts of "sweet nothings" into his ears: "I love you, I love I, love you!," "You're the cutest little man in the world!," and so on. I noticed she didn't just gently kiss his cheeks either, but was planting big, loud "smooches." I guessed that Michael was trying to get away as much from the sounds too close to his ears as from the smothering hugs themselves.

Michael wasn't avoiding affection; he was perhaps avoiding the overstimulating soundtrack that went along with the affection. He wasn't lacking in giving affection either. Like each of us, though, he needed to trust he had autonomy and some control in the exchange of it. As hard as it was for his mother to somehow contain and control her effusive expressions of affection, it didn't take long, about 12 weeks, for Michael and his mother to re-establish a new relationship. Once he experienced softer and quieter hugs and learned that he could freely move away without a struggle, he wanted more and more of his mother's adoring affection.

When we recognize that some children's behaviour is due to sensory perception differences, we become more curious. We take more time to observe before we judge. We begin, like Oliver Sacks, to understand more about the unique differences and capacities of the human body and brain. Rather than working hard, often against a child's will, to make them act like the average person, we could learn how to accommodate their differences. The onus could be on us to learn and to change.

BE OPEN TO NEW POSSIBILITIES

There are literally hundreds of sociobiological factors that could interfere with the process of relating to others. And there are hundreds of sensory-physiological variables too. The assessment and diagnostic process is complex and puzzling. No one has been able to map it all out yet. The human condition is far too multifaceted. For any one social challenge that an autistic child might have, there could be many different causes.

For example, instead of the brain dysfunction that Dr. Baron-Cohen hypothesized, it could be that some individuals with autism aren't properly identifying emotions because of chronic migraine headaches. It is well documented that migraines can cause visual distortions. If you can't see clearly, how would you be able to distinguish the fine nuances between anger and frustration on someone's face? Oliver Sacks coined the term "mosaic vision" to describe the distorted images that can accompany migraines. Sacks writes that the painful vision goes through stages from pixels to mosaic to cube-like images and eventually "becomes impossible to recognize, and a peculiar form of visual agnosia is experienced."[12]

So without lumping this diverse spectrum of people into one-size-fits-all theories, how can we learn what's affecting whom?

First, we have to begin with a new paradigm that acknowledges the individual differences that exist within the autistic population. This means we would stop making broad generalizations when talking about all people with autism.

Then we would engage in many more interdisciplinary teams of researchers to cooperate on multi-dimensional answers that address the needs of the multi-dimensional people with autism.

With these steps forward, we would listen more to what the autistic community is explaining to us; the ways we are conducting research on autism would fundamentally shift.

WHAT YOU CAN DO

Recently while modelling a therapy session for a team of young therapists in Southern Ontario, I spent some time playing with a five-year-old girl who has no language and spends much of her time facing the walls, rocking from foot to foot and waving her hands as she stares vacantly into the space in front of her. At one point in the session, I offered my hands to spin her around in the air. (She loves swings.) After a few spins, I bent over to ease her down to the ground but she kept her arm over the back of my neck. Usually she would walk away, returning to the wall. This time, however, after two years of building trust and respectful physical interactions, she wanted to stay close. I kneeled down with her arm still draped over my shoulder and we stood side by side, two buddies, sharing a moment of closeness and affection.

When we adopt the belief that people with autism *can* be affectionate, we open ourselves to see the little signs of affection that are there. The following ideas can help shift the myth and increase affection.

• First Build Trust

I was leading a team meeting with three therapists to discuss the progress of a beautiful five-year-old girl diagnosed with ASD and seizure disorder. Tilly is developmentally delayed by three to four years in some areas but is beginning to show signs of wanting to learn more every day. Her antiseizure medication is helping control some potentially damaging erratic neural activity, but it also creates a foglike state that Tilly has to work through to pay attention and to focus her mind. She's truly doing her best.

Prior to my work with this family, Tilly had two years of behaviour modification programming. Her mother explained to me that Tilly had been forced to sit for hours and repetitiously perform learning tasks, such as beading and sorting shapes, on command. During the first month of the behavioural program, Tilly rejected the therapists and had had major tantrums. She eventually settled into it, but the family didn't see many gains. Even though behaviour modification has been proven to help many children move forward quickly in their development, it isn't suited for all children with autism. I believe these strategies work best at certain specific times in a child's development. Tilly showed us clearly that she wasn't ready to start such structured and controlled learning.

When the family approached me to run a program for their daughter, based on this background information, I knew it would initially have to be centred on immense fun and care-based relationships. For the first four weeks of her home-based education program, I directed the new team of therapists simply to make their two-hour sessions entirely fun. They were asked not to place any demands on the young student. Tilly was given her choice of games and activities, even if they were repetitious and simplistic. At the staff meeting two months into the program, the therapists shared enthusiastically how their new little friend greets them at the door.

She had made a 180-degree turnaround. Where Tilly had rejected her previous therapists, she now stands at the top of the stairs leading into the family apartment, eagerly anticipating the arrival of her play-friend therapists. She literally shouts "Hi!" when they open the door, then takes their hand, almost pulling them into what we call her "Fun Room." Tilly stays focused and plays in the room for up to two hours at a time. She doesn't turn away or try to exit like she had done in the past.

From this experience, the family learned the importance of building trust with Tilly first. Before we move to instruction and teaching, we use play and fun to build rapport. It was this respectful rapport that built trust and that helped Tilly to relax. Her body was literally less tense and appeared less nervous and less stressed. Tilly's affection blossomed in a stress-free environment and on her terms.

• Accept Difference

Affection flows from acceptance. It's hard to be affectionate with someone who is judging you. Respect and acceptance are the core principles of many of the most effective programs for people with autism. How can we train ourselves to see different, sometimes unusual behaviours and to not judge them as wrong?

If you enjoy hot coffee it doesn't mean that iced coffee is abnormal or inappropriate. It's just different. If you prefer physical activity, it doesn't mean that sitting and reading books is bad and wrong. They're just different activities. But most of us do in fact engage in these kinds of judgments all the time. We judge things and people and choices and behaviours that are different from our own. This is especially true if we don't understand them. We lack empathy for things we can't relate to and judge them negatively. Most people like hugs, so it's hard to relate to those who find them ticklish or painful. We judge this as not normal and develop treatment plans to help them "overcome" this "abnormal" experience of hugs. It wouldn't occur to us, though, to put together a treatment plan for all iced-coffee drinkers to stop this abnormal behaviour and to convert them over to hot-coffee drinking. How do we decide what is "normal"? How do we decide what a "normal" experience of affection is?

One practical strategy you can implement in a school or home-based program to support someone with autism is acceptance. Be more aware of the biases or judgments you have. Different does not have to mean abnormal. Practise (even more) empathy. Like affection, empathy flows from acceptance. Consider alternative explanations for behaviours you think are different. Before you move to change a behaviour, spend a few moments trying to understand it from the child's perspective. When you do these things, you will feel more affectionate and you will find that the child will be more affectionate with you too.

• Communicate Even More

Affection can't be imposed or forced out of someone. Affection is a willing communication between people. Parenting or working with a nonverbal person with autism requires even more attention to communication. When we're in survival mode and mostly focused on just getting through the day, affection from both sides can be miscommunicated and misunderstood.

One parent was pleasantly surprised after just 24 hours of communicating more to her two-year-old son diagnosed with autism. Before our consultation and training, this mother simply went about taking care of the daily routines of bathing, dressing, and feeding her son without his cooperation. With struggles and screams and sometimes complete passivity, he resisted. She didn't tell him directly what the daily agenda was. She had assumed that her nonverbal son couldn't understand language anyway.

Moving forward, I recommended that she get down to her little boy's level, face him, and talk to him in a gentle and inviting way about what she was going to do with and for him. "Talk to him as if he understands you. I'm going to brush your teeth now. Open your mouth, little buddy." She had used similar words before, but not on his level, rarely facing him, never with animated inflection, not slowly enough for him to grasp, and she hadn't ever thought to wait for his response. She hadn't considered he could understand. But within minutes of taking the time to communicate in the ways I suggested, he began to cooperate more. She was amazed. Her son started to hold his mouth open for teeth brushing and to sit still for face washing. Instead of struggling, he cooperated. The lines of communication were opened. Next, the affection between them could begin to be communicated. He started to take his mother's hand for the first time. He smiled more often. He allowed her to hold him longer in her arms.

• Get Curious—Discover Each Person's Unique Needs

I've discussed many alternate possibilities for why some people might pull away from affectionate behaviour. Now it's your turn. Become a detective and investigate any possible underlying reasons your child or a person you're helping is rejecting your affection. Learn about the unique "sensory profile" of your child, for example. Start with sincere and non-judgmental curiousity. Take some time to simply observe. Ask questions if you can, and take time to listen to the answers whether they're typed, spoken, communicated through a journal, or even shown through drawings.

As a person wanting to share your affection, take it upon yourself to learn more about an autistic person's unique perceptions, physical needs, and communication style. A hug may not work, but blowing a kiss might be welcomed and appreciated.

• Ask for What You Want

An important aspect of my work with families is parent and marriage counselling. So much of this work focuses on effective communication. Even as adults we often don't give ourselves permission to ask for what we really want from our partners. Or we wait until we're so fed up that we communicate ineffectively, with anger and judgment. The same scenario often plays out between parent and child. Rarely do parents ask directly for the affection they want from their child. They wait in anticipation, expecting and believing that "if he loved me, he'd show me."

Over a period of several months, I led a team of therapists in teaching a severely delayed 11-year-old girl diagnosed with autism to give gentle hugs. She had an extremely sensitive sense of smell. She sniffed almost every toy, object, and person she came into contact with. Every time I entered her home, when I approached her to say hello, she would lean into my cheek or neck and sniff. She would then giggle and smile. I assume she recognized me by smell and had a happy association to my scents. Her parents and the staff appreciated that this was her way of knowing people and sharing affection. At the same time, we recognized it didn't work socially for her in public and with her peers at school. While we continued to allow her to greet us with a sniff, we used her affectionate gesture to introduce hugs. While respecting her needs, we asked for what we wanted. Instead of breaking trust, lacking respect, and closing down communication by pushing her away, we drew her closer and asked for what we wanted. We were patient. Now, she sniffs much less and hugs us much more.

• Write and Share Stories of Affection and Autism

Too often stories, documentaries, and the media focus on the unusual and stereotypical behaviours of people on the autism spectrum. Head banging, aggression, and kids rocking alone in the corner make for a dramatic story. We can begin to create a new, more humane narrative of autism by sharing our examples of affection. Tell your family members about a little moment when you shared affection with your child. Talk to your class about how affectionate your autistic student can be and how his peers can encourage this important human emotion in socially appropriate ways. Write a short story about how you discovered a unique way to share affection with a neighbour or niece with autism.

If enough people engage in this kind of dialogue, a critical mass for change will be reached and the narrative concerning the myth of affection will be rewritten. Researchers, doctors, therapists, and popular media will follow. By engaging in this dialogue, people with autism might teach us all many new possibilities of what it means to be affectionate.

CHAPTER TWO

THE MYTH OF RITUALS

"Repetitious Behaviours (Stims) Are Bad and Should Be Stopped"

*Day by day we grew more relentlessly demanding of her. No gazing into space,
no teeth grinding, no playing with her hands, no manneristic touching of surfaces,
no anything that looked autistic.*
Catherine Maurice, *Let Me Hear Your Voice*

*The child with autism requires adult intrusion in their play/activities in order to
have experiences which promote learning. Moreover, there is no benefit to a child who
engages in non-productive behaviors (e.g., stereotypical, repetitive play).*
**"General Behavioural/Educational Suggestions for Autistic Children,"
Autism Treatment Services of Canada, www.autism.ca**

Cole flicks his fingers rapidly with precision at the corners of his eyes. It looks like he's playing the piano in his peripheral view. Sometimes his hands and arms also begin to flap in a very specific pattern. He does it over and over throughout the day. People passing by might think that he was having a seizure or that he was really excited. But there is another reason. Cole has autism spectrum disorder (ASD). Psychologists and specialists don't know why Cole flaps his hands. They explained to his parents that it's a maladaptive stereotypical behaviour and a symptom of his autism. They call it maladaptive because it interferes with his ability to pay attention at school and socialize. They directed his parents to stop him from flicking his fingers. Since most people who see Cole don't have an explanation for why he acts like this, they assume he is misbehaving and wonder why his parents don't just stop him.

According to the American Psychological Association, for a child to get a diagnosis of autism, one of the criteria is the presence of restricted repetitive and stereotyped patterns of behaviour, interests, and activities. Hand-flapping, continuous humming, body-rocking, toe-walking, lining up or spinning objects, repeating scripts, echolalia, twirling hair and bits of string, circuiting rooms or pacing, jumping, grinding teeth, and staring at objects are just some examples.

In the field these behaviours are variously called self-stimulations, stims, stereotyped behaviour, stereotypes, isms, rituals, obsessions, fixations, perseverations, and compulsions. The diversity of these labels echoes the range of behaviours. Even though each behaviour is unique and different from the others, they've all been lumped together as maladaptive, meaningless, purposeless, aberrant, and inappropriate.

Similar to obsessive compulsive disorder (OCD), repetitious behaviour appears like a need for routine and a resistance to changes in that routine. Some children with autism often resist any obstruction or interruption of their rituals. For example, a person with ASD might get visibly upset if she can't take the exact same route to school every day. If road construction reroutes traffic, she could have a tantrum and meltdown. One parent told me about her daughter's fixed ritual of wearing mittens outside no matter the weather. Even in the heat of summer her little girl refused to go outside without her mittens and experienced a lot of anxiety if she couldn't find them. For others with ASD, self-care (insisting on always using the exact same bath towel, for example) and play routines (putting the same toy blocks in the same order every time) have to be maintained or the child may feel stress and panic. Some have peculiar habits like holding on to a certain object from dawn till dusk. I knew one young boy who always held on to a specific DVD cover during breakfast, at school, while watching TV, and in bed as he fell asleep. Once when he lost it, his parents had to purchase a second copy to reduce his anxiety and help him get through the day. Others seek out sensory stimulation like opening and closing cupboards, rubbing their fingertips over and over hundreds of times on a carpet, or smelling anything they can. One girl I worked with would greet people by leaning in and quickly smelling their hair.*

---

* Sometimes people with autism also engage in repetitive self-injurious behaviour (SIB) such as banging their heads on the floor or poking their eyes. SIBs can be dangerous and even life-threatening in cases where a child bangs his head to the point of internal

Of all the symptoms of autism, repetitious behaviours are perhaps the most socially awkward and isolating. Most of us are uncomfortable with these unusual routines and rituals. No one really knows why they happen. Some researchers think they are a way for autistic people to manage sensory chaos, by sticking to certain routines and finding comfort in order. We're not sure how to respond or how to help. These behaviours make it seem as if people with ASD aren't in control of themselves. Parents are understandably concerned about how their children will be perceived. They want to help their children fit in, but these behaviours make them stand out.

There is a lot of mystery and uncertainty around this aspect of autism. What is certain, however, is that when we judge a behaviour as bad, our next move is to try to stop it. Most training programs for parents of children with autism have strategies on how to eliminate repetitive behaviour. This reinforces the myth that these behaviours are inherently bad. As a result, most doctors, therapists, and parents work hard to rid children of them.

Many years ago, I was asked by a family to come to their home, observe their child, and offer some advice on what they could do next to help support their son's development. Daniel was eight years old and had been home-schooled in an Intensive Behavioural Intervention program for over four years. He had learned a lot and was especially good at math. By the time I met Daniel, he was fully mainstreamed at school and had tutoring at home afterwards every day. He had some language but was still not very social and was having a hard time making friends with his peers. Daniel's parents were ardent believers in the behavioural treatment but their son

---

hemorrhaging and brain damage. SIBs are almost always repetitive and are therefore often included in research, textbooks and assessments as stereotyped repetitive behaviour. Self-injurious behaviours are extremely challenging for parents and caregivers to manage. They are important to address and can raise ethical questions. However, for the purpose of this chapter I focus on the non-self-injurious repetitive behaviours more commonly referred to in the diagnosis.

still wasn't fitting in socially at school. They had heard good things about my multi-treatment approach that emphasizes socialization and were curious to see what I might suggest.

When I arrived that afternoon, Daniel's mother ushered me downstairs to the basement where they had set up a study room for his tutoring. I stood awhile watching the math lesson. It was highly structured, highly controlled, and conditional on rewards. Daniel loved animals and was allowed to watch a few minutes of a video about animals as a reward. "Okay Daniel, good job. Go take a break. You have three minutes," the therapist praised. Daniel had finished his math exercise. He leapt up from the table and bolted out, whizzed passed me, and jumped into a large overstuffed reclining armchair in the adjoining room. He leaned forward a bit then slammed his body back into the soft chair. He paused, leaned forward again, and turned on a TV that had been set up about two feet in front of the chair. An animal documentary played and Daniel rocked with even more intensity and delight. He rocked forward and back, over and over. When the three minutes were over, Daniel was called back for more tutoring. Five minutes later he earned another break and returned to his favourite chair and animal video. This time I decided to join in. I wanted to see what rocking so close in front of the TV felt like. I wanted to learn more about Daniel's behaviour. Maybe I would discover a new perspective to help his family understand him better. I pulled up a chair, faced the TV, and rocked at the same pace as my little mentor. I really got into it. Stopping at one point, he quickly glanced over at me, grinned, and rocked again, letting out a little shriek of delight. This was the first time, his mother would tell me, that anyone had joined in his rocking. But she didn't share Daniel's delight.

Upstairs, I sat at the kitchen table with his mother to talk about my observations and recommendations. She was clearly annoyed. "What were you doing? Why did you do that with him?" she asked me sharply. I started to answer but she cut me off. She wanted to make her position clear—that his rocking behaviour was *not okay.* They had worked hard for many years to rid him of it. She had banned it and other repetitive behaviours from anywhere but the basement chair and as a reward only. If he started to rock at meal-times, for example, he was sent to his room. "I've told him I don't want to see it. He knows he's not allowed to do it in front of me," she explained. She believed by rocking with him I was reinforcing the behaviour. I encouraged him to do it more, she scolded. With my main goal to support parents and respect their choices for their families, we agreed to respectfully disagree. I shared a few ideas to help with social skills and wasn't invited back.

About six months later I was using the washroom at a bookstore in the same city. Someone walked in while I was in a stall so I could only see his feet. The person talked to himself under his breath and I was startled when he started to pace back and forth across the room. Next, I could see his feet skip and hop. He was literally bouncing around the bathroom. I exited the stall to see Daniel. I don't think he recognized me; he was happily absorbed in his dance. Daniel's mother was waiting outside the washroom for him. I wondered if she knew he was in there doing his ritualized behaviour. She had tried time outs and saying "No." She had banished the rocking and pacing from her sight. But Daniel had figured out how to be left alone . . . by asking to use the toilet. Sadly, public washrooms had become his refuge.

The myth about repetitive rituals begins with the way in which we interpret and judge them. We don't have a clear understanding of why people with autism engage in these behaviours or why they're repeated. For each behaviour there are hundreds of possible under-lying causes, pathologies, and motivations to consider. Is there a bio-logical cause? Could a ritual be the result of an individual's thinking process or sensory needs? Do some serve specific adaptive functions? Could stereotyped behaviour be used in some way as a bridge to more communication instead of a block in the way?

Before we banish all unusual behaviour as maladaptive and purposeless, we could start first to gain more insights into this poorly understood aspect of autism.

WHY DO WE JUDGE AND FEAR AUTISTIC BEHAVIOURS SO MUCH?

First, it's human nature to categorize right from wrong and good from bad. Medicine and psychology are based on identifying "abnormal" with the aim to fix it to "normal." The success of this approach relies entirely on where we draw the line between normal and not. Do autistic repetitive behaviours need to be "fixed"?

In her autobiography, *Nobody Nowhere,* Donna Williams explains how she rubbed her eyes over and over. It was a repetitious behaviour she describes as another beautiful world. "I discovered the air was full of spots," she explains. Williams was just three years old when she discovered that by facing the sunlight and rubbing her eyes she could see sparks of light and floating colours. Looking closely at the sunbeams, she could see the tiny microparticles of floating dust. Pressure on the eyes is translated by the optic nerve into "seeing" spots and patterns called phosphenes. Not yet diagnosed with autism, she had already discovered a variety of ways to shut her family and others out from her attention.

But her parents couldn't see through her eyes. Who could? To them her behaviour was meaningless. She just looked closed off, staring into thin air. They thought she was ignoring them and tried punishment to snap her back to attention. She was slapped. She writes, "There they were. The bright fluffy colors moving through the white. 'Stop that!' came the intrusive gabble. I'd continue rubbing merrily. *Slap.*"[1]

Donna's parents were reacting with the same fear that most parents feel when they see their child shut down and slip into stereotyped repetitious behaviours. It's natural to fear behaviours we don't under-stand. But the more her parents tried to force her away from staring, the more she focused on the spots to shut them out. The coloured spots were more comforting than the world of adults and communi-cation that she couldn't make sense of. For her, the staring behaviour was meaningful.

What is normal behaviour, anyway? Depending on your culture, the country you live in, your age, gender, and hundreds of other factors, normal has an extremely broad range of meaning across our planet. The Sufi dervishes of the Mevlevi order in Turkey can be seen spinning round and round for up to an hour or more, whirling into ecstasy. Known as the whirling dervishes, they are a group of Mus-lims who have practised this amazing traditional dance as part of a formal ceremony known as the Sema. For them, whirling until you are beyond dizzy is normal. I've worked with several autistic children who also love to spin non-stop.

In another part of the world, Don Lerman of New York State set a record for eating seven quarter-pound sticks of butter in five min-utes and another for eating six pounds of baked beans in one minute, forty-eight seconds. For a member of the International Federation of Competitive Eating, this kind of gorging is normal. I've worked with many autistic children who constantly want to eat and have unusual cravings like lemons and salt.

Standing in a circle, the leader in a group of adults starts to laugh. Another person chuckles, which makes a third laugh harder too. Soon, the whole group is laughing out loud for no reason at all but to laugh. The Association for Applied and Therapeutic Humor (AATH) was founded in 1987 by a registered nurse named Alison Crane. Members of her organization get together on a regular basis and start to laugh together for no reason other than laughter itself and the belief that it's healthy. I've worked with several children and adults with autism who also love to laugh for apparently no reason.

In her book *Concepts of Normality,* Wendy Lawson, an author diagnosed with Asperger's, offers us many insights and important views about how society draws the line between where normal ends and autism begins. When she saw for the first time a group of deaf youth signing to each other, Lawson was forced to rethink her own judgment that talking was normal and not talking wasn't: "I felt uncomfortable because I couldn't relate to them. However, they were very much at home with one another and signing was very normal for them!"[2] Maybe little Cole's finger-flapping and eight-year-old Daniel's body-rocking feel normal to them. But we won't likely find out because we've already decided it's not and then work hard to stop it.

There is a wide range of opinions on "normality" and autism. At one extreme is a movement led mostly by people with autism themselves who believe repetitive and self-stimulating behaviours are simply different (not wrong) ways of behaving. People with autism, they explain about themselves, have different sensory experiences and need to move in different, admittedly unusual, ways. This group advocates that society should accommodate these differences and not try to change them.

Of the opposite view is a larger movement led mostly by parents of children with autism, therapists, and academics who believe stereotyped behaviour is purposeless and gets in the way of normal functioning. They advocate strategies to reduce or eliminate any unusual behaviour. (I'm not partial to one side or the other. There's a range of ideas in between and I see some merit in many of them.) So far, throughout the entire history of autism, the anti-stims majority has won favour with most treatment methods, but there are a few exceptions.

Whether you're for them or against them, those of us who aren't autistic don't honestly know that much about the nature of the behaviours. We've been investigating autism since Kanner first wrote about it in the 1940s, but we still can't explain repetitious rituals.

I believe two main theories have contributed to our lack of understanding: Wing's Triad and Lovaas's treatment.

WHY DON'T WE UNDERSTAND MORE ABOUT AUTISTIC STEREOTYPES?

When Austrian-born psychiatrist Leo Kanner wrote about a small group of children in a 1943 paper that would introduce autism to the world, he described some clear examples of ritualized behaviour. One of his young patients lined up wooden toy blocks in exactly the same pattern every time "with the same color of each block turned up, with each picture or letter . . . facing in the same direction as before."[3] All of his patients had "monotonously repetitious" behaviours that he said were "governed by an *anxiously obsessive desire for the maintenance of sameness* that nobody but the child himself may disrupt."[4] Through 60 years of disputes and debates about the nature of autism, the diagnosis has broadened into a spectrum but the restricted rituals and the "maintenance of sameness" are still characteristics of the official definitions. Kanner's original description of repetitious behaviours remains almost unchanged.

In the late 1970s Dr. Lorna Wing and colleague Judith Gould took a turn, like many others had, at redefining autism. Dr. Wing's contributions to the field of autism have been pivotal. She helped pioneer the concept of autism as a spectrum disorder, for example. Wing and Gould wanted to better define autism so that children in England who needed help could be identified. They compared all of the different symptoms from the leading definitions of autism (there were more than one floating around at the time) and studied a large group of children with special needs to figure out what the central deficits of autism were. They settled on three aspects of autistic behaviour they called the Triad of Impairments, which form the basis of our modern notion of autism today. They concluded that people with autism have challenges in 1) socialization, 2) communication, and 3) imagination.* This is the "triad."

But what about repetitious behaviours? Didn't everyone as far back as Leo Kanner agree that they were at the core of autism? Instead of including them in the triad, Wing and Gould proposed that they should be seen as *symptoms* of the other impairments. In other words, children with autism may sit and rock because of their developmental delays. They linked repetitious behaviours to the children's problems with imagination in particular. Without the capacity to imagine, the kids get stuck doing the same thing over and over, Wing explained.

So how did this now broadly accepted theory inhibit our learning about stims? The introduction of the Triad of Impairments in 1979 prompted academics and researchers to develop theories, like Simon Baron-Cohen's Theory of Mind, to help explain the triad. Since repetitious behaviours aren't specifically part of the triad, they haven't been researched as much—the way Wing and Gould framed the definition of autism seemed to push repetitious behaviours out of the core into a second tier of symptoms.

In early 2008, the American Psychiatric Association held a conference to discuss the diagnosis of autism and related disorders. In his address to the panel, Dr. Edwin Cook Jr. of the University of Illinois in Chicago raised similar concerns about how defocused stims have become in autism research. Since stims are now explained as symptoms of other core problems, not much research goes into looking for other possible causes. When we conclude that a child rocks back and forth because he has social, communication, and/ or imagination impairments then we miss out on investigating other possibilities.

---

* I believe Wing's Triad also led to the myth that children with autism don't have imagination, which I discuss in Chapter 7. Wing and Gould have since made it clearer that they meant *social* imagination and have acknowledged that people with autism can "invent their own imaginary world." Nonetheless, the myth lives on in full force.

The second major theory I believe that has contributed to a lack of understanding of stims is Dr. Ivar Lovaas's successful worldwide promotion of applied behaviour analysis (ABA). Lovaas taught that children with autism have an understimulated nervous system and are constantly seeking sensory stimulation. This is why he called them stimulating behaviours or "stims." He trained therapists to systematically stop any that looked "bizarre" and replace them with a toy the child could use for more socially appropriate stimulation. But in concluding that the purpose of all repetitive behaviour is stimulatory, Lovaas and his students have missed considering other physiological sources like genetics, nutrition, and biochemistry.

Additionally, Lovaas's ABA therapy relies on a student's compliance to follow instructions in the lesson. When repetitive behaviours get in the way of the teacher's agenda and the student's learning, they are judged as distracting and the student is pressured to stop them. In this sense, ABA promotes the myth that repetitive behaviours are bad. In his how-to manual, *The ME Book*, Lovaas describes why self-stimulating behaviours are not good and how to stop them:

> *Self-stimulation is like drugs: both are difficult to compete with. What we have to do, then, and what we recommend, is that the teacher actively suppress the child's self-stimulating behavior. . . . This means that if the child self-stimulates when the teacher is talking to him (when she wants him to pay attention to her), she may physically restrain him, or she may give him a loud "No" and perhaps some aversive [negative experience] to stop the self-stimulation.*[5]

How can we possibly learn more about
these behaviours when our focus is so fixed
on eradicating them?

How can we possibly learn more about these behaviours when our focus is so fixed on eradicating them? Behavioural therapists, like other educators and parents, are doing their best to help people with autism achieve their full potential. But when they move too quickly to block and stop a behaviour, they miss the opportunity to learn more about it.

At this point in the history of autism, with a backdrop of "normality," we now have a leading theory, the Triad of Impairments, and a leading treatment, ABA, all of which inhibit us from being more curious and learning all that we can about stereotyped behaviour.

WHAT ARE THE
NEGATIVE CONSEQUENCES OF THE MYTH?

Years ago I was asked to review a short video of a child who had severe repetitious behaviours. The senior staff at a private treatment facility were looking for suggestions on how to handle an eight-year-old student whose repetitious movements had escalated to the point where the staff decided he needed to be fully restrained. The first few minutes of the video showed a sad view of the young student harnessed into a wheelchair even though he wasn't physically disabled and could walk just fine. He was mute and had been assessed as autistic and profoundly mentally retarded. He had good motor skills yet there he was with a body harness, his legs strapped down, a helmet over his head, and with wooden splints taped along his arms. There wasn't much action in the video for me to comment on, since the boy's movements had been intentionally so restricted except for a slight swaying of his head, rhythmically from side to side. One senior staff explained that what I was seeing was the culmination of a whole series of escalating behaviours.

Initially, months before, the young student just rocked his body forward and backward at his desk. He wasn't harming himself or anyone else but they felt the repetitious rocking was disrupting his

learning in class. They implemented a no rocking rule, so his therapists started to interrupt and block him. Within a few days he began
to swing his feet under his chair. Again the teachers felt it interrupted his learning. He wouldn't stop when they asked, so they had
to restrict his legs so he could focus on the lessons. They fitted him
with a torso harness that held him in his chair so he couldn't rock
and restricted his leg swings with a beltlike strap across his shins.
Within a day he started to slap his own head. They implemented a no
slapping rule but he was too fast for them to block. The more they
said "No!" the more he slapped. He upped the ante from slaps to
punches and bruised his own face. They had no choice but to force
a helmet on him. The boy continued to whack his helmet until they
fit his arms with splints to straighten them so he couldn't bend his
fist in to his head. Finally, he was safe. Protected by a body harness,
a shin strap, a helmet, arm splints, and a wheelchair to move him
around without having to strap and unstrap him from chair to chair,
he sat relatively still.

Looking closely at the video, I could see him swaying his head
gently side to side. His eyes seemed distant. "How do we stop his
head from moving?" the therapist asked me. I countered rhetorically,
"And when his body is totally braced, what if he starts dreaming a
scene over and over and over and doesn't focus on his work, how
will you stop his dreaming?"

There was an uncomfortable silence for a moment while we confronted the truth: there's only so far we can go to control behaviour.
In a sense, the student was being forced to retreat to the only part of
himself no one else could control: his own thoughts.

This is an extreme example of restraint. Yet, sadly, it's not
uncommon. It is but one of many negative reactions to the belief
that stereotyped behaviour has to be stopped. In some cases, we
get the opposite of the result we aimed for. We trigger a person
to shut down socially even more than they were before. When we
move against someone, there's also always a risk of physical harm.

I couldn't tell from the video if this particular boy was hurt and I'm certain his teachers took every care they could. I can't imagine that sitting in a wheelchair for most of the day without being able to move his legs would be good for circulation, posture, or muscle tone. In this example, the escalation of restraint resulted in a student who was literally bound and not able to participate in any kind of activities, learning, or socializing. They had controlled his behaviour in one way, but inhibited it in so many others. His need to move was restricted. His freedom was restricted. His dignity was restricted.

An even more intense example of how damaging the myth can be was recorded in an almost infamous article titled "Screams, Slaps, and Love" about University of California (UCLA) Professor Ivar Lovaas's early autism research. For the record, the nine-page *Life* magazine photo essay published in 1965 is not representative of the therapy today. In the article we see pictures of young children with autism being rewarded for good behaviour with food and hugs. We read about some of the new behaviours the students have learned through the then new intervention. Other photos are almost too intense. A therapist screams "No!" just inches from a young boy's face while in a two-photo sequence we painfully witness a raised hand and then a slap against the boy's ear. Pamela, a nine-year-old girl, is seen bending in pain as she's given a jolt of electricity from the wired floor to her bare feet for staring at her hand in an unusual way. At the time, these harsh punishments for incorrect responses and stereotyped behaviour were experimental, and they do not represent how behaviour therapists treat children today. Applied behaviour analysis (ABA) has moved away from punishment toward positive reinforcement. Lovaas therapists no longer slap or shout at students. However, I mention the 1965 magazine article here because the photos *do* illustrate specific judgments that *still exist* today beyond the ABA community. The judgment that all stereotyped behaviour is maladaptive and should be stopped has done much damage in the past and continues to do damage, although in more subtle, less physically harmful, ways today.

Today, physically stopping stims is still a common part of most behaviour modification and other treatment programs. If a student is hand-flapping, therapists will reach across a desk, put the student's arms down and say "No" or "Hands down." I've personally seen many instances where a child's hands are held down firmly to stop hand-flapping, to stop them from covering their ears or twirling their hair. One little boy tried to pull his hands away but the therapist was bigger and stronger and held on tight. I could see the pressure on the boy's hands. It looked forceful. The child's behaviour wasn't dangerous or destructive or disturbing others. But the therapist wanted control. No teacher or parent ever intentionally harms a child or person with autism.* We want to help and the myth tells us this means stopping "socially inappropriate" behaviour, sometimes at a cost: physical restraint and pain can and do happen.

Behavioural therapies aren't alone with these ideas. Nobel Prize winner Nikolass Tinbergen wrote a book called *Autistic Children: New Hope for a Cure* and believed, like Bruno Bettelheim and holding therapy advocate Martha Welch, that autism is caused by a dysfunctional bond between mother and child. In the book, Tinbergen explains that stims are infantile behaviours that the autistic child does over and over because he is stuck in an approach-avoidance pattern. The child reaches out to touch, for example, but is apparently afraid so he pulls back. He does this over and over until a repetitive behaviour of arm-flapping develops. To help the child move past his attachment problems, Tinbergen taught parents to hold (restrain) their child, sometimes for hours at a time, to force them to confront their alleged rage until a catharsis is reached. Once docile, he believed, the child could then be reeducated and would no longer be stuck in repetitious rituals. The methods have no basis in science but continue to exist to this day.

---

* There are some sad documented cases of infanticide by parents who murdered their autistic child, claiming they couldn't handle the enormous stress.

Some theories maintain that children and adults with autism are victims of these behaviours. They aren't in control of the stims, which are attacking them like a virus. From this perspective, restraining them, it's believed, is a way to provide relief from this thing that is happening *to* them. Other strategies that have been used to stop stims include vigorous exercise, stimulating the vagus nerve, and blasting loud music. For Judith Bluestone, founder of the HANDLE program, the idea that people with autism are being victimized by their stims "leads to treatments designed to suppress symptoms, without a clear idea of what is causing the symptom in the first place, perhaps making ASD patients easier to control, but often doing violence to their humanity in the process."[6]

Another negative effect of the myth is emotional hurt. We can feel rejected when we are judged by our body movements. I often wonder how Daniel, who ended up sneaking his stims in a public bathroom, felt about his parents completely rejecting and banishing his behaviours. Some would argue that because he's autistic he doesn't feel emotions. I'm not convinced of that at all. At the very least, the rejection inhibits motivation for building a secure relationship.

Ironically, when we stop stims from interrupting our teaching agendas, we risk triggering negative emotions and stress, which in turn interrupt the very relationship we are trying to improve. The student is less likely to pay attention and less likely to cooperate with a teacher who triggers behavioural and emotional defensiveness. When we move against a person we break trust, we cause stress, and we hinder communication. When teachers block or stop a student's need to move, they become the next boundary for the student to push against. They become less fun and less easy to communicate with or to learn from. How motivated would you be to talk and cooperate with someone bigger than you who blocked your movements *against your will*? Paradoxically, we sabotage communication with the student to get rid of behaviour we think is sabotaging our communication with the student.

Saying "No" and physically stopping a child from spinning objects may limit the behaviour for a short time but it doesn't work in the long run. Ask a therapist who's tried it. Ask any parent. If it was as easy to extinguish as a firm "No," Lovaas would certainly not have experimented with slaps and electric shock.

NEW PERSPECTIVES
ABOUT REPETITIOUS BEHAVIOURS

Repetitious behaviours can be the bridge to insights, to understanding, and to accepting difference. Of all the myths, this is one we can evolve and change most easily and to great effect.

A place to start is to recognize there is no one-size-fits-all theory that explains all stereotyped behaviour. Research shows that there's a broad range of different types of these particular behaviours. It no longer makes sense to lump them all into one big group called "maladaptive." We need more specific distinctions. We need to learn more about their nature and cause. One way to do this is to look at other instances where humans get stuck in repetitious rituals. From typical infant development to other common diseases, there are insights to be gained.

• Repetition Is Human

Jeffrey shook the ring of keys as hard as he could. Up and down. Side to side. He put them in his mouth and then dropped them onto the floor. His mother picked up her ring of keys and handed them back. The two-year-old shook them again and again with a contented smile. He dropped them again too. His mother patiently picked them up and returned them to her toddler. He was enjoying the sound of shaking the keys, feeling them in his mouth, and how fast they dropped to the floor. He did it over and over. Yet Jeffrey isn't autistic. He was just too young to know any better as he purposefully experimented. Like a little scientist, he was learning the physical properties of gravity and weight, about sound, and even social skills like how to get mom's attention.

Many of the repetitious behaviours we see in the autistic population can be found in typical children's play. Children will flap their hands in excitement up to about two years of age, while an autistic adult might do this his entire life. Yet, with autism, we say he hand-flaps for no reason. Neurotypical toddlers mouth objects, line up toy blocks, and often stare off at nothing in front of them. Developmental psychologists explain that repeating behaviours has a purpose in growth and learning. The brain seems hard-wired to practise certain motor movements to help to mature our sensory systems and to perfect complex behaviours like language and walking. Obviously, it's different in autism. Repetitious rituals and fixed behaviour patterns can last for hours at a time and might not change for years. In some cases they stay fixed, unchanged, over a lifetime. I'm not suggesting autistic stims are just part of normal development; I am suggesting they might still be purposeful.

Another reason we repeat things is simply because we like them and want more of them. They make us feel good. A child can ask to be tossed in the air over and over for as long as her uncle has the energy to do it. I often visit a good friend of mine whose son asks me to chase him to be tickled. Almost before I've stepped into their house, the bright-eyed youngster wants the exact same game without fail, and has for more than six months now. Yet he's not autistic. He just knows what he likes. As adults, we continue to return to what we like so consistently that we order the same meal at our favourite restaurant again and again for years and feel disappointed when it's suddenly not available on the menu.

For reasons we don't understand, people with autism repeat behaviours over and over in unusual contexts and with seeming disregard for others. Although they might appear anti-social, these behaviours may still be meaningful to that person. When we remind ourselves that the behaviours we see within autism are human behaviours, ones that we all have done at some point in our lives, we become more compassionate and perhaps more patient.

• Repetition beyond Autism

Dotty sat up in her bed at home when the nurse arrived. The 72-year-old woman was once a national athlete and Olympian. "I want to go home. Can I go home now? It's time to go home," Dotty repeated. Over and over, hundreds of times every day, she asked the same question. But Dotty was already home. "You *are* home, Dotty," her nurses would answer, and then she would ask again. Dotty suffers from Alzheimer's. The cause of the degenerative disease is still unknown. A common symptom is repetitive behaviour. Like Dotty, many people with autism repeat words and phrases again and again. Alzheimer's researchers are looking at genetics and nervous system degeneration. What is the connection between these two conditions?

Repetitive and restrictive behaviours (RRBs) have been studied in several other conditions such as Tourette's syndrome, mental retardation, schizophrenia, and Parkinson's disease. Unfortunately, their connection to autism hasn't been made. A few investigators like Dr. James Bodfish at the University of North Carolina are pioneering these kinds of comparative studies.

He points out that not all repetitious behaviours are equal. Lining up objects repeatedly in a row may need to be treated differently than, for example, a question that is asked repeatedly even when it's been answered. There is little consensus or even any literature on how to classify the broad range of behaviours. Is a particular RRB self-injurious or not? Is it language-based or motor-based? Is it aggressive or passive? Does it involve an object or not? *The Diagnostic and Statistical Manual of Mental Disorders* (*DSM-IV-TR*) specifies the types of RRBs found in Tourette's syndrome (an equally broad range of behaviours as in autism called tics) according to type and duration so that more specific diagnosis and treatment recommendations can be made. In contrast, all RRBs in autism are lumped together into one catch-all category. No wonder misinformation like the myth continues.

• What's in a Name?

"Hand flapping may be described as stereotypic, self-stimulatory, ritualistic, perseverative, gesturing, or posturing by different clinicians," notes Bodfish.[7] The problem is that each of these labels has a slightly different meaning (or what doctors call etiology) and therefore possibly a different cause and treatment. What you call it matters.

Dr. Simon Baron-Cohen of the University of Cambridge warns that the words "obsession" and "compulsion" should be used with caution with respect to autism because these labels usually imply a psychological problem. He argues that we simply don't know enough about the psychology of people with autism except that they likely think and feel emotions differently.

"Self-stimulatory" or "stim" implies that a person flaps their hands to stimulate themselves. This may be true for some, but not for all.

Some might flap their hands to shake out a pain, like when you pinch your finger or hit your thumb with a hammer, and you shake it in the air almost reflexively.

In this case you are trying to *de*stimulate your finger, not stimulate it more. Some children with autism frequently and repetitiously cover their ears with their hands. This is often called a stim. But it's possible they are covering their ears to decrease auditory stimulation. A student may be trying to shut out distracting noises so he can concentrate better, for example. If we pull his hands down we might actually contribute to him being more distracted. For behaviours like this, the "stim" label may be misleading. A more accurate, although awkward, term might be "destim." This would lead us to offer him a set of noise-reducing headphones or to redesign the classroom to have less echo or less sudden sounds. We would "destimulate" the learning environment so that he doesn't have to "destim" himself.

As a solution to the labelling issue when it comes to the myth of repetitious behaviours, more and more, researchers in the field are using the term repetitive and restricted behaviours, or RRBs. This term is purely descriptive and not interpretive. In other words, we can describe the behaviours as repetitive without interpreting (guessing) their function (stimulating versus destimulating, for example). However, this doesn't address the need for more research on different kinds of RRBs.

To date, several different classification systems have been proposed but none of them are used widely yet. James Bodfish and his colleagues developed the Repetitive Behaviour Scale to try to understand more about the motivation and function (arousal, escape, attention, sensorial, stress reduction) of various behaviours. Bodfish hopes the scale will help to answer three important questions: Should we be treating repetitive behaviours? When? And how?

We should also keep in mind the possibility of "no treatment." In some cases there may be no treatment required. If an RRB is not harmful or disruptive, on what grounds do we presume to treat it? Could we not just accept the difference and make accommodations?

A good example of how classifying RRBs more accurately could change how we treat people with autism comes from Simon Baron-Cohen and Sally Wheelwright's Cambridge University Obsessions Questionnaire. Recording the content of RRBs into six categories, they found that many kids focused their RRBs on the mechanics of objects and how things work, such as light switches and toy car wheels. They called the kids superior "folk-physicists" and, contrary to the standard practice of therapists in the field, they suggested the intense interests in mechanics and math might indicate a talent to be nurtured rather than a symptom to be fixed.

Not surprisingly, however, the very people
we are trying to understand better seem
to be left out of the discussion.

Not surprisingly, however, the very people we are trying to understand better seem to be left out of the discussion. Data is collected by either surveying parents of children with autism or by researchers observing. Self-reported insights and information about their own RRBs from people who actually have autism could expand our current limited understanding, but this seems to be a blind spot in the research so far.

MOVING BEYOND TRYING TO STOP RRBS

David was transfixed. He stood still and the room was silent except for the faint licking sound he made. He stood a few feet away facing me but wouldn't let me come near. He avoided physical touch and closeness for the most part. He appeared aloof to his family and therapists except for the special rapport he shared with his mother, Rachel. David was nine years old and diagnosed with severe autism. He lacked social skills and had no language with the exception of one particular word, "chips," which he used ubiquitously to mean everything from "food" to "go away" to "yes" and "no." "Chips!" I noted he had fairly slouched shoulders and held his jaw slightly too forward. His fix was intense. Although he wouldn't look in my eyes, he followed my every step and didn't turn his back on me for even a second. Yet, we remained completely disconnected.

For much of the day, David was fully engaged in his unique repetitious behaviour. He held his hand to his mouth, almost touching his lips, and alternated between licking and blowing on just the tips of his fingers. David spent hundreds of hours doing this, over and over, with the tip of his tongue darting in and out so quickly you had to look for it to see it. He moved his hand across his lips from right to left and back again, as if he was playing a harmonica, licking and blowing on each individual fingertip. By any measure, it looked obsessive and compulsive, like he had no choice but to do it.

David's family chose training at the Son-Rise Program in Massachusetts because the program's fundamental positive attitude was aligned with how the family wanted to treat their son. Rachel was grateful to have found a treatment centre that not only taught them educational strategies but also supported the family through the stresses and intensity of running a home-based program. They started with a commitment to not judge his repetitious licking behaviour and learned a technique called "Joining." The training began with Rachel, her husband, and David's therapists discussing any negative feelings they had about his aloof and unusual behaviours. The goal was to not see the finger-licking and blowing as bad. They believed David was doing it for a reason.

Accepting the behaviour doesn't mean sitting back or walking away, however. Joining is a proactive strategy of doing exactly what the child does, which helps to gain more eye contact, increase joint attention, and promote imitation skills. As if they were a mirror, David's parents and therapists would copy his repetitious ritual. When he raised his fingers to his mouth, they did the same with their fingers. When he started to lick and blow on his fingertips, they did too. They did this for months and months. The therapists practised for so many hundreds of hours with David that they got in perfect sync at times, starting when he started and stopping when he stopped, as if it was choreographed. Sure enough, the Joining built social rapport. It led to increased eye contact and David allowed the therapists to stand closer to him. They established trust by giving David control to do the behaviour and to see others Join him. The family was hopeful.

One of the benefits of doing what someone else is doing is that you learn more about it. When I Joined David by licking and blowing on my own fingertips, I became aware of the cooling sensation. Through my own experience of actually doing it, the behaviour was transformed from unusual and purposeless into a sensation I could relate to.

I reflected a lot on my sessions Joining with David. "Why would a person want a cooling sensation on their fingers?" I asked myself. "If they were burned or *felt* like they were burning," I guessed. David hadn't burned himself, though. I thought back to my basic biology and neuropsychology course work. Some kinds of skin rashes and internal inflammation can feel like burning. A pinched nerve can create a numb feeling like pins and needles, or burning sensations too (doctors call this paresthesia).

I remembered David's posture, his slouched shoulders and protruding jaw. Could there be some chronic compression in his neck that was pinching the nerves to his fingers? He was, after all, nonverbal and wouldn't be able to tell us of any pain or irritation. I jotted down these guesses and shared them with the family the next day. Going through my list, they confirmed there was no sign of rash and there hadn't been any burns that they knew of. Rachel did, however, remember clearly that David's birth had been difficult, including the doctor having to literally pull him out using forceps and potentially irritating his neck.

A few weeks later, they went to a doctor of osteopathy who confirmed that David had chronic tension in his jaw (called temporomandibular joint disorder) and identified a specific area in his upper neck that was misaligned, where the nerves that extend through the shoulders down to the fingertips were compressed. We were amazed that after just a few months of osteopathic treatment, David's finger-licking and blowing decreased from seven or more hours a day to no more than ten minutes. At the end of almost a year of treatment, the repetitious behaviour had completely stopped. Today, David is 27 years old, and his mother tells me he still abstains from licking his fingertips but sometimes rubs his thumb and ring finger together very softly. He explained through typing that it's calming, and he has no problem stopping when asked.

My experience with David illustrates two main approaches to RRBs that can be used in combination: 1) "Joining," or imitation, which addressed social rapport such as eye contact and trust,[8] and 2) analyzing possible physical causes. In my own work, Joining or imitating is just one of many strategies used initially to build more rapport with an autistic student and to learn about the nature of his or her repetitious behaviours. However, Joining on its own won't help a child learn to talk or read or write, or emerge miraculously from his "autistic shell."

In David's case, we all agreed that his obsessive-compulsive-like behaviour was stopping him from living his life fully. He wasn't able to even try to learn to speak because his hands and mouth were locked in the ritual. His family had seen that attempts to physically restrain David or stop the behaviour made him turn away and pay even less attention in a battle of wills for control. Joining was the perfect approach to de-stress the situation, build trust, and learn more about the unusual behaviour. Joining alone didn't resolve the underlying cause but it did lead us to a verifiable physiological solution.

• Joining and Accepting People with Autism

Although not widely accepted in the field as a mainstream technique, imitating is used with great success in several treatment programs such as the Intensive Interaction program in England, the Adam Shelton Center in France, the Floortime program, and Reciprocal Imitation Therapy (RIT). These programs developed independently from one another with their own imitating technique and theories of why it works.

In his chapter on self-stimulation in *Engaging Autism*, the late Dr. Stanley Greenspan, a medical professor at George Washington University and founder of the Floortime program, wrote that "one of the first things you can try is to imitate what the child is doing"[9] and "join in the child's activity to create a relationship."[10]

Howard Buten began to experiment with imitation strategies in 1974. In his book *Through the Glass Wall*, he describes his discovery that "by imitating an autistic person thoroughly, in detail and for long periods of time, we could obtain first hand, *visceral* knowledge of the state in which that autistic person finds himself or herself."[11] Buten founded the Adam Shelton Center in France where he uses imitating as the primary strategy to demonstrate empathy and create rapport, or what he calls a therapeutic alliance with the student.

Based in England, Intensive Interaction is founded on the work of the late Geraint Ephraim, who introduced his approach, including imitating, in 1982. Now practised at Harperbury Hospital School in Herfordshire, they've found that with a "sensitive person" as therapist, imitating leads to more eye contact and promotes "enjoyable and relaxed interaction."

The Joining technique used with David, which led to critical insights of an underlying cause, is described in detail by Barry Neil Kaufman in his 1976 book *Son-Rise*. He also stresses that the effectiveness of the Joining technique hinges on therapists' nonjudgmental attitude toward the repetitious behaviours. Personally, I first learned about this approach to repetitious behaviours during my formative training in the Son-Rise Program at the Autism Treatment Center of America. The founders' innovative merging of an imitation-type technique with the positive attitude of acceptance of the RRBs is, in my opinion, the most effective of the imitation techniques.

Like Buten, Kaufman, and Ephraim, I too have experienced how critical a positive relationship between teacher and student is when addressing repetitious behaviours.

An empathic, sensitive, non-judgmental attitude creates rapport that acts like a primer.

An empathic, sensitive, non-judgmental attitude creates rapport that acts like a primer, a catalyst, and an accelerator, for all other strategies to be most effective. Buten says it best in his book:

"Though I would never go as far as to say that once these relation-ships are established anything is possible, I say that without them very little will be."[12]

Imitation techniques have doubters, although this too is chang-ing. The strongest proponents of ABA continue, for some reason, to be the strongest promoters of the "repetitious behaviours are bad and should be stopped" myth, and the strongest arguers that "imi-tating repetitious behaviours will just make kids do it more." I once stood in a hotel lobby at a conference on autism in Toronto defend-ing the Joining technique. Two ABA therapists were irate that I had just talked about imitating in my presentation to parents. "You're going to hurt those kids and make them do it more," one therapist snapped. I listened to their opinions that imitating encourages and reinforces the behaviours. "How do you know?" I asked. "Have you ever tried it with your students?" "No, of course not. We'd never do that," they answered. "Have you ever seen any research that shows imitating makes kids do their rituals more?" I continued. "No," they answered, more quietly.

A vocal ABA proponent, Dr. Laura Schreibman of the Univer-sity of California, confidently denied any benefit from the Son-Rise Program imitating technique. During a lecture in which she listed it under "bogus treatments" she wondered rhetorically if it works, and answered: "No! Doesn't work! Not one shred of evidence to suggest that it works." Interestingly, Schreibman had published a study a year earlier with Dr. Brooke Ingersoll that showed the positive benefits of imitating (what they called contingent imita-tion). Children who were imitated by an adult showed more social responsiveness, more joint attention, and even more attempts at language.

As behaviour therapy shifts toward a more positive approach, and with good research to convince them, some behaviour therapists are slowly incorporating development-based strategies like imitat-ing. Dr. Brooke Ingersoll is an autism researcher at Michigan State

University and also a Board Certified Behavior Analyst (BCBA, the top level for applied behaviour analysis in autism treatment). She too has met with some resistance from her fellow behaviourists. However, she confidently points to the more than 15 articles, including her own, published on its benefits, none of which have indicated a serious increase in RRBs. Drawing from research on neurotypical play and how imitation naturally develops in children, she developed Reciprocal Imitation Therapy (RIT) and promotes it as an important adjunct technique that can be added to most other therapy programs. Her research recently demonstrated that imitating can increase students' spontaneous imitating of peers and also language learning.

THE BIOLOGY OF REPETITION

In one of the photos projected onto the giant screen, a young boy lay over the armrest of a sofa. In another slide, a slightly older boy was leaning forward, pushing the edge of a table hard into his stomach. I sat in the massive lecture hall along with 700 other participants at the 2004 Defeat Autism Now! (DAN!) biomedical conference in California where Dr. Arthur Krigsman was presenting his research. Dr. Krigsman, a pediatric gastroenterologist, was showing this interesting series of photographs of children who all had the same seemingly purposeless repetitious behaviour. Each photo was taken by parents who came to the doctor concerned about the behaviour. Although none of the kids were related, they all were similarly leaning over and on a variety of furniture, draped over the ends of counters and flopped face-down over the seats of kitchen chairs. "What can we do to stop this?" the parents wondered.

Taking a biological perspective, Dr. Krigsman examined each child, with a particular focus on their guts. Over the past ten years, many of the DAN! doctors, although stirring controversy, have been researching and studying the links between gastric dysfunction and autistic symptoms. Dr. Krigsman found that all of the young patients in this particular group had similar gastrointestinal symptoms including constipation and bloating. He then hypothesized that the children might be finding ways to relieve cramps and bloating by pushing their abdomens into edges like tables, counters, and armchairs. Children who are nonverbal or can't speak clearly are not able to ask for help easily. They can't tell their parents where the pain is or when it started. Many parents have told me this is one of the hardest parts of having a young child with autism who can't talk—not knowing if their child is feeling well or not. Through various treatments, Dr. Krigsman was able to reduce or eliminate most of the gut symptoms. As a result, the unusual flopping-on-furniture behaviour also stopped. The behaviour wasn't "purposeless" at all. In fact, it served an important purpose—a bit of relief and comfort.

There is a large body of research that links repetitious behaviours to underlying biological causes. A few of the leading investigations are looking at abnormal structure of the basal ganglia in the caudate nucleus of the brain, chromosomal and genetic anomalies, head trauma, and chemical imbalances. Dr. Derrick MacFabe, director of the Kilee Patchell-Evans Autism Research Group at the University of Western Ontario, has pioneered compelling studies using propionic acid, produced by a bacteria commonly found in humans, to trigger RRBs. In the US, Dr. Eric Hollander of the Mount Sinai School of Medicine has pointed out that excess dopamine in the brain can lead to RRBs similar to those found in higher-functioning individuals with autism, such as taking apart and reassembling calculators or flashlights, or organizing and reorganizing a purse or closet. Dr. Melvin Kaplan, a behavioural optometrist and director of the Center for Visual Management in Tarrytown, New York, has studied the connection between stereotypical toe-walking behaviour and visual-vestibular problems. Dr. Mary Megson has linked hand-flapping with a genetically induced G-alpha protein deficit.

UTILIZING RRBS IN TREATMENT

Besides imitating techniques and exploring physiological causes, some educators have actually incorporated RRBs into activities and lesson plans. Dr. Mary Baker of the University of California in Santa Barbara used a creative version of bingo that she based on the ritualistic interests of children with ASD. One five-year-old boy with autism crashed toy cars over and over repetitiously, so Dr. Baker designed a car-crash bingo game to encourage more play with his sibling. Instead of calling out numbers like in traditional bingo, the kids rolled a toy car down a ramp and over a jump to land on a large card with a variety of photos of other cars on it. Then they looked to find the same photo on their individual bingo cards. The result was the boy played more socially with his sibling and there was a decrease in the ritualistic car-crashing behaviour. Baker explains that "ritualistic behaviours, typically viewed as problematic in young children with autism, may be considered intrinsically reinforcing agents for positive change and development."[13]

The idea that RRBs can be seen as signs of intelligence and ability is supported by Dr. Simon Baron-Cohen's controversial idea that autism is an extreme form of maleness, or hypermasculinization. In his book *The Essential Difference,* he suggests that certain male-oriented features like ordering of objects and systemizing could be highly purposeful and just a different way of thinking.

Clearly, it's not the repetitious behaviours themselves but restraining and stopping them that is inappropriate. The myth has now been debunked. Looking ahead, approaches combining positive behavioural, social-developmental, and biomedical strategies are most promising.

Given all of the evidence-based approaches to RRBs, it's hard to understand how the myth that these behaviours are bad and should be eliminated is still in circulation. It's hard to understand how we could still believe that RRBs are purposeless and bad behaviours without cause. There are many starting points to begin new conversations about RRBs, new conversations that will lead to more respectful treatment of people with ASD.

WHAT YOU CAN DO

• *Call Them RRBs Instead of Stims*
What's in a name? "Stims," "compulsions," "obsessions," and other labels imply certain characteristics that often aren't accurate. They're loaded labels that might misguide how we approach a behaviour. They're also limited names that don't reflect the huge range of different repetitive behaviours found in autism. The most neutral and most accurate descriptor is repetitive and restricted behaviours (RRBs).

The next step is to put more resources into classifying the huge range of behaviours that fit this label. These would focus on categories that relate to function and cause, not just description. Subtypes like sensory-motor, sensory-vocal, and object-focused can help us to design more individualized appropriate treatment strategies. One subcategory might even be "stimulatory" or "stims," but it would be limited to a well-defined group of behaviours and not a catch-all as it today. With more specific labels in place, research could start to look for specific causes linked to specific kinds of behaviour.

• *Stop Judging RRBs as Bad*
Consider that the autistic person's repetitive and repetitious behaviour has a reason and a cause. This shift in thinking will move you to *look* for the reason or cause. Look more closely, Join and imitate to experience it, and research for more information about that specific behaviour. More importantly, try to be aware of your feelings about the behaviour and the child doing it. Don't judge him. He's likely not trying to make you mad or to bother you but

is just taking care of himself the best way he knows how. When we don't judge, we don't assume or draw conclusions. We stay open to learning something new. Instead of immediately stopping the repetitious behaviour with a drug, for example, David's team stayed curious long enough to explore other possibilities of what adaptive function the finger-licking might have. Most importantly, when supporting individuals with autism, as we did in David's case, we didn't move against him but tried to learn more about his individual needs.

One particularly lively boy I once worked with from Virginia was nicknamed Mr. Snuggles. For his mother, the name represents a paradigm shift for the family, from trying to eliminate the autism, to accepting and embracing the boy's different and unique behaviours. In a letter she recently sent to me she explained, "Before our IMTI (Intensive Multi-Treatment Intervention) program, Colin avoided eye contact by sticking his head in corners of the wall or running away when we tried to talk to him. When I tried to hug and kiss or snuggle him he would, in a panic, move away, pushing and turning his head as if he didn't want to be touched. Yet a minute later he would crash his body into couch pillows, wiggle around in blankets, and slide his body across the wall while walking down the hallway. He wanted physical stimulation, just not from us. I felt rejected and judged his self-stimulation. But this didn't help and I finally decided to try a new perspective. I love my son and wanted to show him that even when he was squeezing himself into the pillows and rubbing along the walls, I was still loving him. So I did it with him. After about three months of Joining-imitating his behaviours, he changed. We saw more eye contact. He paid attention to us more and more. He stopped guarding himself from us as much. In fact, now he actually takes our hands and places them on his body where he wants scratches, rubs, or pressure. He comes to us for snuggles instead of the furniture. And so we started calling him Mr. Snuggles!"

• Try Joining First

Before you criticize someone, walk a mile in his or her shoes. Well-known and wise, this saying reminds us to gain perspective, insight, and empathy by taking on another person's view and actually doing what they do. Joining in a child's behaviour, as long as it's not harmful, gives new perspective and can create social rapport. Without taking this first step, in our rush to redirect and stop a child's behaviour, we close the door on insight—we lose the opportunity to learn about the behaviour.

Imitation is a genetically encoded process infants use to learn social skills and communication. It's a natural process. For autistic children who don't imitate spontaneously, there is good science that shows that if we imitate them there can be many benefits. In my own work, I imitate only repetitive behaviours, then use other strategies to respond to anything else. First we Join to build rapport and hopefully gain insight about any underlying biological imbalance, as well as insights into motivations, skills, and needs. If there is no obvious physical trigger, then I design activities to expand on students' restricted interests while at the same time teaching and strongly reinforcing alternate social skills. Joining is a good starting point with new students as an entry into a positive student-teacher relationship. Walk the mile.

• Consider Biological and Sensory Causes

Most children can tell us when they have a sore stomach or a headache. Since children with autism can't often communicate the help they need, they may instead try to take care of themselves by moving in ways that relieve pain or maintain balance, for example. In medicine there are many catalogued examples of repetitive behaviours and their known causes. From abnormal levels of oxytocin and propionic acid to conditions like Alzheimer's and Tourette's syndrome, science has discovered that chemical imbalances and genetic differences can result in ritualized repetitive behaviour. Less scientific, but equally compelling, are the insights about sensory differences recorded by people with autism themselves. They explain that some RRBs are used to stimulate certain senses and others are used to de-stimulate the senses. There really is so much anecdotal and scientific evidence to justify much more thorough investigations into the biological and sensory causes of repetitive behaviours.

Meanwhile, before I jump to conclusions and put a treatment plan in place, I try to take the time to observe and to consider what physiological imbalance could lead to that particular behaviour. I've seen extraordinary cases where a specific biological cause was identified—the stereotype was a symptom of ill health. The child needed some medical attention, not a behaviour modification program, to extinguish the behaviour.

• Change Your Thinking from "Maladaptive-Purposeless" to "Adaptive-Purposeful"

Start with the belief that a repetitive and restricted ritual has a purpose. Through this belief, you will notice more details in the behaviour than you would if you thought it was useless. In other words, try not to be too quick to categorize and label a behaviour. Try not to assume one RRB is like all the others.

Working with one little boy, I got a wonderful reminder to not make assumptions. It happened in the middle of a therapy session with a four-year-old diagnosed with global developmental delay. Ricky's parents had originally contacted me to help him with his autistic tendency of shutting down from communication and into his repetitive behaviours. He used to spend up to 20 minutes at a time by himself, shutting the family out, lining up his Thomas the Tank Engine trains on tracks, not looking up or responding to his mother's interjections to play. We had been working with Ricky for just four months but he had already shown us his capacity to change. Even though he didn't speak very clearly, he was motivated to communicate with his family and friends, and was enjoying the new social skills and independence he was gaining. But Ricky still had what looked like some autistic tendencies.

This particular week, Ricky was going through a period of repeatedly talking about helicopters. He wanted to draw pictures of helicopters and sometimes cut them out to tape onto the wall. He was at times so highly focused on this subject that the therapists were finding it difficult to introduce other activities. They were able to divert him but only briefly before he would return to the subject of helicopters again. I watched as one of the therapists worked diligently to gain his interest in a pretend cooking game, but just when she asked him to sit for pretend tea, he walked away talking about helicopters. His fixation on them was stifling.

When it was my turn to be with Ricky, I wanted to model to his mother and therapists how to get deeply involved in his interest in helicopters, instead of trying to redirect him. I decided to use his motivation for helicopters to respectfully and playfully expand it into a more interactive activity. After a few minutes of talking about helicopters with him and looking at the pictures he had drawn earlier, I showed him how we could stand up, hold our arms out like propellers and spin around like helicopters. He watched my demonstration with eyes wide open. I'm sure he thought he hit the jackpot with an adult who wanted to do even more helicopter stuff! We whirled around the room together and it soon turned into a chase game. He laughed. It felt that we had connected and were interacting. Next, I made some sort of helicopter sound effect that made him stop and take notice once again. Ricky was showing how focused he could be when he was interested and having fun. He was much more motivated to listen and to look at us when we took time to sincerely learn more about his interests like helicopters. Then, all of a sudden, having just been whirling around the room, Ricky stood still and quiet in front of a large floor-length mirror.

Ricky hadn't said anything to me. He just stopped running and stood looking at his mouth. He concentrated on it and didn't look at me even once as I walked over calling his name. He just looked straight ahead, peering into his mouth and moving his tongue from side to side. I assumed he had switched over from play into fixation mode again. So there we stood, side by side in front of the mirror. I opened my mouth too to imitate and figure out what he was doing. I watched closely, assuming Ricky was just visually distracted or fixated on his mouth. But then I noticed he was trying to flick the tip of his tongue on the roof of his mouth. He leaned closer in to the mirror and became even more focused. I too leaned forward and copied his movements. Then he finally glanced over at me through the mirror and saw my tongue moving too. He smiled. I used the moment to ask him, "Hey, whatcha doin'?" "Blueberry," he said. "Huh?" I looked even closer. At this point he poked his finger into his mouth and pushed it around. I asked if I could see inside his mouth. He opened wide for me and that's when I saw a very small piece of blueberry skin stuck up on the roof of his mouth. It must have been distracting him since lunchtime 30 minutes earlier. Ricky hadn't been trying to shut me out and wasn't fixed in a ritual. He was just intent on trying to dislodge the blueberry but he didn't really have the language to tell me that. The experience was a good reminder that in many cases a child's autistic-like behaviour has an underlying purpose and cause. It should be up to us to find out what that is.

In many cases, a child's autistic-like behaviour has an underlying purpose and cause. It should be up to us to find out what that is.

• Reallocate Resources from Stopping RRBs to Teaching Social Skills

Teachers and parents feel extra pressure to stop unusual behaviours in public spaces where RRBs can be disruptive to other students and people. Understandably, a lot of energy and resources are put into controlling these behaviours. But with limited time, this means less training and support of alternate social skills.

When a child is prevented from doing an RRB it stops in that moment, but the child is not likely to be any more social than before. For children with autism, stopping one behaviour doesn't necessarily trigger an alternate. So the new desired behaviour, of being more social, has to be taught. This is a two-step process. A more efficient strategy than moving against the child is to focus almost entirely on teaching the alternate pro-social behaviour as the first step, with very little focus on stopping the RRB.

It turns out that when children with autism learn a new social skill, like how to shake hands or how to play a game, the amount they interact with others goes up and the amount they engage in RRBs goes down. In other words, teaching more social skills brings about the positive side effect of decreased repetitive behaviour. So it stands to reason that perhaps we don't have to allocate so many resources—therapists, time, and money—into stopping them.

Whenever a parent asks me how they can stop their child from doing a particular behaviour, I always answer with a question: "What do you want them to do instead?" The answer is often a long pause and silence. They are certain what they *don't* want, but not clear about what they *do* want. It doesn't take long for them to make the shift from "don't" to "do," especially when parents and teachers see the positive results. Children are taught skills that work better for them, repetitious behaviours decrease as a side effect, parents feel more positive about their children's progress, and the process is less stressful for everyone.

Pick one of these strategies that you haven't considered before. Try it with an open mind. You may quickly find evidence that challenges the myth of repetitious behaviours.

CHAPTER THREE

THE MYTH OF SOCIALIZATION

"Children with Autism Should Be Pushed to Socialize as Early as Possible"

You're doing a disservice to your daughter by being
a stay-at-home mother. . . . If you really want to help your child,
you'll go back to work full-time and put her in full-time daycare.
Diagnosing psychiatrist, The George Hull Centre, Toronto

I paid a small fortune having him in a Montessori school with an educational "shadow"
for a year. . . . The idea was that he would get something out of other kids. NOT!
Mother of child diagnosed with ASD, Mexico

The grade three class was unusually quiet. Students sat in pairs, heads down, focused on math problems, except for Marnie. She was in the back of the rows, separated out just slightly on her own and monitored by an educational "shadow" assistant. She was the tallest eight-year-old and by far the strongest. She had been diagnosed with autism six months before school started and her mother had worked hard with the district to get the right placement and resources. The day I was there to observe, Marnie was restless and tried to stand up a few times but the assistant gently guided her back to her desk. I sat at the very back of the room taking notes as part of a school assessment the family had requested.

The students worked while the teacher made her rounds quietly up and down the rows of desks. Marnie's assistant was whispering, trying to guide her autistic student through the numbers. But Marnie clearly wasn't ready to learn math that morning. She tried to stand up again but was stopped. She screeched at the top of her lungs. This was her hallmark—an ear-piercing sound that irritated her parents, the other students, and anyone within range. Then, as the assistant tried to push Marnie's chair closer to the desk, she suddenly stood up again, flipping over her desk—Crash!—onto the kids in front of her. All the students' eyes were on Marnie. The assistant took Marnie's arm, pulling her out into the hallway. She didn't resist. As if rehearsed, she was reprimanded, then led back into the classroom and given ten minutes of "cool-down time" at the computer . . . one of her favourite things to do.

It was obvious to me and the teacher that Marnie's outbursts were being reinforced. She was rewarded with attention and computer games. But the school staff were lost: "What else can we do? We've tried a bunch of other ideas the regional special-education support gave us, but nothing works. The principal made it clear that her safety and the other students' safety is the number-one priority, so we feel we have to separate her out and calm her down with computer games," the assistant spoke honestly. She pushed up her sleeve to show me scratches and pinches she had endured from Marnie in the first three months of school. Her eyes filled up with tears as she explained that she was trying to do her best but felt she was failing. She clearly cared for Marnie, but she didn't have adequate training or support to deal with her student's special needs.

Before arriving at school that morning, Marnie's mother also spoke frankly to me. She wondered aloud if school was the best place for her daughter to learn. She had been told by everyone on Marnie's professional-care team—the school staff, the psychologist, and local autism services—that getting Marnie into school as early after the diagnosis as possible was the best thing she could do for her daughter's socialization. "She needs to be around her peers so she can learn how to play," her family doctor assured confidently. With so many trusted professionals pointing in the same direction, the parents had no reason to think otherwise. Marnie was enrolled in school and by the twelfth week had already been sent home five times. Her parents wondered if their nonverbal daughter with autism would ever learn to socialize and make friends at school.

Many years before I met Marnie, I had learned about autism at university in an Abnormal Psychology class. The core challenge for people with autism, the textbook explained, is socialization. They find it almost impossible to understand and learn the skills and rules of relationship. From as young as six months of age they can have difficulty with eye contact and don't respond typically to social stimulation. The text added that toddlers learn social skills by watching other toddlers, therefore kids diagnosed with autism should be placed as early as possible into groups of other kids to learn from.

Although up to that point I hadn't ever met anyone with autism, I was convinced that children with ASD who had problems playing and forming relationships with other kids needed to be around lots of other children to learn how to do this, and that school and play groups were the best places for them. This myth of socialization I had learned was challenged as soon as I left academic theory for work in the field.

Immediately after graduating, I started training as a play-therapist and was introduced to many new perspectives. During eight years at the Son-Rise Program at the Autism Treatment Center of America in Massachusetts, I witnessed first-hand how isolation of kids from larger peer groups (versus inclusion) worked well for hundreds of children to at least jump-start the learning process. The centre teaches families to set up home-based therapy programs of play with just one adult at a time. The model seriously challenged what I had learned at university. I listened to families explain how their children were withdrawn, stressed, and simply not learning well at school with so many kids around.

"Unfortunately, the answer to socialization isn't that easy," a parent once told me. "If my son could learn social skills just from being around other kids, then why are the leading treatments for autism all intensive, adult led, and one to one? If school and play groups are so good for socializing then all of the private intensive therapies out there would be out of business. There simply wouldn't be the need." I admit I was confused, like most parents, between what I had read and what I had personally witnessed and learned from parents' personal experiences. Are all of the professionals who push autistic students into social groups as early as possible, wrong? I wondered.

HOW DID THIS MYTH
GET STARTED IN THE FIRST PLACE?

Around 1923, a Swiss psychologist named Jean Piaget* spent hundreds of hours watching his own kids and recording their behaviour. He had three children and he began almost from their birth to write volumes of notes about how they played and learned from each other. Later, he published his observations, which formed the basis of modern social development theory (literally, how humans learn social skills).

Piaget discovered that children have an innate internal motivation to be social. We are genetically programmed to make social connections, to observe others, and to imitate social behaviours.

Meanwhile, enter autism, which, in 1943, Leo Kanner identified mostly as a social-skills disorder. The children he diagnosed didn't make social connections and didn't observe or imitate social behaviours. Today, the modern diagnosis of autism includes "qualitative impairment in social interaction" as the first criteria.

And so, the myth begins to take shape. Piaget said children learn social skills from other kids. Kanner said children with autism lack social skills. Therefore, we conclude, children with autism should spend lots of time around other kids.

The disability rights movement that followed added momentum to the myth. Starting in the early 1960s, there was a massive shift away from segregation in institutions and special-education class-

---

* At the time, Piaget taught at a boys' school in Paris that happened to be run by Alfred Binet (the developer of the Binet Intelligence Test, which plays an important role in the myth of mental retardation in autism).

rooms toward including people with disabilities, such as children with autism, in mainstream classrooms. Inclusion is a human right that sadly didn't get written into the Canadian Charter of Rights and Freedoms until as recently as 1981, and has had to be enforced by law.

Nevertheless, the myth of socialization gained strength: Inclusion gave students with autism access to mainstream classes where lots of neurotypical peers could model social skills. Thousands of success stories of children with many types of disabilities in mainstream classes make inclusion hard to question.

Dr. Josh Harrower, a professor of special education at California State University and Dr. Glen Dunlap, research professor at the University of South Florida, agree, as I do, that the trend of recommending school for socialization "has stemmed largely from theoretical arguments related to [Piaget's theory of] social development and legal issues related to the civil [including disability] rights movement."[1]

SO WHERE'S THE MYTH IN THESE GOOD IDEAS?

Will screamed and screamed. It was just after eight in the morning and his mother had tried all the tricks she knew to calm him down. He was inconsolable and she was exhausted. It seemed as if her son had been crying non-stop for years. "Could he be sick? What's constantly upsetting him? Is he in pain?" Natalie searched for answers and wondered all day long from the time she woke up until the time she finally fell asleep, often not until the early hours of the morning. Will was diagnosed with autism spectrum disorder at two and a half years of age. He was completely nonverbal, flapped his hands, and showed no social connection to family or other kids. It was as if he ignored the people around him.

No one had answers for Natalie about the constant crying. The diagnosing pediatrician recommended early intensive behavioural intervention (an applied behaviour analysis program in Canada) and put Will on the 18-month waiting list for the government-provided program. The doctor stressed the importance of early intervention, starting therapy as early as possible, and also the importance of putting Will into peer groups to learn social skills.

She contacted a local centre that offered half-day special-education programs for junior kindergarten–aged students and Will was placed into a small class with four other children, all with autism. The director of the centre explained that the class was designed to promote communication, socialization, and group participation. Natalie wondered how her son would be able to interact with other nonverbal children with autism when he didn't even relate to her, his own mother.

The staff in his class were qualified and caring but Will didn't make any gains in communication or socialization. Natalie sat in the room and watched her son ignore the other students as they ignored him. She saw the sincere effort the teachers made to facilitate interactions between the kids but few of the students had the attention span or motivation to participate. Natalie was anxious they were losing valuable early development time, and the staff couldn't explain to her how being in a class with other autistic students would teach her son to play. After six months of the class, she contacted me for a consultation to learn about other options. I listened to Will's parents tell a familiar story of trying a school- or centre-based socialization program without success. The pediatrician wasn't wrong to suggest peer groups, but Will wasn't ready in his development, and evidence-based peer group facilitation strategies weren't in place at the centre.

During our first consultation, I tried to help the family understand Will's learning needs, the treatment options, and why the play group wasn't working. I explained to Natalie that the evidence for teaching social skills with groups of non-verbal children with ASD is thin (although there are many centres in Ontario and in the US that use this approach).

How is a socially challenged child supposed to learn social skills from another socially challenged child? Dr. Phillip Strain of the University of Colorado has done extensive research comparing mainstream classrooms to segregated or special-education classes. He found that there is little social benefit gained in placing an autistic student with other students with autism or other disabilities. He concluded that this just resulted in "pro-social behaviour extinction, with non-trained, socially non-responsive children ignoring target [autistic] subjects."[2] Although some parents report some gains, students with autism can't provide adequate social behaviour to model from and they don't give each other enough social reinforcement either. How can a beginner piano player teach another beginner piano player? It's not uncommon, however, for autistic students to pick up "bad habits" from their autistic peers. Even Dr. Ivar Lovaas, the pioneer of behaviour therapy for autism, recognized that when his autistic students were in the presence of other autistic children, any pro-social behaviour they demonstrated usually disappeared within minutes, presumably because it was not reciprocated.

Social-skills training in groups mixed with neurotypical peers, like Pamela Wolfberg's Integrated Play Groups (IPG) model, work much better. In her book *Play and Imagination in Children with Autism*, Wolfberg underscores the importance of pairing autistic children (whom she calls "novice players") with more capable experienced play partners ("expert players"). Wolfberg explains that children learn "first in the context of social interaction with adults and more capable peers."[3] Autistic students aren't assumed to be able to socialize simply by sitting next to their peers during activities either. In the IPG model there is an important role for well-trained adult facilitators. Neither Marnie's educational assistant nor Will's teachers had had enough training to facilitate social learning. "When he's ready, the right kind of play groups with the right kind of facilitation can be excellent places for Will to learn social skills," I confirmed for Natalie, "just not yet." "What do you mean 'when he's ready'?" she wondered.

Natalie and I each sat with a cup of tea and kids' toys scattered on the floor. She hadn't slept for weeks but she was eager to learn all she could. We talked about the stages and processes of socialization. Will had been put into a social group to play, but he hadn't yet developed the first steps that most babies go through. For example, infants as early as six months of age *watch* the social life around them. From birth, babies begin to "track" their parents' eyes, their mouths, and faces. They watch people's movements, and begin to turn their heads to see adults approach and walk away. The key social-learning process at this early infant stage isn't actually playing with other kids; it's *observing* people. Children learn a huge amount of social behaviour including basics for language just from observing. A child with autism who isn't spontaneously observing her peers is not likely going to benefit from being placed in a group of her peers.

One University of California researcher who has done some work on socialization in autism is Laura Schreibman. She agrees: "We know that just placing autistic children in proximity to typical peers does not automatically lead to increases in social interaction."[4] Will was pretty good at observing the details of his fingers or the plastic wheels of his toy cars and other objects, but he wasn't tuning in to observing social behaviour. He studied objects instead of people. Until Will starts to watch others more, along with several other social-learning behaviours, he isn't likely to learn many social skills in school.

"What are social-learning behaviours?" Natalie asked. That's what I call the behaviours young children do naturally, like watching and imitating, that help them learn social behaviour from others. I talked about Jean Piaget's theory of socialization and how neurotypical children don't have to be taught to observe, to imitate, or to join in with peers. But children with ASD seem to have different motivations and different learning styles. Genetic and neurological differences, and biomedical complications may block or hinder typical social-learning mechanisms. The results of these differences are summed up by Dr. Richard Simpson, professor of special education at the University of Kansas, who wrote that "children with autism lack many of the language, learning, and social skills that a child needs to function and learn within a typical education environment."[5] Will was one of these kids.

Natalie wrote notes in a way that helped her understand why her son wasn't benefiting from the kindergarten social group at this stage in his development.

Neurotypical Social-Learning Behaviour	Will's Autistic Behaviour
✓ *Observes peers and adults:* Stares at and watches others. Makes eye contact and pays attention to social behaviour around him.	x *Observes objects:* Avoids eye contact and prefers to pay attention to objects versus people.
✓ *Imitation:* Imitates language, facial expressions, play, and other social skills.	x *Lack of imitation:* Doesn't follow peers, or imitate. Does routinized repetitive behaviours instead.
✓ *High social motivation:* Moves toward others, participates, and wants to be part of peer groups.	x *Low social motivation:* Moves away from others. Happy to play alone. Feels stress in groups.

The idea that kids learn from other kids is true and we tend to think the more, the better. This might be true for neurotypical children at certain stages of development. However, larger groups can overwhelm many students with autism. For most infants socialization begins just one to one with a parent. Most often this is true for autistic children too. The best initial social contacts happen between an autistic child and just one adult or child.

I suggested that the type of strategies we could use for her son would depend on his current level of social ability, communication, and physical needs. "First, it's paramount that you address any physical pain or discomfort Will might be having. Your notes to me said he's a picky eater and often has a bloated stomach. If he's suffering from any food allergies or indigestion, he won't be in a physical or emotional mood to enjoy much play. Think about the last time you had a stomach ache or headache. Did you feel like going out with your friends to socialize?" She hadn't connected physical well-being with socialization before but admitted that Will was definitely more social when he was feeling better and happier. Finding a doctor to investigate some of these underlying issues would be an important first step in a socialization program.

"We just have to back up a little bit from social groups and help Will with some basics, one to one. Then, when he's ready, he could go back into a social group and ultimately school to really socialize more naturally with his peers," I recommended.

Socialization was just one group of skills we wanted to teach Will. We also discussed self-help skills, fine-motor and gross-motor skills, and communication and language-based goals, among others. However, we had decided to pull Will from the all-autistic play group and focus resources in a home-based adult-led education program. The suggestion made sense to Natalie. We would draw upon evidence-based strategies, consult with other professionals, and commit to making it fun and full of love for Will. When I left that day Natalie was smiling for the first time in a long while.

Over a year of many intensive hours of play and fun, learning and practice, Will had more language, he enjoyed being with people, and his general physical health was much improved. He no longer had a bloated stomach and his constant crying was down to a typical four-year-old's level. Will was ready to start playing and learning with his peers. We arranged play dates with neighbourhood kids using Wolfberg's Integrated Play Group strategies, among others. We gave the peers some training and had a skilled adult facilitate and guide the play.

Following his unique development timeline, when Will was ready, he attended summer camps and other social groups. These natural play environments were rich sources of socialization and natural positive reinforcement for interaction and communication. Peers are great because they play and interact more naturally than adults and it's better for generalization purposes too. They provided exactly what Will's parents were told years before they would. The difference now was that Will was able to observe, listen, follow instructions, and communicate. Eventually, Will's behaviour had changed enough and he was comfortable enough with his peers that we planned for his transition into a mainstream classroom at the local school.

> Eventually, Will's behaviour had changed enough and he was comfortable enough with his peers that we planned for his transition into a mainstream classroom at the local school.

Recently, I telephoned Will's mother for an update on her son's development. I could hear kids in the background talking and laughing. Will had a friend from school over to play for a few hours before dinner. "What are they doing together?" I asked. "Well, they were outside for a while on the trampoline and then they were wrestling a bit and running around. I think they're now upstairs playing with cars and toys," Natalie answered, seeming almost carefree. It had been several years since her son's tantrums and aggression had worn her down and kept her up late. When I first met her, she almost didn't allow herself to imagine that Will would have friends at school, friends who would ask if they could come over and play. Once the pressure was off to surround him with lots of kids, he was able to begin to focus on the basics, step by step, and without stress. Will is quirky and is still learning about socializing, but we believe the careful timing of putting him in social groups made all the difference.

"I've gotta go now, Jonathan. Will and his friend are calling me to come and see something they've built." Natalie was supervising play instead of a tantrum. "Mom!" It was music to her ears and mine.

Even though Piaget observed that children learn to socialize through other children, and even though the disability rights movement provided access to classrooms of peers, neither the theory nor the movement were based on the unique challenges and needs of children with autism. Without basic learning skills in place, together these approaches add up mostly to a myth for children with ASD.

WHY DOES THE MYTH PERSIST?

Autism is still very much an enigma. New ideas for treatment are few and far between. One of the biggest challenges in treating autism is the different severities of symptoms, the range of learning challenges, and the complex multitude of likely intertwined causes. It's a spectrum disorder and "no single intervention has been shown to deal effectively with problem behaviors for all children with autism."[6]

Despite the spectrum nature of ASD, institutions like the medical and school systems have to settle on only a few treatment options. Since the practice of socializing autistic children in peer groups is deeply rooted in widely accepted notions of developmental psychology and disability rights, it satisfies the medical, educational, and government policy status quo.

Inclusion laws are in place and families expect schools to treat their autistic children with equal access. Teachers honestly try their best, but with limited resources and expertise, like any single-intervention program, they simply aren't able to deal effectively with all of the various needs of students with autism. The resources it takes for such individualization are almost impossible for systems like public schools to implement.

An in-depth study of inclusion by Richard Simpson and his colleagues showed that many mainstream classrooms don't provide the necessary modifications and supports students with autism need for success in school.[7] Many schools work hard to create accepting inclusive environments. However, is inclusion always the best policy for *all* students with autism, no matter their needs and no matter their level of functioning?

In Alberta, one lawyer has wrestled with the myth of socialization for years. Yude Henteleff has dedicated over 30 years to the disability rights movement. He is a Member of the Order of Canada and was presented with a Lifetime Achievement Award by the Learning Disabilities Association of Canada. Acting as the solicitor of the Association of Parents of Children with Autism in Manitoba, and on behalf of individual families, Mr. Henteleff has argued at legislative levels as high as the Supreme Court that not all children with ASD are ready for or can benefit from full-inclusion classrooms. In a paper he presented at the National Summit on Inclusive Education, "The Fully Inclusive Classroom Is Only One of the Right Ways to Meet the Best Interests of the Special Needs Child," he argues that for some students "total inclusion is a discriminatory concept because it limits the environmental choices, which groups of children and youth with differing difficulties have the right to make in their best interests." He supports this argument by pointing out that "there is no longitudinal, validated research available that full inclusion can provide superior services for all children with disabilities regardless of the nature of the disability. There is, indeed, much research to the contrary."[8]

Mr. Henteleff makes it absolutely clear, like I do, that he is an advocate of public education and of inclusion for children with autism. Yet, he also insightfully points out that full inclusion shouldn't be applied as a one-size-fits-all-children-with-disabilities policy. When a student with severe autism feels stressed and can't learn in a classroom or social group, then that full-inclusion placement is no longer in the best interests of that particular child. I would add that, in the same way, programs that isolate children to learn exclusively from adults should also not be promoted as the right choice for all children on the spectrum.

This chapter is not meant to argue against inclusion as an ideal, nor in favour of private, home-based programs. Rather, very specifically, to challenge the widely held idea that all children with autism can learn social skills simply by being placed in groups of kids. The universal application of inclusion policies has strengthened this myth by adding "equal rights" and "equal access" to the list of reasons why students with autism should be in school. But gaining these equalities doesn't address their wide range of socialization needs. Our focus on the individual needs of students with autism may be distracted by the noble societal goals of inclusion.

Like most questions about autism, there is no one-size-fits-all answer. It's good that there are home-based programs and school-based programs because this variety of options accommodates the immensely wide range of abilities, challenges, and needs of people with ASD. Unfortunately, as a field we aren't clear enough about which children will benefit from which programs for socialization, at what age, or for how long. As a result, the myth of socialization, to get children with autism into group environments as early as possible, has become a rule of thumb in public institutions looking for clear guidelines.

Doctors play a role in the myth too. Autism is not defined as a medical disease per se but rather as a mental and behaviour disorder.* As such, for the past 60 years, autism has been primarily diagnosed by doctors, but treated by educators and behaviour therapists. Arguably, therapists and teachers who work directly with children and families have an intimate knowledge of the challenges and strengths of people with ASD. They know what works and what doesn't to help kids learn. However, doctors (including

---

* This may change as we learn more about the biological nature of autism and find medical interventions that can help.

psychiatrists, pediatricians, and GPs), not therapists, are usually the first point of contact for parents. They make the most important first decisions including assessment, diagnosis, and initial treatment recommendations.

Doctors can have a wide range of training from diagnostics to treatment options, but very few have hands-on experience in autism therapy. It's simply not their role or expertise. There is a disconnect in knowledge and experience between the professionals who diagnose and the professionals who treat. The US National Research Council's 2001 report *Educating Children with Autism* concluded that "while research in developmental psychology, child psychiatry, and pediatric neurology has become increasingly well integrated, there is a need for more effective communication between professionals in these disciplines and the educators and other professionals who carry out the bulk of treatment and inter-vention-oriented research."[9] As this communication increases, it will begin to bridge the gaps of knowledge that parents are left to sort through.

Recently, I interviewed a psychiatrist who works at a major hospital and a senior-level developmental pediatrician who directs one of the largest hospital-based child development clinics in her city. As specialists, they had both learned about research like the National Research Council's report that concluded most children with autism do best in adult-directed one-to-one programs (excluding those who are higher functioning or with Asperger's). They explained that medical students are taught that applied behaviour analysis is the treatment of choice, and that children with autism should be placed in groups of other kids so they can socialize.

The psychiatrist went on to describe a nuance that is fundamental to this discussion. For children who are higher functioning with language and little to no stereotyped behaviour, she recommends social-skills groups and school. But for lower-functioning, nonverbal children she first and foremost recommends intensive behaviour intervention along with language therapy and many other supports. Although she couldn't articulate a specific framework for this distinction, it is mostly in line with best-practice trends in the field. "So why is it then that so many parents hear from doctors to put even their lower-functioning autistic children in school?" I asked. She answered thoughtfully, "It's true that we probably have a push to get the kids to be around other kids quickly, but even if we wanted to use a more tiered model, there simply aren't enough resources to get every lower-functioning child who is diagnosed with autism into full-time, one-to-one therapy. And what about single parents and low-income families who can't afford private behaviour therapies while they're on the waiting lists? We often only have one or two short visits with families to do the assessment, the diagnosis, and treatment recommendations. It's very difficult in such a short time with the child in our office to figure out the finer details of what's best. So we have to make choices: either we recommend daycare or many children sit at home with grandparents in front of the TV all day. Surely, being in school is better than TV, even if the kid isn't fully ready for school, don't you think?"

Interestingly, her remarks echoed the findings of a study completed by medical residents at the University of Toronto that showed there is often a gap between what doctors know about autism and the real-life decisions they make in diagnosis and treatment recommendations. As well as training their clients to use best practices, sometimes doctors make recommendations influenced by a sense of urgency, and take into account patients' (families') agendas and the barriers to services they are helping them navigate.[10] What the study called the "knowledge-behaviour gap" is perhaps better described as doctors simply taking human factors into account.

Although, more and more, the medical profession is refining its understanding of autism and evidence-based treatments, and schools are finding ways to provide more one-to-one behavioural training, too many young children with severe autism are being prematurely placed into social groups and schools, with negative consequences.

We still need to more clearly understand at what time in a child's development they can benefit socially from school and how best to facilitate this. Which children can benefit from social groups and which aren't ready? What's the best way to prepare children to benefit from social environments like school? What factors determine successful transitions into social groups and school?

NEW PERSPECTIVES ON SOCIALIZATION IN AUTISM

When a child is put into an environment they aren't ready for, it's stressful and can isolate them and their parents too.

It was a cold morning on the playground of the daycare centre. I jotted down notes in between sips of hot coffee with my coat collar buttoned to the very top. I was there to evaluate if the preschool placement was working as a socialization strategy for one particular little girl. A small group of three- and four-year-olds chased each other around the enclosed yard. Three-year-old Madison, recently diagnosed with autism, was walking by herself along the fence. She stood looking at the ground and then quickly glanced at the kids who had huddled around one of the teachers. Madison wandered by herself over to the kid-sized playhouse and sat alone on the little bench inside. One teacher helped a student zip up her jacket while another staff refereed an upset about whose turn it was next on the tricycle, but Madison wasn't involved in the social beehive buzzing around her. One friendly little guy came right up and asked something about her jacket. I couldn't hear well from where I stood, but I saw that Madison didn't respond. She simply didn't have the ability in that moment to interact. The boy ran away back to the group and to playing chase.

I knew Madison had some language and could do some limited pretend play. However, in 30 minutes of recess she hadn't had any meaningful contacts with her peers. It was clear that she wasn't benefiting much from being on her own in the cold.

Many students with autism aren't able to manage larger play groups. They deal with sound and light sensitivities, communication disorders, and often stick to the same routines over and over. They can experience stress in unpredictable environments like social groups. "Hello" and a handshake for most of us are automatic and welcome behaviours but they may be startling or simply not understood by a person with autism. In extreme cases, busy environments can trigger sensory overload, increase repetitious behaviours, and cause stress, tantrums, escape, and flight-or-fight reactions. As a result, their peers don't get enough positive feedback for friendships to grow, and the children are often excluded from school social life.

Even higher-functioning students with ASD who can manage school routines and the busy environment don't make friends easily, and some who are aware of their differences can feel isolated and even depressed. One study looked at the social networks of students with Asperger's syndrome and found they "experienced lower centrality, acceptance, companionship, and reciprocity."[11] In the worst cases, peers can be judgmental and bully the autistic child. Dr. Digby Tantum, professor of psychotherapy at the University of Sheffield in England, found in a survey that as many as two-thirds of students with Asperger's syndrome were bullied at school.[12]

An alternative to the belief that autistic children will naturally pick up social skills by being around other kids is acknowledging that many benefit from being taught directly by adults first. This notion is echoed by Phillip Strain, a professor of educational psychology who has done a lot of research on this topic. He writes, "autistic children require explicit instruction from trained tutors on how to interact with their peers."[13]

Parents themselves can feel alienated when they choose one-to-one, adult-led programs, and are made to feel bad for "isolating their kids." Whereas parents who keep their child home with the flu are seen as acting responsibly by taking care of the community and the child, our zealous commitment to mainstreaming children with autism blinds us to the possibility that isolating a child with autism for some structured social-skills learning is possibly the most appropriate learning environment for that child.

One mother angrily told me how she had been judged by her psychiatrist for wanting to keep her toddler-aged daughter at home. She had fond memories of her own mother being at home during her elementary years and had dreamed of providing that for her own child someday. When her two-year-old daughter, stressed and anxious in public places, was diagnosed with pervasive developmental disorder, she felt even more certain she wouldn't return to work. However, she was confronted with the full force of the myth of socialization by a psychiatrist at a specialist centre who scolded, "If you really want to help your child, go back to work and put your daughter in full-day child care. She won't learn social behaviour at home, and you're only doing a disservice to her by keeping her there." Although she felt dismissed, she had read enough to know that her daughter was not likely to start speaking and making friends by spending her days in the sandbox or colouring at daycare.

Getting children with autism ready for less stressful and more successful transitions into social settings through adult-led, temporary or interim preparatory "skill building" is a good idea that works.

TEACHING SOCIAL SKILLS OUTSIDE OF SCHOOL

Not everyone agrees with my perspectives. Most educators and therapists believe that it's by being in social groups that a child will start the socialization process. Some educators are strongly influenced by an early Soviet psychologist named Lev Vygotsky. Pamela Wolfberg cites him often and argues that children with autism develop social abilities differently in the context of natural play with peers versus with adults. Wolfberg explains, "According to Vygotsky, play (particularly pretend play) is a primary social and cultural activity through which children acquire symbolic capacities, interpersonal skills, and social knowledge."[14]

It's a bit of a "chicken or the egg" debate: Do children with autism need to play in order to learn social skills, or do they first need to learn some social skills in order to be able to play (and learn more complex social skills)? Keeping in mind Vygotsky's ideas weren't based on the unique differences of children with autism, and may be more applicable to typical development, the debate is another example of how the field of autism is divided about what is best.

In fact, there are several debates in the field of autism surrounding the best strategy for socialization: inclusion versus segregation; home-based versus centre- and school-based; and adult-led training versus peer-led play. Lots of professionals and brand-name programs passionately defend one versus another.

An alternative to the one-size-fits-all notion that pushes kids as quickly as possible into social environments is a more customized, more nuanced approach to socialization. We need a more sophisticated understanding of socialization, one that recognizes varying degrees of social skills and their corresponding degrees of necessary support.

I personally believe that no one theory or method works for all children on the autism spectrum but that each has some merit for some kids some of the time. To this end, the most important questions I've been researching for over 20 years are, "Which strategies, for which children, when, and for how long?"

One main reason parents are interested in my Intensive Multi-Treatment Intervention (IMTI) program is that I don't subscribe to any one particular strategy or theory, but instead pick and choose the right fit for each individual child's needs.

When we step away from the debates, we can recognize there is a logical continuum, from an adult working one to one with a child, to play with just one other neurotypical "expert player" peer, then progressing to small groups, and eventually a successful transition into a mainstream, fully inclusive classroom.

Since many therapists recommend isolated one-to-one therapy as a starting point, parents are often concerned about how they will teach socialization if their child is just with adults most of the day. "What's the best way to teach social skills?" is a common question I'm asked.

There are many methods and strategies that focus specifically on teaching social skills to choose from: Barry Prizant's SCERTS model, Pamela Wolfberg's Integrated Play Groups (IPG) model, Steven Gutstein's Relationship Development Intervention (RDI) Program, the Son-Rise Program, Dr. Greenspan's Floortime Model, Pivotal Response Training, Carol Gray's Social Stories, Project LEAP, Recess Buddies, and social-skills training videos are just a few among many others.

Many of these different approaches span various environments too, from in-home therapy rooms or small classrooms, to larger gymnasiums and outdoor camps. Some programs offer primarily one-on-one, adult-led therapy to teach social skills, while others include two or more peers. Peer groups and school settings seem to work best for higher-functioning students with ASD. For children who are nonverbal with apparent physical issues and frequent behavioural outbursts, and who avoid groups of peers, the one-to-one model may be the right fit to start with.

An alternative perspective to making parents choose one socialization program strategy over another is to present all options, along a continuum, for example, with key decision-making information that addresses at what developmental stage each strategy works best, for how long, and in what order.

WHAT TEACHERS AND SCHOOLS
CAN DO DIFFERENTLY

Several years ago, I worked with a team of teachers at a private school during their annual in-service training day. The staff had prepared and forwarded a list of questions about autistic students they wanted my help with. I began the day by pointing out that the entire list was focused on stopping "inappropriate" behaviours like acting out and lesson disruptions. Good behaviour makes sense, I agreed; however, the core challenges of autistic students aren't inappropriate behaviours but social and communication skills. Without these, the whole premise of classroom learning (paying attention to other people), following good peer and teacher role models, and being motivated by social inclusion can't take place. The more students with autism have social communication skills and positive relationships with peers, the less they tend to act out.

Schools don't primarily teach social skills per se. The main curricula focus on academics and students are expected to listen to the teacher, work independently, speak only when they are called on, and wait until recess to play. Starting from grade one, schools are not designed to implement social-skills training programs that promote a lot of peer interaction, conversation, and play. Whenever I am invited into a school to train teachers on autism, I make sure to discuss socialization strategies and how they really are a main key to success in school.

Years ago, I presented a seminar on autism to a group of special-education schoolteachers. After reviewing the definition of autism and highlighting the core social challenges, I began to discuss the myth of socialization. This ignited a spirited and passionate reaction. I shared my observation that many young children with autism aren't ready to be social learners or students because they have weak prerequisite social-learning skills, like observing their peers. I explained that unless the teachers were specifically teaching their autistic students how to socialize, the kids would not just socialize through the mere experience of being in a classroom with lots of kids. And before I could suggest solutions, their hands launched in the air, almost all of them at the same time, ready to defend inclusion. One by one, they gave examples of how neurotypical students benefited by having an autistic peer in the class because they learned about accepting diversity. They gave examples of how most of the students with autism had been able to learn school routines like sitting on the carpet for storytime, lining up in the hall to walk in single file, and hanging their coat on the right hook under their name. Some of the teachers stressed that the students had received special resources like speech therapy and reading instruction at school.

I listened sincerely to each comment. They were right, of course. These were good examples of some benefits of school. Then, in the most diplomatic way possible, I pointed out that none of the benefits included socialization for the autistic child specifically. Even though their autistic students eventually learned school routines, they still played alone at recess, didn't have friends to talk to and laugh with, and were rarely invited to birthday parties.

"The core social deficit isn't being addressed," I said. Once again, I triggered a defensive reaction from the group. Hands waved in the air like students eager to be picked first. "We can't take the time to work with them one on one. We aren't trained to do this. We don't have enough support. We have to stick to the academic curriculum. We spend a lot of time doing behaviour management so we can all just get through the day . . ." they called out. They were, of course, right again. "I agree," I said. "You're not trained or supported properly in school to address the social learning needs of students with ASD." What followed was an honest discussion of the benefits and the limitations of school and social groups. In the end, they realized they didn't have to defend themselves against the limitations of school but instead simply acknowledge the evidence against a myth they could let go of.

With this point made, there are good resources available to facilitate optimal transitions and inclusion into mainstream classrooms and social settings. A few national autism associations in several countries have developed strategies and protocols that every teacher and educational assistant should read thoroughly. For example, the Australian Advisory Board on ASDs posted an excellent position paper in 2010 that clearly outlines the considerations and discussions that need to take place for successful school placements. It underscores that "Educational Services should therefore address the core impairments of ASDs: social competencies, communication skills and learning style."[15] Schools need to develop and adopt specific strategies to teach social skills and make sure they are included in students' individualized education plans (IEPs).

One of the most comprehensive resources for educators is the Autism Spectrum Disorder Inclusion Collaboration Model developed by Richard Simpson and Brenda Smith-Myles at the University of Kansas. The model includes key components like "attitudinal and social support" and "coordinated team commitment." A central concept to this model is collaboration (not just consultation) between school and home and outside experts. I especially appreciate the authors' focus on positive attitude. They highlight the importance of teachers, school staff, and all students learning more about autism to foster greater acceptance and generally more positive feelings about including students with ASD. Looking specifically at social-skills deficits in students with ASD, the Autism Spectrum Disorder Inclusion Collaboration Model emphasizes best practices including direct skill instruction, peer-initiated training strategies and peer tutoring, and adult-prompting methods. The authors warn that "without such support students with ASD are vulnerable to rejection and isolation, which could destine them for failure in an otherwise successful inclusion program."[16]

Instead of inclusion focused on appropriate behaviour, consider positive collaborative inclusion.

WHAT YOU CAN DO

• *Think of Socialization in Stages*

Social development happens in steps across stages. Children typically begin to socialize just by watching and observing others. Then they imitate and begin to experience the reciprocal back-and-forth nature of interaction and shared attention. Infants don't begin socializing by playing in groups with other infants. Following this natural course of development, children diagnosed with autism should not be expected to take their first social steps in groups of kids. First, they should experience and learn to observe, to imitate, and to enjoy back-and-forth sharing with just one other person. Adults and peers act differently. Both are good to learn from in manageable environments that set the child with autism and the playmate up for enjoyable social interactions.

Children typically acquire social skills in an order that builds one upon the next. Although development in ASD doesn't seem to follow a certain pattern, we can appreciate the importance of smaller skill-building steps that lead toward a greater chance of success in more demanding complex social settings, like peer groups and school. In the IMTI program the steps begin first with just one well-trained adult specifically focusing on what I call the "pre-social" skills or social-learning behaviours. Then, peers are trained and introduced, one at a time at first, and guided by an adult. Eventually, a child with autism is introduced to small groups of peers and is finally transitioned into mainstream school. Groups of peers and larger social settings like classrooms have a place in the stages.

If you were to build a socialization program in stages, you could start with the Son-Rise Program methods, then add Robert and Lynn Koegel's Pivotal Response Training,* followed by more structured applied behavioural analysis methods still focused on social

---

* Koegel Autism Center at the University of California, Santa Barbara

skill learning and practice. Next, add Pamela Wolfberg's Integrated Play Groups model for peer group socialization practice, and ultimately the ASD Inclusion Collaboration Model for transition into school, with an emphasis on stress-free social experiences. It may *not* be helpful to push a child as early as possible into social groups at the same time as helping them learn more basic social skills. I've found that completing one step before taking the next works best.

• *Understand That Lots of Kids Doesn't Equal Lots of Socialization*
"Get your child into lots of social groups and around as many other kids as possible so they can be exposed to socializing." This common notion can be easily interpreted as "the more kids, the better." But I've found that for a lot of children with ASD it's often the opposite.

When an environment is so overwhelming that a person with ASD shuts down to take care of himself, that environment is no longer inclusive. Arguably, it's isolating.

There are many considerations when designing social environments with an aim to promote socialization, including the number of people invited to be a part of the group. However, more people do not necessarily make a space more sociable. More children do not necessarily help a child with autism learn social skills better or faster.

Every parent I have ever talked with has wanted one same goal for their child with autism—to have friends. Interestingly, most parents are not thinking about dozens of friends at first, but about one or two really good friends that will appreciate and enjoy their child's wonderfully unique character. For many of us as adults, we may name just a few, two or three, people whom we consider our closest friends. This is our core social tribe. Many of the children I've worked with get more enjoyment and gain more benefit from time spent playing with one caring and interested individual as opposed to the over-stimulation and stress they experience in larger social groups.

There are infinite ways that a child with autism can be included in common childhood experiences that can develop socialization without triggering stress. When we let go of any push for a child to have to be with lots of kids, we can plan equally social experiences that are more manageable and enjoyable for the child and attending adults alike. Enjoyable and stress-free social experiences motivate the child to want more of them.

• Ensure Social-Learning Behaviours Are in Place

The deep end of a pool is not usually the best place to learn how to swim for the first time. Even with supports, the deep end presents overwhelming challenges. Likewise, I've witnessed many situations where the push to socialize a child with ASD in a group of peers is simply overwhelming for the child. The child is not ready for those social depths.

Social readiness is a debated concept in the field of autism treatment. Who's to say what "ready" is? I have worked with hundreds of children across the spectrum and observed that the *timing* of varying levels of social experiences can make a difference. In other words, the children I've worked with can manage and even enjoy groups of peers and school when they have learned certain social basics first, that is to say, when the timing is right. Most peers aren't trained, lack an understanding of autism, and can have less patience or attention span for a child with autism than trained adults. Left on their own, the social pool of classrooms and playgrounds is enormously challenging for autistic students. For many children, inclusion in and of itself is not necessarily a socialization strategy. Let's reframe the discussion about social groups and school from "either in or out" to "in, but when and how?" To ensure a positive experience in social groups with peers, parents, therapists, and teachers can work toward ensuring that the basic social-learning behaviours of observing, imitating, and social motivation, among other skills, are in place.

• Let's All Agree on a Common Set of Basic Social Skills

As a profession including researchers, academics, policy makers, and educators, we need to develop a consensus of clear behavioural measures that can help determine a student's readiness when making school placement decisions. With a strong emphasis on socialization as a turnkey area to develop in children with autism, there should be more consensus between treatment programs on how we define socialization and social skills. Imagine if there was agreement across the hundreds of treatments and early intervention programs about which specific social-learning behaviours should be in place before transition into school. We could all be working toward similar socialization goals. Parents wouldn't have to bounce from program to program trying to bridge the gaps. When students are prepared and practised with the basics, they have smoother transitions into larger social groups, more enjoyment, and greater social success.

• Implement the ASD Inclusion Collaboration Model

There is no need to reinvent the wheel. Several researchers at the University of Kansas have created a comprehensive and sensible model. It details evidence-based practices to design learning environments that promote inclusive education and positive socialization for students with autism and other disabilities. The information is accessible and can be followed like a map. The Autism Spectrum Disorder Inclusion Collaboration Model works with willing school superintendents, school principals who have positive attitudes toward students with disabilities, and flexible teachers prepared to learn new strategies and to modify classroom environments and lesson plans. I recommend reading the article "*Educating Children and Youth with Autism: Strategies for Effective Practice*" by Richard Simpson and Brenda Smith-Myles, who authored the model.

• Empower Schools and Peers to Be Social

In social settings and in school, children are generally expected to act "appropriately." This usually means paying attention to a teacher or a coach, not speaking unless asked to, letting the teacher be in control, and not distracting other students. In many ways, that appropriate behaviour in a class is contradictory to appropriate typical child play and interaction, which is filled with lots of impromptu commentary, sharing joint attention, and exploring reciprocity. Ironically, I've observed that children with special needs are often required to act even more appropriately than their typical peers. They're often more closely monitored, asked not to fidget, and told to keep their eye on the teacher while their neurotypical peers fidget and look off without the same level of scrutiny.

Can classrooms really be rich environments for socialization? Yes. If socialization is written into the core curriculum as a subject or a learning module then teachers would surely begin to find creative and dynamic pedagogy to support the social goals. Somehow we need to train school systems and teachers to be good at teaching and facilitating social skills.

I sat at the back of a grade two class last year to observe a seemingly shy and soft-spoken little girl whose treatment program I had directed for over two years. The desks were arranged in pairs. When she turned to her desk partner and commented on the other student's colouring, my heart filled with joy—she was initiating interaction! Within seconds the teacher called out for my little friend to "be quiet please and work on your own." My heart sank. After class, I was granted a small window of time to speak with the teacher. She was open and eager to learn whatever she could to help her autistic student. I gently renarrated the scenario from my perspective. "As you know, she usually doesn't speak much to other students but today she turned to watch her desk buddy colour. This is a pro-social behaviour. And on top of that, she made an effort to comment. She took the first steps to start a conversation. It wasn't a talking activity, but that's less important than her social development. A strategy in this scenario could be to walk closer and first acknowledge and reinforce the social behaviour: 'Wow, you noticed your friend's drawing. That's exciting. And it's so nice that you told her what you were thinking. Next time you can whisper so that other students aren't disturbed and can keep drawing too.'"

Not all treatment programs focus equally on social skills. As professionals we can educate parents with a wider range of choices to inform programming decisions, while parents can stay focused on socialization to ensure it remains a primary aspect of any therapy. Teachers, therapists, and parents can work in collaboration to include social development in evaluations and reports. Is a particular social group, daycare, preschool, or classroom actively fostering social interactions? Is a child making friends, playing with others, and included by their peers at recess, initiating and responding to social interactions with classmates and teaching staff, and demonstrating social motivation to want to be included in groups without prompting?

Like parents of children with autism, teaching staff in preschools, play centres, and mainstream schools need ample training and support. When teachers are given training and positive feedback, they become empowered. When peers are educated about autism and trained to be social "experts," they too become empowered to engage students with autism, helping to transform them from peers into friends.

CHAPTER FOUR

THE MYTH OF EVIDENCE

"Applied Behaviour Analysis (ABA) Is the Only Evidence-Based Treatment for Autism"

The only evidence-based treatment that currently exists is ABA.
Jason Oldford, board of directors, Autism Society of New Brunswick

I am dismayed and appalled at the ludicrous position taking [sic] by many other supporters of ABA, who claim that ABA is the only scientifically validated treatment for autism. Not so! That position is not only false, it is absurd.
Dr. Bernard Rimland, founder, Autism Society of America

When Talia was diagnosed with autism and seizure disorder at a young age, her parents launched immediately into finding the right treatment. Her mother, Annie, combed the internet, called different specialists, and met with a case worker at the local autism services centre. Everyone pointed to applied behaviour analysis (ABA) as the best option because, they said, it was the only treatment that had any scientific evidence to back it up. Surely it would be unwise, even foolish, to consider anything unproven.

Her parents did more reading about ABA and learned that behavioural treatments teach children by reinforcing behaviours you want to increase and by not reinforcing or even punishing behaviours you want to decrease. The process is called behaviour modification and therapists are trained to follow very specific principles and rules of learning theory. Applied behavioural analysis, simplistically speaking, is a scientific method of systematically defining a learning goal, making sure a therapist is using the right techniques in a logical and consistent way, and measuring any changes in behaviour. People mistakenly think ABA is an autism intervention, but it isn't. ABA methods are used to change human behaviour in corporate business, in sports, and in mainstream education. They're used to train animals and to design computer programs and to treat hundreds of mental and behavioural disorders. It was the late Ivar Lovaas, professor at the University of California, who was one of the first to use applied behaviour analysis in the treatment of autism. His 1987 study caught media attention and popularized ABA as a favourable treatment for the condition.

Annie soon learned that ABA-based programs can differ enormously from one to the next even though they are all working from the same principles. She read books, surfed websites, and talked with professionals about other (non-ABA) interventions too. There is a range of biomedical approaches including special diets and supplement regimes, developmental and social-pragmatic approaches that focus on socialization and communication, and the list goes on. What stood out to Annie, though, was how split the field is. She noted that everyone, from other parents to professionals, goes to great lengths to make it clear that they are *for* or *against* behavioural treatments. It seems as important to some as wearing a team jersey to identify what team you're on. And for many, their jersey is imprinted with the slogan "ABA is the only evidence-based treatment."

Annie's decision about a treatment for Talia was confused by the number of programs that claimed to be "the only" program or that there were "no other" ones. It seems to be a worldwide phenomenon. No matter what country they live in, families researching about treatments see the same message. A parent in the United States looking through Florida's Beyond the Spectrum, Inc. website reads: "Applied Behavioural Analysis (ABA) is the only therapeutic program known to be effective in improving verbal and communication skills." A parent in Canada who attends an informational presentation by the staff of the Behaviour Institute in Hamilton, Ontario, may be told that ABA is the only medically approved, scientifically proven therapy for kids with autism. A parent in England will see the Autism Partnership UK website has devoted an entire page to warning parents about other non-ABA approaches and, without providing a single alternative to ABA, ends by claiming, "What the research consistently shows is that [only] one approach meets this scientific standard. . . . There is no other treatment that has been shown to be more effective." Many parents accept these claims at face value.

In Talia's case, her pediatrician and the autism services centre reinforced the message and strongly recommended behavioural treatment, along with some speech and occupational therapy, as the only option for her autism. Annie had no reason to doubt these professionals and followed their advice.

Annie watched her daughter learn to sort coloured beads and do puzzles in ABA sessions. But Talia often cried and resisted being forced to learn. Annie thought it didn't look like fun and her daughter wanted nothing to do with the sessions. The therapists provided charts to show that Talia was learning and prove the behavioural treatment was effective. The data points told one story, but Annie felt her daughter's functional behaviour outside of the sessions told another. Talia was still very autistic with little language development. After over a year of giving "the only evidence-based treatment" a fair try, she began to wonder if her daughter would perhaps benefit more from a different approach. She was ready to consider other methods beyond ABA.

Simply put, ABA is not the only
evidence-based treatment for autism.

It's not uncommon for me to hear from parents who started with an ABA program, saw some initial benefit, and then got curious about what else might be added to help further. After all, with such a wide range of challenges and abilities in the autistic population, we all agree that no single intervention can address all of their needs. When parents ask, I confidently reassure them not to worry, there are indeed other evidence-based options. Play-therapy techniques, development-based programs, and social-pragmatic strategies are all non-ABA-based and each has scientific research to back it up. Simply put, ABA is not the only evidence-based treatment for autism.

HOW DID ABA GET CROWNED "THE ONLY EVIDENCE-BASED TREATMENT" ANYWAY?

In 1987, Ivar Lovaas sparked a wave of hope for parents around the world as news that half of the students in his ABA treatment study had "recovered" from autism. As a well-respected professor at the University of California in Los Angeles, Lovaas added credibility to the ABA claims and gained media attention. Almost immediately, parents and professionals, including the late Dr. Bernard Rimland, founder of the Autism Society of America, promoted the Lovaas Method through support groups and newsletters, while parent-led lobby groups used this new compelling evidence to ask governments to fund ABA treatment programs. As increased research funding led to more studies and even more evidence of its effectiveness, ABA became the treatment of choice for thousands of families.

In contrast, around this time, there were few scientific studies supporting any other autism program. Even though individual non-ABA treatment strategies had been shown to be effective, research on other comprehensive programs didn't meet the same scientific rigour as the Lovaas Method. These combined factors led to ABA being known as "the only evidence-based treatment."

Over the past 20 years, there have been hundreds more studies published on the benefits of ABA treatment. So it's also now true that ABA is the *most-* and the *best-*researched treatment for autism. What most professionals and parents don't know, however, is that over this same 20 years, research on non-ABA treatments has also flourished. There are now dozens of excellent quality scientific studies that provide substantial evidence for a whole range of treatment programs and strategies beyond Lovaas's ABA method. The phrase

"ABA is the only evidence-based treatment" has become much like a mantra and might have been true 20 years ago, but today it's a myth that stands in the way of progress.

Fourteen years after I first began teaching people diagnosed with autism, I returned to university for graduate studies. I had worked primarily with non-ABA-type strategies at the time and, despite having witnessed hundreds of successes, I too had accepted the belief that only ABA had evidence supporting its effectiveness. Then one day while browsing through a stack of academic publications like *The Journal of Autism and Developmental Disorders,* I decided on a whim to look up one of the play-therapy techniques I used. I searched the journal for a therapeutic technique called "imitating" and there it was: a well-designed scientific experiment. My jaw dropped open. Imitating really was an evidence-based autism treatment strategy. I felt butterflies in my stomach like I had stumbled upon a little-known secret. I quickly looked up another technique, and another, and soon found many fascinating studies on non-ABA techniques that reported significant positive results. But I had to wonder: Why doesn't everyone else in the field know about this research?

Obviously, I hadn't uncovered any secrets. These were all well-reviewed and established academic articles that others in my field read. But I was stunned that this important information hasn't found its way into parent groups or policy meetings or into the popular media. Why did Lovaas's 1987 study get so much worldwide media attention while most of these promising studies seem to be hidden in dusty academic journals?

Even long-time supporters of ABA have spoken out to challenge the myth. As a parent of a son with autism, Bernard Rimland, ABA advocate and autism researcher, has fought to empower parents. He recognized the wide spectrum of challenges in autism and believed parents need to be given as much information and as many options as possible about *all* researched strategies, not only about the *most* researched. In an open letter to his fellow ABA advocates titled *The ABA Controversy*, Rimland wrote:

> *The "ABA is the only way" folks are wrong, not only because of their lack of information about research on the validity of other interventions, but because of their failure to recognize that parents have a right and an obligation to consider all possible forms of intervention.*[1]

More recently, Barry Prizant also has questioned the credibility of the beliefs that ABA is the only way by challenging many of the assertions used to support these beliefs. To be clear, ABA-based treatments are the most researched and they've even been shown to be more effective than some other approaches. But the *most* evidence does not mean the *only* evidence.

• Why Does It Matter?

It matters because parents are being misled. It matters because children are being short-changed. Remember, half of the children in Lovaas's research improved. That means the other half of the children in the study didn't. For thousands of children like Talia, development-based, play-based, and social-pragmatic-based strategies unlock the door to learning in ways that ABA doesn't. Sadly, parents may not consider these strategies and programs because they've been led to believe there is no evidence showing they're effective.

The scientific research and real-life anecdotes of "recovery" in non-ABA programs are overly criticized and diminished while the "ABA only" mantra gets louder. This means that many therapists are trained to do ABA only, and shun other methods. It limits the range of treatment choices parents are offered and ultimately limits children who don't respond well to ABA. Other options that allow autistic children to develop and learn in different ways aren't readily available. Here are four ways I've seen the "ABA only" movement hinder what's best for children with autism:

1) The myth contributes to competition between different treatments instead of cooperation and collaboration.

Behavioural and non-behavioural programs alike waste energy and resources promoting their "only" status instead of sharing expertise and inviting dialogue about other kinds of treatment. During my own study of as many different educational strategies and treatment options as I can find, I've been discouraged by the number of websites and books that go out of their way to criticize and diminish other treatments beyond ABA. This is often done under the guise of protecting vulnerable families.

Combining approaches doubles the benefits for the children.

In my work with autistic children, I use strategies from a variety of methods because combining approaches multiplies the benefits for the children. The various methods can be more complementary than either side seems to understand.

2) The myth limits the variety of strategies therapists learn and that kids receive.

Peter was diagnosed with pervasive developmental disorder and was considered high functioning. I remember his quirky humour and keen memory. Over two years, I designed and directed a multi-treatment program for him including peer play dates and daily recess at the local public school. He was almost ready for a successful transition into school when the family was offered some speech therapy through the local government ABA agency. Even though he no longer needed intensive therapy, his mother was curious about what the speech therapist could offer. I went along to observe the first session through a two-way mirror.

Within the first five minutes, Peter spotted a favourite toy on the shelf and asked, "Can I have the pirate ship?" The therapist responded to his perfectly clear verbal request by grabbing a communication board, holding it in front of him, and asking him to point to the plastic laminated "I want __ please" word cards. Peter did this easily then looked up at her again and asked, "Can I play with the pirate ship now?" Peter's mother and I couldn't understand why she used a communication board with such a highly verbal child. Afterwards, we asked her directly about it. She explained that even though she fully understood Peter's request for the toy, she had to follow the ABA baseline protocol. She was obliged to make sure Peter could do the preverbal communication steps of pointing to words first, and check them off on her list, before she could begin to respond (appropriately) to his clear verbal communication.

I use this example not to judge this therapist or the ABA methods she used but to illustrate how the belief that ABA is the only effective method can seriously restrict therapists' abilities to interact and respond in ways that don't require scientific evidence to act on. Her ability to respond effectively to Peter's natural communication was limited by a belief that she should only follow the planned protocol. Training therapists to use methods that are exclusive of any other ideas is limiting to both the therapist and the child. A zealous play-therapy program, for example, may not recognize a child's need for structured ABA-style learning. Opportunities for development are missed and children lose out because therapists cling to just one approach.

> Children lose out because therapists
> cling to just one approach.

3) The myth puts parents in uncomfortable situations. They're made to feel guilty and to keep their choice of non-ABA treatments secret.

The idea that ABA is the only evidence-based treatment for autism leads some therapists to refuse to work with any non-ABA strategies and therapists. I've personally had some families ask me if I would work with them in secret for fear that their ABA therapist would refuse services if she knew.

One family was forced to make an unfair decision when, after two years of seeing their son, Will, thrive in my program, his name reached the top of the ABA-service waiting list. They were finally going to get funding they desperately needed for their home-based program. It was perfect timing, in my opinion as the program director, because Will had already learned to cooperate and to follow instructions. He was ready for ABA-style structured learning. I would typically provide this for a family, but of course, it made sense for them to get whatever public funding they were offered.

I naively thought I could work together with the designated directing ABA therapist. During my first meeting with her, I expressed my willingness to collaborate and to customize the ultimate program for Will. I talked about the approaches and strategies that had been extremely effective from the previous two years I had spent working with Will, and shared my excitement that we could learn from each other. I left the meeting feeling hopeful that the added funding and her skills would really help Will. The next day, however, the family received a difficult phone call. I didn't have the right ABA credentials, the directing therapist told them. The strategies I had talked to her about, although effective with Will, weren't allowed in her ABA approach and public funding was strictly reserved for ABA-based interventions, she explained. Bottom line: If they continued to work with me, she was not interested in the contract and they risked losing their funding. The family was devastated and angry. They felt backed into a corner, forced to make unreasonable compromises for their son's development. They desperately needed the funds, but resented the conditions attached that showed more commitment to the myth than to really helping their son.

4) When ABA treatments don't have the expected effect, the myth that they are the only evidence-based treatment can cause parents to lose hope.

I have spoken with many families who feel deeply disappointed that their children didn't recover from autism through ABA, even though they'd read that many others had. The "ABA only" myth can leave parents with little hope. After all, they are told there's only one evidence-based treatment and they've exhausted that *only* hope.

Other professionals in the field have witnessed this trend too. One professional whose work I've studied over the years is Barry Prizant, professor at Brown University and founder of the SCERTS model for individuals with autism. He has long been a vocal critic, challenging the myths of autism. In an essay titled "Is ABA the Only Way?" he writes, "We hear repeatedly from parents of older children that in the early years, they were led to believe that ABA was the only credible approach that was available. They add that they wish they were exposed to the broader range of practices for children with ASD, as they could have made more informed choices for their children."[2]

This chapter is not about judging one approach over another. It is not meant to diminish the ABA movement or the thousands of ABA therapists who are sincere in their efforts to help kids. Rather, it is about shining a light on the evidence that exists for interventions *other* than ABA so that more children can be better supported and parents can be optimistic.

WHERE'S THE EVIDENCE FOR OTHER TREATMENTS?

Consider the research reviews produced by leading autism specialist panels through governments and private agencies. Expert panels gather all of the best research on any autism treatments they can find and then determine which ones should be rated as "evidence-based" or not. Reviews from the New York State Department of Health,[3] the US Surgeon General,[4] and the Maine Department of Health and Human Services[5] are three of the most cited documents on autism treatment. Even though these reports are often misquoted as supporting the myth, while they all conclude ABA is the most researched method, none of them claim that it's the *only* evidence-based treatment for autism.

In 2009, the National Autism Center (NAC) based in Massachusetts published one of the most comprehensive summaries of evidence-based treatments to date. Their expert panel gave 11 treatments their highest "Established Treatment" rating. Not surprisingly, of these 11 treatments below—

1. Antecedent Package
2. Behavioural Package
3. Comprehensive Behavioural Treatment for Young Children
4. Joint Attention Intervention
5. Modelling
6. Naturalistic Teaching Strategies
7. Peer Training Package
8. Pivotal Response Treatment
9. Schedules
10. Self-management
11. Story-based Intervention Package

—approximately one-third are *not* exclusively behavioural-based treatments.

The experts confirm there's enough "compelling scientific evidence to show these treatments are effective"[6] and that some of the scientific evidence came "from the non-behavioral literature emanating from the fields of speech-language pathology and special education and story-based interventions."[7] So there we have it. Based on this information alone, the myth falls apart. There are unequivocally other evidence-based treatments besides ABA.

If this isn't enough to convince you, though, the NAC report lists a further 22 treatments in their second-highest-rated "Emerging Treatments" category. Nineteen of these are not considered traditional ABA-based interventions. Even though the report calls for even more research to back these up before they can recommend them with absolute certainty, all of these interventions have at least one scientific study that demonstrates their effectiveness. At this point in the history of autism research, one has to be in serious denial to continue to promote the myth that ABA is the only evidence-based intervention.

• Need More Evidence?

Thousands of families have reported seeing positive learning and development in their children using non-ABA-based intervention programs. Here are seven of the most prominent development- and social-pragmatic-based treatments and some of the evidence that supports them.

1. The late Dr. Stanley Greenspan, MD, clinical professor of psychiatry and pediatrics at George Washington University Medical School, founded a development-based program called the Floortime Model. Similar programs like the Son-Rise Program and Relationship Development Intervention share common play-therapy techniques. Many of these strategies have been individually studied and are shown to be effective. Thousands of families report beneficial results from using them. A large two-year study showing the benefits and effectiveness of Floortime is due to be published by a group at York University in Canada.

2. Dr. Barry Prizant, Ph.D. (see page 132), professor of child and adolescent psychiatry at the Brown University Program in Medicine, and

professor of communication disorders at Southern Illinois University and at Emerson College, founded the SCERTS (Social Communication, Emotional Regulation, and Transactional Support) model. This social-pragmatics-based intervention for autism has been used in school systems and has demonstrated measurable gains in students' skills and learning. Prizant, his collaborators, and staff have recorded hundreds of successful case studies.

3. Dr. Brooke Ingersoll is a professor of psychology at Michigan State University, a Board Certified Behavior Analyst who founded Project ImPACT (Improving Parents as Communication Teachers). This cutting-edge program combines developmental and naturalistic behavioural intervention strategies to teach social engagement, language, imitation, and play. All of the methods and interventions are evidence based, supported by published research.

4. One of the longest-running non-ABA-based programs was founded by the late Dr. Eric Schopler, a professor of psychiatry and psychology at the University of North Carolina-Chapel Hill. His TEACCH (Treatment and Education of Autistic and Communication-Related Handicapped Children) program is widely used in England and has been adopted by several school boards as a comprehensive education program for people with ASD. Schopler and the long-time director of TEACCH, Gary Mesibov, published numerous studies and have recorded hundreds of cases of developmental gains, positive changes in behaviour, and learning in their students. Many parents and professionals attest to the gains they have witnessed in their children from this program. The National Autism Center's study lists four research studies that support TEACCH.

5. The Hanen Centre is a Canadian program that focuses on language and social communication training. Founded in 1975 by Ayala

Hanen Manolson, a speech-language pathologist, the Hanen More Than Words program provides parents and educators with strategies to teach communication. It was one of the first programs to empower parents to be at the centre of their children's language development. The program has been taught and used around the world in many countries for over 20 years and has helped thousands of children with autism take their first steps in learning to talk. Hundreds of people in the field have personally witnessed the benefits of this non-ABA-based program and recommend it. They have documented success stories, and there are several studies on its effectiveness.

6. Dana Weise-Brown founded the PACT (Pediatric Autism and Communication Therapy) Institute located in Minnesota. It's a development-based program that focuses on teaching social and communication skills. They emphasize parent training and highly customized curricula through play and real-life activities in a variety of environments. Several high-quality studies have demonstrated the PACT program's effectiveness.[8] This is widely considered a non-ABA evidence-based intervention.

7. The Early Start Denver Model is an offshoot of one of the comprehensive intervention programs listed among the top ten in the National Research Council's 2001 treatment review. It's a naturalistic play-based model developed in 1981 by two leaders in the field: Sally Rogers, professor of psychiatry at the M.I.N.D. Institute at the University of California, and Geraldine Dawson, formerly a professor of psychiatry at the University of North Carolina at Chapel Hill and currently Chief Science Officer at Autism Speaks. They combine contemporary ABA strategies and social-developmental approaches with great results. As rigorous researchers, Rogers and Dawson have published numerous studies on various aspects and techniques used in the Denver Model.[9, 10]

Each of these programs, and many others not mentioned here, was developed by professionals with extensive education and qualifications including medical doctors, Ph.D.s, speech-language pathologists, and researchers. Behind them stand thousands of families who insist the programs worked for their children diagnosed with autism. But anecdotal testimonials aren't scientific evidence. Even if a program is founded on good theory, it doesn't count as scientific evidence. The ways that many intervention programs are implemented, recorded, and then reported don't follow scientific methodology. They are designed to help children, and are not designed as science experiments. While scientific studies produce one kind of evidence, no one can deny the sheer volume of positive gains that children have made in the seven programs, among others, listed above.

Some argue that even though scientific evidence is an important pursuit, there can often be long lag times between innovations in treatment and science catching up with evidence. ABA advocate and autism researcher Dr. Bernard Rimland often pointed out that, when he began an ABA program in the early 1960s for his son, Lovaas hadn't even published his landmark study. ABA wasn't yet an evidence-based treatment but his son benefited from it nonetheless:

I can't help but wonder how the ABA-only folks would view my efforts to have ABA accepted between 1964 and 1987. Though there were no control group studies, and certainly no double-blind studies to point to, the evidence was clear enough to compel me to fight for ABA. Should I have abandoned my efforts for more than two decades while waiting for a control group study to appear? I'm glad I didn't. [11]

AN IRONIC TWIST
THAT PERPETUATES THE MYTH

More and more, the field of ABA-based treatments is merging with play-, development-, and social-pragmatic-based strategies into what is called "naturalistic behavioural approaches."

Behaviour therapists are discovering the benefits of moving beyond rote learning drills.

Behaviour therapists are discovering the benefits of moving beyond rote learning drills to techniques for engaging students in play and socialization. They're adopting what developmental therapists, play-therapists, and socialization-communication therapists have been using with success for decades.

As "new" treatment techniques are adopted into ABA, behavioural researchers set about testing them. They've developed an entire science to measure and study behaviour. Ironically, behavioural researchers are generating the scientific evidence to back up originally non-ABA interventions. However, it seems that, in the process, any intervention that they study using behavioural analysis is then reclassified as an ABA treatment. Once a treatment is published in a behavioural journal it's considered a behavioural strategy. The problem is that when the same strategy is used in a non-ABA program, behaviourists dismiss it as not evidence based (even though they've been using the strategy with success for decades before ABA treatment was even discovered, and behaviour therapists are now themselves using it).

I've been using play as a way to motivate children with autism to learn for over 20 years. In the early '90s I was reminded by many ABA therapists at conferences and in books that play-therapy techniques such as "incidental teaching" were unproven and not effective. Now that behaviourists have recently studied and published scientific evidence of how effective incidental teaching can be, it's considered an evidence-based ABA strategy. Today, play- and ABA therapists both claim "incidental teaching" as an important treatment technique but only one of these groups claims it's exclusively effective and evidence based when used in their program.

In my own practice, I've seen the most positive benefits from using a blend of both ABA- and non-ABA-based methods. Mine is a multi-treatment approach.* Combining different types of strategies affords more choices for the individual learning styles and needs of people with autism.

> Combining different types of strategies affords more choices for the individual learning styles and needs of people with autism.

So I sit comfortably in the middle, advocating for evidence-based intervention and knowing this means choices well beyond the confines of ABA.

WHAT YOU CAN DO

• Take a Cue from Lovaas

Applied behavioural analysis is the practical application of the science of learning behaviour. ABA and behavioural science don't necessarily specialize in autism, or in children or childhood development. What this means is the principles of ABA alone are not particularly able to address the specific challenges and needs of people with autism. It is

---

* Recent research studies have demonstrated that what is called "eclectic" treatment is less effective than a single intensive intervention. This is misleading insofar as it is only one specific model of multimodal intervention. The Intensive Multi-Treatment Intervention (IMTI) program is not an eclectic approach that combines separate services delivered by independent therapists. I distinguish a multi-treatment program as a comprehensive package delivered by therapists who are trained in an eclectic variety of strategies and methodologies while supervised and coordinated by a single directing therapist and an overriding set of principles and consistency measures.

only when ABA is informed by and combined with an understanding of children and their development needs that ABA-based strategies begin to become effective.

Dr. Ivar Lovaas is the researcher who originally connected applied behaviour analysis specifically to autism treatment. Interestingly, he himself wrote about the lack in ABA principles alone in addressing all of the needs of children with disabilities. In the introduction of his formative instruction manual, *Teaching Developmentally Disabled Children*, he warns readers that "no one approach will solve all the problems of developmentally disabled persons. Rather, the persons who try to help these individuals need to draw upon a variety of concepts and teaching techniques."[12]

A colleague of mine in California once saw a video of Lovaas modelling his therapy with a young child. He described Lovaas as an intuitive therapist who had a natural playfulness with kids. It seems Lovaas brought more to the therapy sessions than he was able to express through the principles of ABA. Lovaas ends the "Words of Caution" section of his introduction with a powerful metaphor: "Keep in mind that, just as a physicist needs to know more than the laws of gravity to transport a person to the moon, you need to know more than the laws of operant behavior to move a person to more adequate functioning." [13]

• Reboot and Stay Current

As the *Ontario Health Report on Autism Treatments* points out, "Treatment guidelines are based on a body of knowledge at a point in time, and need to be re-examined and revised periodically."[14] Practitioners, therapists, and counsellors have a moral and professional obligation to provide parents with current information. ABA websites and promotional materials could begin to acknowledge the research base that now undeniably exists for other kinds of treatments.

• Use Facts, Not Fear

Parents have been duped into paying thousands of dollars for bogus treatments. Interventions with little or no effect waste limited resources, including irreplaceable early-learning time. There are a large number of autism treatments that are mostly untested, lack scientific evidence, and that often make questionable claims of recovery and cure. Doctors and professionals are right to be protective of families who may be vulnerable and desperate to help their children.

Unfortunately, fear of bogus treatments is used as a deterrent to parents exploring options outside of ABA. Parents learn to suspect non-ABA treatments as harmful by default. After all, if ABA is presented as the only evidence-based treatment, everything else must be bogus, right? However, as we've seen, the facts tell a different story. Parents should be told that there *are* evidence-based interventions that fall outside of the ABA approaches, run by caring and skilled therapists, that aren't harmful. Parents need more facts, not more fear.

• Cooperate and Educate

Surely it makes sense for us to move beyond the "ABA *versus* other" paradigm to an "ABA *and* other" model of treatment.

Without taking away from the success or importance of ABA as a leading treatment option, more and more ABA researchers and therapists enjoy the benefits of working on teams and learning from therapists representing different methods. In her paper *Teaching Social Communication,* Dr. Brooke Ingersoll outlines the similarities and differences between behavioural and other autism treatments. She concludes that in some ways there are more similarities than either side of the treatment-divide acknowledges. She attributes this to old stereotypes and a lack of education about how interventions have changed, especially in the last decade.[15] Contemporary ABA programs behave and feel dramatically different from Lovaas's original drill-styled discrete trial training. Some have rebranded themselves as "naturalistic ABA" (NABA) using play and positive behaviour support. One NABA clinic in Singapore advertises, "It is only when a trusting and warm relationship is established that the child will be motivated to work through therapy."[16] These are words that could have been lifted right out of a play-therapy brochure from the Son-Rise Program or Floortime Model. On the other hand, as Ingersoll points out, there is more structure and well-defined learning goals in developmental and play-therapies than most ABA therapists know.

The way forward is for therapists and researchers from different disciplines to go out and proactively learn about methods other than their own. The rich libraries of research and theories on childhood development, language acquisition, socialization, and many other disciplines can inform ABA therapists to modify and improve their techniques. Likewise, the science and research behind ABA provide a wealth of proven effective strategies and experience that developmental, play, and other types of therapies can incorporate. Ingersoll writes, "Graduate and professional programs that prepare professionals to work with individuals with autism (e.g., special education, psychology, speech pathology) should consider offering interdisciplinary courses that cover both the behavioral and developmental literatures as they relate to autism interventions."[17] Unfortunately, even though there's enough evidence-based research beyond ABA to fill an entire course, most college ABA certificate programs in Canada don't introduce students to many other evidence-based treatment options besides ABA. This only perpetuates the myth. If we can teach the next generation of autism therapists and researchers about the range of evidence-based options that exists, we can foster innovation that combines the best and that merges into even better. Cooperation will help more children than competition.

CHAPTER FIVE

THE MYTH OF IQ

"Most Children with Autism Have Mental Retardation"

Atypical autism arises most often in profoundly retarded individuals.
"Atypical Autism," International Classification of Diseases (ICD-10)

Most government hospitals in the state are still signing the health certificates
of autistic patients as "mentally-retarded."
"Autistic Patients Labelled 'Mentally Retarded' in State,"
Indian Express News Service

A	hmad's mother sat across from me in her tiny living room. The furnishings were sparse. She had been forced to hide away any precious decorations, picture frames, trinkets, vases, and keepsakes for her son's safety because of his extreme hyperactivity. He would bounce across the floors, leaping onto chairs and the sofa for hours. This was our first meeting. She told me the details of her struggle with the Ontario health system, which took 18 months to get a diagnosis for Ahmad. They finally told her he had severe autism. She told me this in a matter-of-fact way; autism is what she had suspected all along. But the assessment report didn't stop there. She paused, looking down, and admitted softly that Ahmad had also been labelled mentally retarded. It upset her to say this out loud. In her mind, at just four years old her son had been written off as uneducable. She had read in books about the low expectations for any meaningful development. Compared to the more optimistic prognosis of autism, to her, mental retardation was an added curse.

Many parents lose hope when the mental retardation label is tacked onto an autism diagnosis. Their children will be judged twice, they fear. Mental disabilities are still poorly understood and stigmatized. For some it means little optimism and even shame.

Dr. Laura Schreibman, director of the Autism Research Program at the University of California in San Diego, is a leading expert in the behavioural treatment of autism. In her book *The Science and Fiction of Autism,* she examines controversies in the field of autism and how to determine whether something is fact or fiction. In it she claims that the majority of the autistic population is mentally retarded.[1] During a 2003 lecture she claimed as fact that "about 75 to 80 percent of these individuals have some degree of mental retardation and in many of them it's severe." Unfortunately, Dr. Schreibman is repeating a misguided myth that can be found in most textbooks on autism, in hundreds of articles and research papers, on websites, and in official government reports.

Unfortunately, in neither her book nor her lecture did she give her audience all of the information available for us to understand the nuances and criticisms about these often-cited numbers. For example, the US National Research Council's 2001 report on autism, cited in her book, adds that "children first assessed in early preschool years are likely to show marked increases in IQ score by school age."[2] In other words, the younger a child with autism is tested, the lower their score is likely to be. There is evidence that as a child with autism gets older, her IQ score will likely increase. There are a good number of studies that suggest the percentages Schreibman and many others cite may be more fiction than fact. These are important nuances that should accompany a sentence of MR on so many people with autism.

Sadly, when parents and therapists hear these "facts," they are more likely to treat autistic people as less intelligent. They are less likely to look for the strengths, creativity, and communication that's possible. It's imperative that academics in positions of influence consider the negative implications of this serious label on the people on whom they stick it.

Mental retardation (MR) and autistic spectrum disorder (ASD) are separate conditions. To be clear, IQ scores and measures of intelligence are not even used in the official diagnosis of autism.

IQ scores and measures of intelligence are not even
used in the official diagnosis of autism.

Yet the commonly repeated myth that upward of 70 percent of
people with autism have mental retardation leads many people to
speak as if MR is an inherent part of autism. Most in-field therapists,
educators, and parents don't formally measure intelligence. Compared to most of the other myths, this myth in particular has been
both created and promoted almost exclusively by researchers and
physicians. But the way IQ tests have been interpreted, and their
validity for the autistic population, is up for serious debate.

HOW DID IQ SCORES AND MENTAL RETARDATION GET ASSOCIATED WITH AUTISM?

Alfred Binet is often cited as the grandfather of the modern-day
intelligence test. Just as the famous developmental psychologist
Jean Piaget studied his own children, it was Binet's children that
interested him and inspired him to study human development,
which ultimately led him to research intelligence.

At the time, around 1900, the French government passed a law
that all children be enrolled in school. This meant they would also
have to find ways to accommodate children with disabilities. Binet
and a group of psychologists were invited to form a committee to
determine an efficient way to identify which students had special-
learning needs. The plan was to group all of the students with special needs into separate classes. Along with his doctoral understudy
Theophile Simon, Binet assembled a series of tasks that he felt typical
children at certain ages could do. The theory was that a typically
developing child would be able to complete all of the tasks for his age
group but not above. A child who couldn't complete the tasks for
his or her age group was identified as mentally retarded and placed
in a class for remedial instruction. Eventually, the test was formally

called the Binet-Simon scale. Hundreds of children in France were identified with one of Binet's scores—a number that quickly became either a mark of pride or one of embarrassment. In later writings, Binet presciently argued against segregating children into "special education" classrooms, and insisted that teaching strategies for special needs would be helpful for children at all levels.

About ten years later, at Stanford University in California, Professor Lewis Terman revised Binet's test and re-released it as the Stanford-Binet Intelligence Scale. Today, it's simply called the IQ test. Around the globe, this is the most commonly used test to measure intelligence, including that of autistic children. However, the test was never designed to measure intelligence in people with autism. It was never meant to account for people with communication disorders like reading, writing, and attention challenges. A person who is blind may not be able to read the questions on a test, but they might be very intelligent.

> A person who is blind may not
> be able to read the questions on a test,
> but they might be very intelligent.

A person with cerebral palsy may not have the muscle control to hold a pencil to complete the questions on a test, but they might be keenly smart. A child with hyperactivity disorder may find it almost impossible to stay focused long enough to complete a lengthy intelligence exam, yet they might be the brightest student in the class. There are many hundreds of possible reasons a child might score low on a test besides a perceived lack of intelligence.

In spite of world-wide use of the IQ test, many debate its validity and reliability, especially for people with disabilities. Since the test's debut in the early 1900s, neurobiology and psychology have taken giant leaps forward. We now know there are many different kinds of intelligence and ways of thinking. Does the test measure all of what we know intelligence to be? The inventor himself, Alfred Binet, cautioned against using his test as a definitive measure separate from other kinds of behavioural observations. Still, the allure of identifying students with an IQ score seems irresistible.

THE GREAT IQ SHIFT

Autistic children were once considered bright, with above average intelligence. Psychologists believed that the intelligence just wasn't obvious because the children's social and communication delays got in the way. Back then, in 1943 when the famous Austrian physician Leo Kanner first popularized the diagnosis, he wrote in detail about his young autistic patients' cognitive strengths: "The astounding vocabulary of the speaking children, the excellent memory for events of several years before, the phenomenal rote memory for poems and names, and the precise recollection of complex patterns and sequences, bespeak good intelligence."[3] He went on to say that his original 11 case studies were "all unquestionably endowed with good *cognitive potentialities*."[4] Around the same time, Hans Asperger was studying a similar group of children and, like Kanner, he also found his patients had strong intelligence. So, in the beginning, Kanner's autism and Asperger's disorder were both associated with bright intelligence.

Unfortunately this positive association didn't last long. In *A History of Autism*, Adam Feinstein describes how researchers in the 1950s were mostly interested in measuring social skills because that's what Leo Kanner emphasized in his original study as the main deficit of children with autism. Then in the 1960s, cognitive psychology became the trend. Psychologists shifted away from analyzing social relationships and instead focused on how people think and solve problems. That's when autism researchers started to focus more on cognitive deficits in autism.

• *If They Score Low Doesn't That Mean They Have Mental Retardation?*
A client family of mine several years ago described a visit to the city's top psychologist for an intelligence test. Their five-year-old, nonverbal

son spent most of the 45 minutes exploring the doctor's office and avoiding the test questions. The room was full of distractions, including lots of his favourite things—papers and pens on the desk. He liked to draw and write various letters, words, and even phrases he had memorized from television. At home in his therapy program, he was doing grade one-level curriculum. But on this day, the test day, he was hyperactive and distracted. Even though he drew some pictures, wrote some words, and had sophisticated nonverbal ways to get what he needed from his parents (including showing how much he wanted to leave the office), the psychologist gave this lively little boy a score below 70. The psychologist hadn't in fact been able to get many responses from the autistic boy. He was "untestable," so he just decided this was evidence enough of low intelligence.

This is not an uncommon practice. During the 1960s and '70s, some researchers such as Dr. Michael Rutter of the Institute of Psychiatry in London, equated children they deemed "untestable" with MR. This unscientifically gained data was included in published calculations and would have falsely bumped up prevalence rates of MR at the time.

Test environments and procedures can be unmanageable. Children and adults on the autistic spectrum deal with many physical and sensory differences like hyperactivity, attention-deficit disorder, graphomotor (writing) difficulties, and sound and light sensitivities. These issues may make it very difficult to focus on thinking tasks. Many with ASD need time to acclimatize to new environments, new people, and new routines. I have worked with children who speak well but only to those they are very familiar with; otherwise they act mute. Most intelligence tests are administered in buildings and rooms that are unfamiliar, by professionals who are strangers, with materials and procedures that can seem foreign. Unfamiliarity can be unsettling for people with autism. I've heard often from parents, "If only they would have come over to our house and given my son the test there, they would have seen what he's capable of." But accommodations and modifications are rarely made. Testing procedures and environments are definitely factors that led to lower IQ scores for this special population.

> Testing procedures and environments
> are definitely factors that lead to lower IQ
> scores for this special population.

Unfortunately the MR label is now strongly associated with autism. It stereotypes an entire population that, as it turns out, has remarkably varied patterns, and arguably a wider range, of intelligence than the neurotypical population. The stereotype has negative implications yet continues to be promoted by physicians, researchers, and popular media alike.

DUBIOUS DATA

Meredyth Goldberg Edelson, professor at Williamette University in Oregon, pieced together over 200 sources that mentioned intelligence in autism to plot the history of autism's association with mental retardation. The earliest reports put rates of MR in autism between 30 to 40 percent. But she cites a 1961 research paper by E. Mildred Creak about childhood schizophrenia (autism) as the first to claim that "serious retardation" is actually a defining characteristic of autism. Even though Creak didn't give any data to support her claim, Goldberg Edelson points out that, from this point on, "shortly after Creak's publications, researchers began finding much higher rates of MR in children with autism"[5] and many of them didn't have any data to back up their claims either. It seems an association between autism and MR was echoed over and over until it became accepted as fact.

What Goldberg Edelson found was astonishing. Out of 215 articles linking autism and MR published between 1937 and 2003,

74 percent were from non-empirical studies (i.e., they didn't actually use testing or have data to back up the claims), and almost half of these didn't even have a proper citation to support their claim. This means less than 30 percent of the studies had any

Less than 30 percent of the studies had any scientific evidence.

Even more alarming is that almost a quarter of the studies that did provide a source for their data had actually reported prevalence rates of MR inflated higher than the original data they cited from. Goldberg Edelson's findings put 70 years of research supporting the myth into serious question.

Through the 1960s and '70s, reports claimed on average that about 86 percent of people with autism have mental retardation. This was a big jump from the 30 percent reported in 1958, and an even bigger leap from the "good intelligence" Kanner wrote about ten years before that. In other words, if we were to believe all of the research that is published, it appears that the average IQ of people with autism has plummeted over the past 50 years with no explanation and in many cases no data.

In the past, IQ scores have been used to negatively target various minority groups including autistics. In 1918 in Alberta, for example, a major report by the National Committee for Mental Hygiene concluded that "feeble-mindedness" was directly linked to immorality and crime. Many of the people identified with low IQ may have had autism-related disorders. Acting on this report, in 1928 the Alberta Eugenics Board was formed and forced sexual sterilization of people identified as mentally retarded. They wanted to eradicate low intelligence out of the human gene pool. The thought of forcing all of our autistic population to mandatory sterilization is shocking to us today but this practice actually continued in Canada up until 1972. In discussions, on blogs, and at conferences within the autism community itself, some condemn genetic research in autism in a similar light, fearing it's the prelude to identifying fetuses as autistic and ultimately their abortion.

Many parents talk openly about their fears for their autistic children's futures. Many wonder, "Who will take care of my son when I'm deceased?" Images of hospital-like residential facilities haunt their minds. In our recent past, people labelled morons, imbeciles, idiots, and feeble-minded were locked away in penitentiaries. Rejected to unsanitary institutions and abused, hundreds of children and adults with autism have been sentenced with mental retardation.

Thankfully these kinds of conditions don't exist in most countries any longer. But they are powerful examples of how a low IQ can lead to poorer treatment, lack of respect, and loss of dignity. Conditions have improved, but the prejudices haven't.

Today, nonverbal children with ASD who score low on intelligence tests are still denied equal access to learning opportunities and are resigned to behaviour management and life-skills programs in segregated classes. Expectations are set lower and opportunities are limited. Today, the autism community still fights against these prejudices.

In his well-researched article on autism, David Wolman of *Wired* magazine interviewed Dr. Mike Merzenich, a professor of neuroscience at the University of California San Francisco, who feels strongly that the characterization of the majority of autistic people as mentally retarded is "incredibly wrong and destructive." Merzenich too underlines the negative impacts of this misplaced myth. "'We label them as retarded because they can't express what they know,' and then, as they grow older, we accept that they 'can't do much beyond sit in the back of a warehouse somewhere and stuff letters in envelopes.'"

SILENT INTELLIGENCE

Intelligence isn't always immediately obvious. Physical disabilities can limit a person's ability to share and express their innate intelligence.

Sadie had cerebral palsy and was diagnosed with autism. She had poor eye contact and spent a lot of the day slumped in her wheelchair, unmotivated to interact with others. Her parents told our group of therapists that they weren't sure about her intelligence level, since she was virtually nonverbal. On a recent IQ test, she scored 68. (Any score below 70 is considered mentally retarded.) They explained she could say a few words, but inconsistently, and described how, oddly, she would sometimes silently mouth words. Despite having had some speech therapy, her communication was still a mystery.

Our team's first goal was to find games and toys and activities that interested this little girl. We weren't trying to teach her anything yet except that we were friendly and interested in whatever she was interested in. We presented a whole range of activities including some physical play like tickle and wheelchair dancing. Sadie showed us quickly that she could understand most of what we were saying. When she was motivated by something, she did her best to gather energy and, with great effort, she'd try to play with us. She was gentle and genuinely sweet. The best reward for our efforts was the huge smile she beamed when she liked a game, arching her head back and looking right into our eyes.

After the first two days of play sessions, we felt we had made a connection with Sadie and she was watching us more and more. She seemed happier, but we still weren't certain about her cognitive abilities. What kind of intelligence did she have? Could she learn to speak, for example? Then, during a therapy session on the third day, a therapist had heard Sadie say several words very clearly. He sang and did the actions to "Head and Shoulders, Knees and Toes" while she moved her body as much as she could, looking straight at him the entire song. At the end of the song, Sadie said, "Again!" Afterwards, our senior therapist asked for more details. "How did she say it exactly?" "Kinda breathy . . . it was really soft . . . but I heard it. She definitely said the word," the therapist explained.

During the next session the senior therapist watched more closely for other clues. Then he saw it. Each time Sadie whispered a word, she was sitting more upright. This seemed to happen when she was highly motivated. At the peak of a game, her body was less slumped in the wheelchair, and she held her head up straighter. "That's it!" he thought. "She's in a better position to make vocal sounds." When she wasn't slumped on her diaphragm, her airway opened up more.

Working with another staff member, the senior therapist kneeled down in front of the wheelchair. He told Sadie he had an idea that might help her talk more easily. He asked her if they could hold her under her arms to help her sit up straighter. She nodded and smiled yes. With her torso no longer slumped, he asked her to tell him how that felt. She mouthed a word but no sound came out. From his position kneeling in front, he studied her behaviour very closely and noticed she hadn't taken a breath before speaking. Even though her airway was more open now, for some reason she wasn't taking a breath before trying to speak. Her breath control (the breathing-talking cycle) wasn't coordinated. Reaching forward, he put his hand lightly on her diaphragm. "Take a breath, Sadie," he coached. She followed his cues and took a deeper breath. "How does that feel now?" he asked. "Good," she answered out loud. It wasn't a whisper either. And for the next few minutes, with the other therapist supporting Sadie to sit up as he reminded her to take a breath each time before she spoke, they had a little conversation. "How do you like the games we're playing with you?" he asked. "It's fun!" she said clearly. Her parents stood nearby with tears rolling down their cheeks. Sadie was talking. With more breath-control training and posture strengthening Sadie would go on to show, and tell, her family and teachers how smart she really was. Along with her posture, her IQ scores surged upward!

It's absolutely true that many children diagnosed with autism have scored below 70 on the IQ test, but how accurate are intelligence tests for children with language delays? If a person doesn't have language skills to physically answer the questions, how valid is the test?

HOW ELSE CAN WE MEASURE INTELLIGENCE IN AUTISM?

Jasmine is a beautiful bundle of joy. I met her when she was five years old and already diagnosed with autism. She had some language and a peaceful manner about her. She would sit quietly alone staring out the living room window, highly focused, able to shut out people around her, even when her mother called her name. Over the past three years I directed an education program for Jasmine. It was a pleasure to work with a family who prioritized accepting their daughter's differences first, and then persistently and creatively supporting her development. This is one of the working principles I teach in the Intensive Multi-Treatment Intervention (IMTI) program. Jasmine has come a long way and is now a mainstream student without the need for an assistant at the local public school. With some in-class support and accommodations, her future looks bright. Despite the myth of mental retardation in autism that they have read about over the years, her parents choose to believe that she is intelligent. They speak to her in intelligent ways. They provide opportunities for her to develop her intelligence while allowing space for her unique intelligences to be expressed. Recently her parents shared with me an insightful example of her keen thinking. She had been asking about God (and war and death and heaven and all kinds of things). Looking for a meaningful explanation that would satisfy an eight-year-old and fit the family's beliefs, they told her, "God is love and God is everywhere." The next day, Jasmine turned to one of her favourite teachers and, with a little impish smile, asked, "Do you God me?"

Spurred on by their own observations, similar to mine, of intelligence in autism, a small group of researchers has been challenging the myth of mental retardation. They're re-examining long-accepted conclusions and considering new approaches to measuring intelligence in autism. More philosophically, some are even rethinking what we call intelligence and what "normal" is.

Professor Laurent Mottron at the University of Montreal and his colleague Michelle Dawson are two of the pioneers trying to answer these questions. They argue that the most commonly used tests like the Stanford-Binet and the Wechsler scales are too dependent on good verbal ability. Test takers have to sit and listen to many of the questions read out loud and then answer verbally. So people with a communication disorder fail even though they might know the answers. In other words, these types of verbal-based tests measure communication skills as much as they do intelligence. Interviewed by Sharon Begley for *Newsweek,* Michelle Dawson explained, "Testing autistic kids' intelligence in a way that requires them to engage [verbally] with a stranger 'is like giving a blind person an intelligence test that requires him to process visual information.'"

Instead, we should use tests that don't impose limitations on those with known language barriers. Mottron and Dawson, among others, propose that we use different kinds of intelligence tests that are more valid for the autistic population. They use a visual-oriented test called Raven's Progressive Matrices to measure what is called "fluid intelligence." Thirty-eight children with autism tested on average 30 percentile points higher than they did on the commonly used Wechsler Intelligence Scale for Children (WISC).

Dr. Goldberg Edelson tested almost 300 children diagnosed with autism using the Test of Nonverbal Intelligence (TONI) instead of the conventional Stanford-Binet. Surprisingly, the kids in her group on average scored around 90 (an IQ score that is about average in the general population). Of the 297 children in her study, only 19 percent scored in the mental retardation range—vastly lower than the myth of 70–90 percent. The kids scored higher, she believes, because the TONI doesn't require verbal responses and isn't timed, unlike the most commonly used tests, which can be stressful and limiting for people with language deficits or attention-deficit disorder.

A different way to measure intelligence that doesn't require verbal responses is to see how fast someone can process information. These speed of information processing tests measure inspection time (IT). Some researchers have found that autistic people who scored low on the IQ test process information as fast, or faster, than their high-IQ neurotypical peers. The researchers, Wallace, Anderson, and Happé, concluded, "It may be that IT scores reflect good intellectual potential in ASD that is not expressed in typical IQ tests because of the social, communication, and/or linguistic demands."[6] What this suggests is that different kinds of tests can measure different kinds of intelligence.

The Stanford-Binet intelligence test is actually made up of ten subtests that each test a different kind of thinking skill. There are verbal and nonverbal sections, for example. One important study by Dr. Susan Dickerson Mayes and her colleagues at Penn State University Medical School found that as many as 75 percent of the children with ASD they tested did much better on the nonverbal sections. Discussing her findings with me through email, Dr. Mayes explained that instead of using the total IQ score (even if it is below 70, in the MR range), she looks at the ten individual subtest scores to more accurately describe a child's strengths and challenges. Depending on the cut-off score for MR and which set of scores was used, Mayes reported that approximately 85 percent of the children evaluated in their autism clinic have normal or higher intelligence.

> Approximately 85 percent of the
> children evaluated in their autism clinic
> have normal or higher intelligence.

Her findings stand in stark contrast to the myth of 70–90 percent having mental retardation.

INTELLIGENCE BEYOND IQ

For one young boy born in Germany in 1879, it took almost 20 years for the world to discover his genius. "Initial indications were that this newborn had been born mentally impaired" and he was "slow to talk, slow to read, [and] slow to learn."[7] Some who knew him, including his own family, described him at times as in his own world. The young boy struggled with school. He was disinterested in his lessons and didn't follow teachers' instructions well. But at home he was a curious little guy with a special kind of intelligence. He was a keen observer, asked questions of his parents, and wanted to understand how things worked. His parents fed his appetite for books and the arts.

At school the headmaster reportedly told the boy's father, "He will never make a success of anything."[8] At home on his own terms, he read scientific books at age 10, and by 11 he started on his career path, reading about the mathematical laws of geometry echoed in the natural sciences. Meanwhile, he resisted school where his intelligence went unrecognized. He was even expelled from his secondary school, the Luitpold Gymnasium. Despite his bright mind, he failed the entrance exams for the Swiss Federal Polytechnic School in Zurich. His parents never gave up on him, though. They found ways to support his interest in learning, provided materials, and believed in the intelligence they had seen at home.

When he finally graduated, he couldn't even find work as a teacher, so he worked in a patent office and in his spare time sketched out many of his world-changing theories. One of his most famous equations was $E=MC^2$. The young man was Albert Einstein.

Some believe that Einstein was on the autistic spectrum. Professor Michael Fitzgerald of Trinity College in Dublin reviewed and analyzed the biographies of dozens of famous people using the ASD diagnostic criteria. He believes Einstein fits the higher-functioning Asperger's syndrome. Of course, there are hundreds of examples of above-average-intelligence inventors, artists, Nobel laureates, and leaders who, like Einstein, didn't do well in school or on IQ tests.

For decades, psychologists have debated the definition of intelligence. What is the nature of intelligence? How do we define it? How do we measure it? Our modern understanding of intelligence has expanded as we've measured the brain's functions and capacities. Yet, despite these advances and despite the dozens of different tests designed to measure different levels of intelligence, IQ score is still a golden standard used in autism research. In his book *The Mismeasure of Man*, Stephen Gould writes critically about the IQ test. "The scale, properly speaking, does not permit the measure of intelligence, because intellectual qualities are not superposable, and therefore cannot be measured as linear surfaces are measured." [9] That means intelligence has many dimensions and levels and angles but most tests measure just one limited piece. Tests measure a fairly narrowly defined range of thinking ability. Therefore they don't capture some of the remarkable intelligence in the autistic population.

There are many children who don't score well on intelligence tests but are intelligent nonetheless.

There are many children who don't score well on intelligence tests but are intelligent nonetheless. Professor Howard Gardner of the Harvard Graduate School of Education is the world leader in researching many kinds of intelligence beyond the IQ. His theory of multiple intelligences (MI) has influenced educators and entire school systems around the globe. Just like the definition of autism has evolved into a spectrum disorder, Gardner has proposed a group of different kinds of intelligences that make up a spectrum. For example, many people in sales, politics, and the social services are good at understanding other people and are comfortable speaking publicly. They have what Gardner calls interpersonal intelligence. Others have bodily-kinesthetic intelligence, like the famous basketball star Michael Jordan, who had a genius for launching his body high into the air while manoeuvring around others on his way to a slam dunk. Howard Gardner has identified eight different kinds of intelligence so far, which help to explain diversity in ability and performance in the human population. In my own work, I've witnessed logical-mathematical, musical, spatial, and bodily-kinesthetic intelligence, in particular, in children with ASD. Indeed, these seem to be common strengths in the autistic population.

• Savants

There are diverse types and levels of intelligence within the autism spectrum. In this worldwide population there are some with severe cognitive deficits at one extreme and some with rare savant abilities on the other. A small number of people with autism or Asperger's syndrome have exceptional and unusual intelligence in one particular area of interest like math, visual arts, music, or memorization. One person might be a world-class musician, another a human math calculator, with neither able to socialize or form relationships very well.

Sometimes referred to as "savant syndrome," this special group displays extraordinary talent and ability in ways that are seemingly unexplainable. Any one individual's superability is usually isolated to just one particular area, called "islets of intelligence," while in other areas they function at typical or below-average levels.

Years ago at a special-education conference in Boston, I listened in awe as then nine-year-old Matt Savage led his jazz trio on piano. Matt taught himself to read music at age six. Even though he had sound sensitivities when he was younger, he picked up piano very quickly. Now, almost 20 years old, he has produced several albums, has appeared on the *Late Show with David Letterman*, and tours the world performing his music. Matt has what Howard Gardner calls musical intelligence, but he still has some significant functional delays and challenges. Nonetheless, we should talk about Matt as intelligent, not just as a savant. Sadly, instead of using this example as intelligence in autism, it's discounted as the result of abnormal brain function.

The movie *Rain Man* was based on a real-life savant named Kim Peek, portrayed by actor Dustin Hoffman, who in the movie memorized half of the phone book and vast amounts of baseball trivia. In one scene he calculates in seconds the number of toothpicks spilled on the floor. This movie, along with documentaries about other savants, linked autism with unusual intelligence for the general public but in a way that framed and diminished it as a circus-like talent.

Author Stuart Murray of the University of Leeds in England points to the history of the label "idiot savant" in his important book *Representing Autism*. In one breath, the remarkable intelligence is dumbed down and reduced to fool status: "In popular representations of autism the idea of the idiot and simpleton remain in certain forms."[10] Even though the term isn't used often, intelligence in autism is still qualified as quirky and a sideshow to the "real dysfunctions."

I train parents and therapists to recognize the potential intelligence in every step forward.

Not all savants have autism. Many people with savant syndrome have autism but only a very small number of all people with autism are savants. For most autistic children, intelligence is not so spectacular nor usually so obvious. In my work, I train parents and therapists to recognize the potential intelligence in every step forward. It's critical to challenging the stereotypes that delayed development or differences in function signal a deficiency in intelligence.

The spectacle of a nine-year-old autistic boy who can play piano like an accomplished jazz virtuoso grabs media attention; stories of more average intelligence in ASD don't, leaving the general public with a polarized view. It's as if people with autism are either mentally retarded or strangely genius but nothing in between. At social events, in conversations about my work, I'm often asked if all the kids I work with are supersmart like *Rain Man.* I use the opportunity to debunk both the myth of the savant and of mental retardation: "Definitely some of the children I've worked with are exceptionally good with numbers, and a lot of them have great memories, and some have unusual ways of thinking, and some really struggle cognitively to communicate and function. People with autism can be smart in one area and not so smart in another." Isn't this true for most of us?

UNCOVERING INTELLIGENCE

Aidan was a bright spark. His eyes were always darting about, exploring his environment. He was busy but he was most often unfocused, dealing with hyperactivity and attention deficit disorder. He couldn't manage kindergarten and sometimes experienced so much frustration communicating that he would be aggressive with other kids. The school staff had recommended his parents seek a professional opinion from a speech therapist and possibly a diagnosis of PDD. There was also talk of some kind of medication for his hyperactivity.

Aidan was a classic case of a young boy whose intelligence was masked by his developmental and behavioural challenges. If he stayed in school, they would have to implement a behavioural management program for the aggressive behaviour, using time outs and other consequences. Aidan very likely would have ended up in a special-needs unit. His individualized education plan would have been focused on self-control, self-help skills, and communication. As a result, we might not have discovered his keen intelligence.

During the first year I worked with his family and therapists in a home-based therapy program, I noted several indications he might have dyslexia. Aidan often mixed his words and sentences up. He would regularly switch the placement of words in a sentence. Explaining who will be "it" first in a game of tag, he might say,

"Then you're . . . after it. . . . I'm first . . . okay?" I also observed his immense difficulty and frustration with reading. He avoided even trying. At the young age of four years, he had already experienced so much frustration with reading and fine-motor tasks that we could hear him mutter under his breath, "I can't do this," and "It's too hard!"

His parents firmly believed that Aidan was a smart kid. In the biweekly trainings, I talked a lot about patience.

> In the biweekly trainings,
> I talked a lot about patience.

Aidan needed to learn patience with himself and we needed to model patience in our work with him. We used calming voices and offered ample breaks from table work. I taught the therapists a variety of mini-activities that I called "sensory snacks." These gave Aidan a rest from focusing, released tension buildup in his body, and helped to ease any mounting frustration too. To work directly on his reading, spelling, and speaking challenges, I borrowed from a range of sources including some focusing and hand-eye coordination exercises from Ron Davis's innovative strategies in *The Gift of Dyslexia*.

We also enrolled Aidan in Interactive Metronome (IM) therapy. IM was originally used to help athletes improve their performance. The gross-motor-visual coordination benefits have also been shown to help children with attention deficit disorder. During an IM therapy session, the child hears beats at various speeds and tries to clap or step to the beat. Visual and auditory cues help to motivate and provide instant feedback. We felt this helped to improve Aidan's attention span, his confidence, and his willingness to sit and try the reading exercises. As he improved his reading and writing skills, his communication also improved. He rarely mixed up words anymore. His thinking seemed to follow straight and cogent lines. We could understand his requests and meet his needs, so his frustration subsided and his aggression disappeared. He shared his creative ideas more easily, inviting us into his play and asking lots of questions to try to satisfy his curiosity to learn. Our unwavering belief in his intelligence and our patience were rewarded.

A year after he graduated from his IMTI home program, Aidan's mother invited me to attend his dance school's final performance. Throughout the two-hour performance, I sat with a big grin each time Aidan danced in routines across the stage. He was the lead role in at least four of the acts. Fully confident, he stood at the front of the stage reciting his lines and singing happily, tap dancing, spinning ballet twirls, and doing some modern hip-hop moves too. The audience of at least 100 parents cheered. I felt so proud of my little buddy. That night I saw the challenges that once blocked his intelligence had definitely been lifted.

We have a choice. We can limit the definition of intelligence to the IQ test and consequently label the majority of the autistic population mentally retarded. Or we can acknowledge the diversity of thinking skills and different types of intelligence in the autistic population and, with acceptance and patience, support them to let their individual intelligences shine.

WHAT YOU CAN DO

The following are new perspectives and strategies you can use to better understand and support a person with autism:

• Remove Barriers and Look for Intelligence

Actively look for intelligence in the autistic population by removing barriers. Focus your mind and your eyes on ability. I'm not suggesting we pretend people with autism don't have cognitive, communication, and social challenges. These impairments and differences are usually already apparent and part of the observations and conversation. But oftentimes, we focus so strongly on the "problems" that an individual's capabilities aren't discussed and explored enough.

Barriers to education need to be removed for us to fully discover intelligence in students with autism. School-based programs and individualized education plans often limit autistic students' access to peer-level curriculum, and they end up focusing too much on special treatments. Anne Martin, a primary school teacher in the US, wrote about how, in many cases, she saw special education become a barrier to learning. Even though assessments and IEPs "may work well in some cases of physical and other extreme disabilities," she stated, "I think they have had a demonstrably negative influence on our views of children and teaching altogether."[11] When our main focus on a child is through the lens of disability, we can easily miss opportunities to see and support skills and talents. Therapy and education teams can instead place a student's intelligence at the very centre of evaluations and programming discussions. When we notice what children can do, they become more motivated to work with us. When we make time for students to build on their strengths, they also build their confidence and are more motivated to try new things.

Next, we can remove testing barriers. Tests and measures of intelligence that accommodate communication differences should be automatically included as standard for students with ASD. More and different tools could be developed to help identify a variety of intelligences. There already are many tests available. How do we get these into the mainstream so we can uncover the full range of intelligence in our students? For students already in school, we can allow for more accommodations at exam time so that they are able to demonstrate fully what they learned, so they get a fair measure of their intelligence. Dr. Thomas Hehir, professor of education at Harvard University, points out that while many school systems make accommodations for learning differences to help students with autism access curriculum, these same schools rarely offer the same accommodations when it's time for testing. Writing about digital assistive technologies, he explains, "Students with disabilities have demonstrated that there is not one way to walk, speak, read, or write. New educational technologies have made this possible. Therefore, it is only fair that the assessment of what they have learned should allow for them to demonstrate their knowledge and skills in the way most appropriate to them."[12] For example, a student who needs to use a keyboard to learn his lessons should be allowed to use a keyboard to demonstrate what he's learned when tested.

Looking ahead, to ensure we continue the focus on ability rather than disability, we can remove barriers in research on intelligence. Research could focus more on how people with autism *do* think instead of on how they *don't*.

• Adopt the Concept of Multiple Intelligences

We might describe a good number of children with autism as "high intelligence, low IQ score." This is the conclusion of some researchers who used processing speed to measure intelligence. There are many other kinds of intelligence too. How fast a child can process information, how well they can tie their shoes, how quickly they can figure out where mom hid the cookies or how to turn on the TV and use the DVD player all represent different kinds of intelligence.

Some children with good intelligence don't do well in school, scoring low on tests. But, like the IQ score, school marks and labels often miss the full story of children's intelligence. For some bright students, formal structured teaching methods just don't inspire or motivate. When inflexible education systems don't accommodate learning differences on tests, for example, these students fail because the system fails them. They can lose interest in school and, most unfortunately, they get labelled as slow learners and poor students. I've met many autistic students who fail in school yet whose parents can list all the ways in which the child is smart.

Intelligence in autistic persons exists beyond the limited boundaries of formal school and IQ tests. Often the intelligence is hidden behind communication disorders and physical challenges. Teachers in schools can ensure tests accommodate these challenges and they can find ways to support autistic students to demonstrate their intelligence. We could take cues from Einstein's mother and focus less on fact-cramming with flash cards and more on recognizing and nurturing the interests and strengths that each child with autism has. Teachers bound by school curriculum can recognize student interests and motivations while working in collaboration with parents who can best nurture the unique intelligences of their child.

• *Accept and Accommodate Cognitive Differences*

When we talk about different ways people on the spectrum perceive and think, we could drop the judgments. Compared to the neurotypical majority, differences definitely exist. Instead of calling these differences in autism abnormal, dysfunctional, or wrong, we could simply call them atypical and unique. Instead of judging the different kinds of thinking processes and intelligences found in autism as abnormal or lesser than, we could include them in a larger, more inclusive definition of human cognition and behaviour.

Discussions about differences lead to discussions about accommodations. Some families find creative ways to accommodate the unique needs of their autistic children. For one young boy, the annual Thanksgiving dinner with over 20 family members was too overwhelming. Chris couldn't bear the mixed sounds and unpredictable movements of the crowd. Forced to stay at the table, he would eventually tantrum and run away into a quieter room. His parents and most of the family felt uncomfortable with the tension. After failed attempts to fit their child into Thanksgiving, the parents finally accepted to accommodate his different needs into Thanksgiving. The following year a smaller room in the house was set aside for their son to dine in. It was decorated equally as the main dining room. A small table was set with special attention and two chairs. A list of family members was drawn up in order of appearance so everyone could take a turn sitting and eating with Chris. It was fantastic. Chris was reported to have a big grin on his face during the entire evening. He had special focused time with each of his family members and he was able to sit and enjoy the tasty food that in years past he had been too overwhelmed to even try. Uncles, cousins, and grandparents felt they had spent some quality time with him too. Like Chris, in the smaller room they were less distracted and could really focus on talking to him. They felt they got to know him better. By choosing acceptance and accommodating his needs instead of forcing him to fit their norm, the battle was over. The parents, their son, and the rest of the family all looked forward to Thanksgiving next year.

• Establish Communication First; Assess Intelligence Second
"Not Being Able to Speak Is Not the Same Thing as Not Having Anything to Say," announces a poster on the wall in classroom 210 of Poplar Tree Elementary School.

There can be hundreds of physiological and environmental impediments to accurately measuring intelligence. Dyslexia can act as a blind between a person's intelligence and communicating their intelligence well. Hypersensitive hearing can act as a major distraction from a child following instructions while taking an intelligence test. Before we can determine the intelligence level (or IQ score) of a person with autism, we should do all that we can to establish good communication skills. As obvious as this strategy is, it is not often followed. Thousands of children with autism have been given IQ tests by clinicians they don't have rapport with in environments they aren't familiar with, while dealing with physical disorders ranging from indigestion and migraine headaches to seizures.

In some ways, *assessing* intelligence should perhaps be of far less priority and importance. First, we should ensure the healthy functioning, supports, and accommodations for people with autism so that they can ably communicate and share their intelligence.

CHAPTER SIX

THE MYTH OF THE "FIVE-YEAR WINDOW"

"Children with Autism Lose Their Chance to Change Once They Turn Five"

Intervention should start before the age of three, and certainly by the age of four. After a certain point, you can still teach an autistic child certain things, ameliorate destructive behaviors, but you're not really going to change the developmental pathway that they're on.

Dr. Deborah Fein, professor of psychology, University of Connecticut

If you have a child with autism who's not wired correctly, and we allow that to continue without intervention, those neuropathways will become fixed, and it becomes far more difficult to undo that tangled mess.

Dr. David L. Holmes, president, Eden Institute, Princeton, New Jersey

"He punched a hole in the wall again," his mother said, searching my face for answers. "And he hit his brother yesterday, for no reason . . . just out of the blue," his father added. Their eldest son, Adriano, diagnosed with autism, was fixed in repetitive behaviours and a controlling personality. Despite some early intervention, he still had limited verbal language consisting mostly of memorized phrases and scripts from movies. Listening closely, anyone familiar with *Thomas the Tank Engine* could recognize the names of the characters that he muttered under his breath—Percy, Henry, and Emily. He was now almost six years old and still resisting any form of interaction. He was fortunate, I thought, to have such a caring family who extended patience to his energy and defiance.

At the diagnosis, the pediatrician had stressed that early intervention was critical. This meant starting therapies and treatments *before* five years of age. After that, the pediatrician explained, learning slows down and his window of opportunity to change will close. Adriano was already three years old, so his parents instantly felt the pressure of the two-year window they believed they had left. Family counsellors at a local autism resource centre reinforced the push for early intervention, warning, "You need to get him signed up for treatment right away while the learning window's still open."

Supporting children's development as early as possible is a good idea.

Everyone, including me, agrees that supporting children's development as early as possible is a good idea. The Autism Society of America website states: "Studies show that early diagnosis and intervention lead to significantly improved outcomes." The earlier a child's specific delays are identified and diagnosed, the earlier appropriate treatment can begin. It makes perfect sense.

Adriano's parents took the early intervention prescription seriously, enrolling him in part-time daycare for socialization soon after the diagnosis, hiring a behaviour therapist, and signing up for a research study that offered some play-therapy training. A year later, they became interested in my multi-treatment approach. One year into the program, we sat at the kitchen table and talked about him punching the wall. As Adriano's sixth birthday approached, their fears mounted. The early interventions hadn't worked as well as they'd hoped. They wondered if I had worked with "older" kids: "Have you seen other kids around his age still improve?" they asked anxiously.

One of the most debilitating effects of the myth of the five-year window of opportunity is the fear and pressure it places on parents. From the moment Sabrina first learned about the five-year window, she felt the pressure that was reinforced by books she read on autism. Even the poem "All I Really Need to Know I Learned in Kindergarten" confirmed her fear that they had limited time. The worry kept her up at night searching the Web for answers, for more that she could do for her son before time ran out. Adriano was only five years old but his parents were already feeling anxious that he was perhaps "too old" for significant development.

To move forward effectively with the therapy program, we needed to alleviate the fear and doubt. Families facing a lifetime of caring for and parenting a child with autism need hope and support, not fear and panic. I presented a different perspective to Sabrina and Lenny, confirming that learning and development definitely continue *after* the age of five. I explained there really isn't any good research to prove that autistic children older than five stop improving at a certain age. To the contrary, there is ample research and many real-life stories of autistic people learning throughout their lives. This knowledge gave them more hope and recharged their patience and energy to continue with the program.

> There really isn't any good research to prove that autistic children older than five stop improving.

The importance of having hope and taking action is paramount. Adriano is now eight years old and known in his family as a courteous, affectionate, and intelligent young boy. When I first met him he had a limited vocabulary of mostly single words and parroted movie scripts. Today, he has an extensive vocabulary, speaks in sentences, and is beginning to initiate some amusing conversations with family and neighbours. At age five he was unable to follow even simple kindergarten-level worksheets and instructions. He couldn't do math and only wrote letters he had seen on television. Today, Adriano is above his peer grade level in math, is an excellent speller, and enjoys journalling for his mainstream classes. Like any eight-year-old child, he fidgets and gets restless at times during longer lessons, but unlike many of his peers, we taught him to ask for what he needs to refocus, like a break or stretch or sip of water.

I smiled as I read Sabrina's most recent email to me:

By the way, Jonathan, we had friends over for brunch and Adriano ate with us and stayed a while then went upstairs to play. When he heard our guests leaving he came down and said goodbye to each one individually. He thanked them for coming, told them to have a nice day and then, of course, reminded them to put their seatbelts on. Very cute! Oh, and I almost forgot, when they said "Thank you" back to him, without missing a beat, he replied, "No problem! See you soon."

The myth pronounced Adriano's window for significant learning closed at age five. Yet, *almost all* of his development, including learning to speak, happened between five and eight years of age. We don't dare imagine the outcome had we believed in the five-year barrier and lost hope. Instead, we challenged the myth.

OF ALL THE MYTHS OF AUTISM, THIS ONE CAUSES THE MOST ANXIETY

One mother posted a plea for support on an internet forum about autism. Her intimate and honest words express the raw emotions she felt under the pressure of the five-year window.

Things are just getting much, much worse with my poor boy. I just feel horrible that all this time was lost to us to do some massive intervention, and I look at him now and he is just so big and old to me now. I feel like I let the "magic window" close on him and it's all my fault. Is it too late to see incredible results starting so late? (He just turned 5.) [1]

What kind of messages are we giving parents for them to feel "horrible" because their five-year-old children are deemed too old for any meaningful developmental improvement? Thankfully, this particular parent found some support and encouragement from others in the online forum. For those who don't see beyond the myth, depression is not uncommon.

Anxiety caused by the myth can negatively impact parenting and even marriages. Stress, pressure, fear, and guilt can lead to impatience and irritability. One study showed that mothers feeling high stress are more likely to interpret neutral situations involving their autistic children as problematic.[2] In other words, the more stress you feel, the more you see the cup as half-empty . . . and ultimately lose hope.

The myth can also lower expectations for older children. Most education for autistic children over five years old is less intense, based on the myth that the window for significant learning has closed. One six-year-old boy had just started first grade where they implemented a picture communication system since he wasn't fully verbal. As I watched him point to picture cards for things he wanted, I knew from the history I had collected from his parents that he could actually say some of those words. The picture system wasn't designed to help him learn new language, but was used anyway, the teachers told me, because he was past the time when he was most likely going to speak.

Lowered expectations become a self-fulfilling prophecy when young children are given less intense intervention with less sophisticated goals facilitated by less hopeful educators.

The myth affects education and funding systems too. It limits what's available for kids after the early-intervention years. The major public focus on early treatment for autism means less attention, research, and funding is available after the three- or five-year mark. There are fewer opportunities for "older" children with autism past the age of five because of the disproportionate funding earmarked for early intervention. School boards are left to do what they can with limited funding and limited expertise.

While there is an extensive amount of evidence and research supporting the popular treatment of applied behaviour analysis for children in the early years, there have been few studies with older children. The consequence is that insurance companies are reluctant to fund the treatment without evidence even though thousands of success stories concerning children six and older exist. Some states mandate coverage for ABA up to 21 years of age, but most still don't. In the province of Ontario, so far, no funding is available for ABA (outside of school) past age six. The answer isn't to decrease early-intervention funding but to recognize the importance of continued intensive input and resources all the way through the primary years of education and beyond.

In her heartwarming book *A Regular Guy Growing Up with Autism,* Laura Shumaker chronicles life raising her now 23-year-old son with autism. Despite their conscious effort to choose a positive outlook whenever they could, at times they too ran into the negative effects of the myth. When her son was five, for example, they asked their developmental pediatrician if they should begin a behavioural treatment program for him. They were discouraged to even try because, they were told, it only works within the one- to three-year window. While researching this chapter, I came across a letter that Shumaker posted on Facebook that describes the family's initial race against the five-year mark and, at the same time, shows that the possibility for growth and learning doesn't end at five or even at 25.

"People with autism of all ages are capable of making significant progress through the lifespan."

When my husband and I suspected that our 3-year-old son Matthew might have autism, we believed we could "nip it in the bud." We felt like we had to do something in a hurry before Matthew was ready to start school and real autism "set in." By the time Matthew was 5 years old, though, we could see that we hadn't done enough.

I was reminded of our cockeyed view of autism when I attended the Easter Seals Bay Area Autism Community Forum in Oakland last month. The message of the forum—that "People with autism of all ages are capable of making significant progress through the lifespan."—was an epiphany for me. Matthew is 23 years old now and making progress, but until I went to the Autism Community Forum last month, I still believed early intervention was the only real time that treatment mattered.

Remarkably, Shumaker learned after 23 years of believing the myth that there are alternative ways to think about learning and autism. She says it best in the title of her online post, "It's never too late to learn as we grow."

WHY IS FIVE THE NUMBER WRITTEN IN STONE? WHY NOT SIX OR EIGHT OR TWELVE?

Not so long ago, in 1986, the US government provided financial incentives for states to expand early intervention services for infants and toddlers with disabilities (from birth to age three). The added funding spurred innovation as hundreds of new intervention programs were launched. Research dollars followed the policy and proved that early education can make a significant difference. MSNBC television news anchorwoman Sue Herera said it best in a report on autism on February 23, 2005: "One of the few things everyone in the autism community agrees on is the value of early intervention—the earlier the better."

Government policies and funding support early intervention more than training past age five. Across North America, Europe, Australia, and other countries, funding for intervention programs is usually restricted to birth through age three, and in a few places up to six years of age. Consequently, the bulk of research on learning in autism has focused on children under five years of age. There is some good research with children older than five, but not half as much as for early interventions. Kids older than five are usually enrolled in school where special-intervention programs are inevitably less intensive and less funded with less specially trained staff.

In some very tangible real-world ways, children with autism may in fact often have the best chance for the most learning before the age of five simply because that's when the most intensive services are provided. The line in the sand may be drawn at five years of age simply because that's when funding for early intervention stops and public education starts.

FACT VERSUS FICTION, ACCORDING TO SCIENCE

What's true and what's not about children's development? I have yet to see a study that demonstrates how learning slows down when children with autism turn five. Where's the research to support this? In fact, there is no evidence strong enough to warrant parents' hold on this belief. But we continue to buy into the old idea that the brain sets after the first few years and becomes less flexible, and less able to learn, as we age. That's the difficulty with challenging a myth: it exists because on the surface it seems to make sense. But when we poke it and examine it a bit more deeply we find it doesn't stand up to its claim.

One man who has methodically poked systems of education and the science of early learning is Dr. John Bruer. In his book *The Myth of the First Three Years,* he discusses concepts from science that are used to support the three- and five-year window of opportunity myths. The science behind the myths is very real and fairly accurate, but the assumptions and conclusions that educators often extrapolate aren't.

Here are two real-science concepts and the false conclusions we've drawn from them:

1) Infants have an enormous amount of nerve endings or synaptic connections that link to form pathways when they learn something new. Young brains are so fertile for the huge amount that they have to learn in the first few years to survive that they, in fact, have an

abundance of synaptic connections. They have millions more than they need or will ever use. However, nature is so efficient that we have a built-in "pruning" system that gets rid of nerve connections that aren't being used by about three years of age. It's like pruning the dead and extra branches on a bush or tree. Early education and intervention, it is said, rely on the abundant supply of synaptic connections before they shrivel up. This early period of synaptic growth followed by pruning is where the "use it or lose it" pressure on parents comes from. This is the science.

The fiction is that scientists used to believe this abundance of synapses happened just once in life from birth to three years of age. However, we now know that there are *several phases* during development when an explosive growth and abundance of nerve synapses happens. Dr. Jay Giedd of the National Institute of Mental Health in the US pioneered game-changing research to show there is a second wave of brain growth in adolescents between ten and thirteen years of age. Therefore, the window of opportunity to establish synaptic connections and learned pathways doesn't close at three, or five, or even at ten years of age. According to Dr. Giedd's work, there may be compelling reasons to create adolescent intervention programs for autism, when science tells us they have a second surge of brain growth.

Moreover, science hasn't been able to demonstrate that learning for autistic children is any faster or easier during these abundant synaptic phases. In fact, on average the rate of learning remains fairly stable throughout youth and into adulthood. Learning doesn't slow down at age five. For many, learning feels easier, not harder, over the years. The more you know, the easier it is to learn more.

2) A cousin to the first concept is the scientifically proven fact that providing stimulation increases synaptic (nerve) growth in the brain. The more a child's senses are stimulated (with activities, language, socialization, sounds, sights, smells, etc.), the more neural pathways and connections are made. It's true that infants and young children

benefit from all of the rich sensory input and "brain food" that their natural social and play environments provide. In fact, John Bruer even questions whether typically developing children benefit from or need extra input like Baby Mozart and flash cards. However, it seems to make sense to provide lots of extra stimulation and input for children with autism who aren't naturally exploring their environments or naturally paying attention to the social world around them.

Science tells us stimulation increases synaptic growth. The fiction is that there is a time limit. Actually, sensory stimulation, input, and cognitive exercise will stimulate brain development at *any* age. There are now dozens of books on the plasticity of the brain. In recent years we've learned much about the brain's amazing ability to regenerate and learn even after stroke and brain damage later in life. One compelling example is *The Mind and the Brain: Neuroplasticity and the Power of Mental Force* by UCLA professor Jeffrey Schwartz and science writer Sharon Begley. Neuroplasticity describes the brain's ability to change based on sensory input, experiences, and our behaviour. The book details examples of adults with obsessive-compulsive disorder who changed their maladaptive behaviours by learning to think differently, and in doing so actually changed their brain circuitry.

As with each of the myths, however, there are important nuances to the discussion that can't all be addressed in a single chapter. Individuals with ASD are indeed individuals, each with unique strengths and challenges. Our science and understanding of the brain and learning is still not sophisticated enough to account for all of the individual differences and nuances that occur in the human spectrum. For some, it may be that the *rate* of learning certain kinds of skills like language slows down at age five while it speeds up for other kinds of learning like math. It's not uncommon to hear that a child with ASD started to make more friends in middle school between eight and twelve years of age, for example. For others there may be biomedical issues that stand in the way of learning. Geraldine Dawson, professor of psychology and director of the University of Washington Autism Center, offers her opinion that "for all we know, a child with a developmental delay may have a longer window of opportunity for growth. I think it's not helpful to alarm parents. I've seen kids who start late and quickly catch up—a lot of kids with intensive early intervention who progressed slowly and then took off in elementary schools." No matter the reason for delayed development, five is an arbitrary age that has more to do with children's age during the first year of school than with learning or science.

> Five is an arbitrary age that has more to do with the first year of school than with learning or science.

Well-established concepts in neuroscience show how ready the brain is to learn early in life but there is no evidence that learning stops or slows down at three, or five, or at any specific age. There's a scientific basis to tell parents that lots of learning can happen in the early years, but not one for suggesting it stops at five or gets more difficult later on.

NEW PERSPECTIVES

Over the past two decades of helping families to accept and live with autism, I've witnessed children older than five make tremendous developmental gains. I've seen seven- and nine-year-olds learn to talk, for example.

I'm often asked what to do differently to help an older child. There's no special trick. I use all of the same strategies that are known to work with younger children. There's no reason to believe they won't work for older kids too. The scientific principles of human behaviour used in applied behavioural analysis programs, for example, aren't age restricted. It is, of course, wise to choose activities and learning materials that are age-appropriate. Play-therapy strategies can be highly motivating for children five and up but I wouldn't use the children's song "Ring-a-Round the Rosie" with a 13-year-old. Maybe we'd play a board game or trade baseball cards instead. Almost any intervention and therapy can be modified for any age with a little bit of knowledge about the age group and some creativity.

It's time to adopt a new narrative about learning and autism. Early intervention is important and so is intensive education beyond age five. I propose two key perspectives to parents and therapists to help keep them motivated and persistent beyond the five-year mark:

1) Be open to the fact that lots of learning can and does happen after age five.

Thankfully, there has been a good deal of research into ABA, which is where we can find studies that specifically look at how older children with autism learn. One team of researchers measured the gains of children who started an intensive ABA program at school sometime between four and seven years of age. The students demonstrated significant increases in IQ and other skills.[3] It is important for parents and educators to hold hope and positive expectations for children with autism through all the years of primary school.

Learning beyond primary school happens. Believe it. For example, one experiment with 13- to 17-year-old teenagers used a parent-assisted social-skills program to help improve their friendships.[4] The teens improved their knowledge of social skills and increased the time they spent with friends. They learned new skills in their teen years.

At age five, Karla still couldn't say more than a few words. She couldn't pay attention or sit still long enough to learn basic skills, and she spent most of the day waving anything she could find in front of her eyes. I remember the first time I met her: she was still in diapers and standing with a toothbrush in each hand that she waved back and forth near the tip of her nose. She fixed her gaze on the waving objects as she avoided looking in people's eyes. When others approached her she turned away. If they moved to try to see her face, she would turn away again. Her parents struggled to calm her restless energy and to find something that would motivate her besides food.

When she was eight, I directed her multi-treatment intervention. That year, her language was assessed to be at a three-year-old's level. After running home-based programs for five years, Karla's parents were still fierce believers that change is possible at any age given the right input and persistence. Of course, they realized, as I do, that trying doesn't mean change will necessarily happen. There's no guarantee how any child will develop or how far they will go, and most families simply can't continue with intensive therapies into the school years.

Their Intensive Multi-Treatment Intervention included structured learning segments balanced with lots of physical activities and social-skills building. We used music and sensory activities, which Karla really enjoyed. These calmed her down and motivated her to stay focused longer. While I designed the curriculum and trained therapists, the program was supervised by a skillful and dedicated senior therapist named Rebecca. Every day, Rebecca observed Karla and found ways to make learning activities motivating and accessible for this eight-year-old. Karla had never before been able to use scissors, for example, but there she was learning to cut along the lines of a circle for the first time at age eight. Rebecca was brilliant at finding creative ways to implement each of the strategies I taught like using an FM personal listening system to amplify speech, following a very specific order of activity rotation, and using a lot of social praise, which seemed to really motivate Karla.

It was during this time, between eight and thirteen years of age, that she began to speak in sentences, became more affectionate and curious about others, learned to follow instructions, and showed more interest than ever in sitting down to learn. Now, at school, she participates in various mainstream classes with an educational assistant who facilitates her participation. She has learned to ski and canoe, and participates in all of her family's outings. Karla has not "recovered" by any definition, but she did make most of her important and impressive developmental gains *after* the "age-of-five window." Now, at age 15, she continues to mature socially and speaks using multiple complex sentences. We believe she can still learn even more and we will continue to provide all of the opportunities for her that we can.

2) Be open to the fact that some children can learn to talk after five years of age.

There are many benefits that come from learning to speak as early as possible. Studies have shown children with autism who learn to talk before five often do better socially and throughout their school career.[5] Children who learn to talk early usually experience less stress because they can communicate their needs and get what they want without a struggle. It's important that we do all that we can to find ways to help children with autism to communicate easily and as early as possible. However, even with speech therapy and early intervention, many children with autism don't learn to speak by age five. This is not the time to believe they never will. It's not the time to stop speech therapy or to lose hope.

Remember David from chapter two? He was not yet talking at age nine, and only used the single word "chips." He had a repetitious ritualistic behaviour of licking and blowing his fingertips all day long that seemed to block him from learning more language. After five years of working to help their son in various ways, his parents finally found a doctor who helped identify some pinched nerves that were causing chronic discomfort in David's fingertips. With treatment, the ritual decreased enough for him to begin learning language. Within six months he acquired about 100 new words. With continued effort, he has built his vocabulary bit by bit. Although he still doesn't speak in sentences, the vocabulary that he learned from age ten onwards has made an important difference in his life.

It turns out that there are hundreds of documented examples of children who have acquired speech well after five years of age. One very compelling report honoured as one of Autism Speaks' Top 10 Scientific Achievements in 2009 reviewed 64 different studies about speech therapy that included 167 children who started to speak after age five. The authors of the report found that most of the late talkers began to speak between five and seven years. A majority used only single words, although some used sentences. What's more remarkable is that 11 of the children learned to speak for the first time at 13 years of age.[6]

> Eleven of the children learned to speak for the first time at 13 years of age.

Therapies that were involved included behavioural therapy, computer-assisted training, and sign language, among others. Speech therapy seemed to help even after other treatments didn't.

I am, however, always careful about not building up expectations and never promising that a child will definitely speak if only a family keeps trying. There are, of course, thousands of children with autism who never learn to speak or only ever use a few single words.

Each family has personal decisions to make each day to hope more or less, to work harder or rest, to stay the course or change direction. When I began working with Adriano, Karla, and David, I didn't promise their parents that they would learn to talk or guarantee any other specific goals. I don't believe it's helpful to sell parents a future that no one can predict. I *do* think it's helpful to educate parents and professionals with perspectives that I know are real and can make a positive difference. Parents come to the table with so many questions and confusion due to misinformation and myths. I listen to what's important to them and then provide knowledge based on research and evidence I have personally witnessed. Parents ask me if there is still hope after five. I answer them honestly and justifiably when I say "Yes."

WHAT YOU CAN DO

• *Change Your Beliefs about Learning*

The beliefs we hold affect how we feel, how we make decisions, and how we behave. Parents who believe there is a time limit on their autistic child's learning may feel more anxious and lose hope. A parent who says "I feel like I let the 'window of opportunity' close on him and it's all my fault" needs support to change what she thinks about learning. Belief in a "magic" window can be changed to belief in lifelong learning.

We are more likely to make an effort when we believe it will make a difference. Parents who believe there is a time limit on their autistic child's learning become increasingly reluctant to try new treatments over the years. Even though Laura Shumaker continued to provide intervention for her son, she admitted, "Until I went to the Autism Community Forum last month, I still believed early intervention was the only real time that treatment mattered." When Laura adopted the belief that her efforts could still impact her son's learning, she says she "felt energized realizing that there was so much I could do to continue to improve the quality of his life."

As therapists and educators, we too need to be aware of our judgments about the learning capacities of autistic students. Beliefs influence our behaviour like the kinds of goals we set and the opportunities we provide, or not. Speaking to a group of parents and professionals at a national conference on outcomes for adults with autism, Dr. Patricia Howlin, a professor of clinical child psychology, stated insightfully: "We really need to focus on changing other people's understanding and behaviour just as much as we try and change the individual with autism."[7]

Perhaps the easiest and most impactful strategy we can implement immediately is to change our own beliefs about learning.

• *Look for Evidence That Learning Is Happening*

As children get older, we settle into daily routines and stop looking for new daily developments as we do with infants.

While working with a family in Alberta, I was reminded of the importance of keeping focused on their daughter's specific needs each time the local school authority reminded us what other students her age were doing. Julie, diagnosed with severe autism, was seven years old at the time, and her peers were all attending grade two. I sat with the family and compared the grade-two curriculum with Julie's level of functioning and her most immediate developmental needs. Julie couldn't yet hold a pencil. She had no motor coordination, did not read, and had almost no attention span. We agreed that she wasn't ready for grade-two mathematics, writing, or the physical education classes that the school was suggesting she participate in. The local autism service representatives were concerned that Julie was not keeping up with the steps other children were taking like being in school and all of the activities there. But her parents were more concerned with what the most immediate next steps in her own unique development should be. Julie needed intensive physical and occupational therapy–type training to support her fine and gross motor development, in order to catch up to her peers. School wasn't able to provide these types of therapies but without them, we felt she would be lost at school.

I remember one therapy session in particular when I laid a hula hoop on the floor in front of her. I modelled how to jump with both feet into the circle. It was a very simple movement but it wasn't simple for Julie. I invited her to try but she just sat on the floor without moving. I raised my enthusiasm, waved my arms, acted silly, and jumped in and out of the hoop several more times to entice her. Eventually, with some prompting, she stood up, next to the outside edge of the circle. Standing with her hands down at her sides, her eyes darted about the room. She seemed to have no clue as to how to coordinate her arms and legs to make the mini-hop into the circle. But we believed she could learn and we looked for small pieces of evidence. We provided lots of encouragement and reinforcement and she eventually learned to jump. Over several years, including some school-based education, Julie has gained control over her movements and the independence that comes with it. She now skis and rides a bike on weekends with her family. She plays soccer, swims, and participates in running races at school. Julie is now writing and is an avid reader. She has play dates with friends from school and will bend anyone's ear willing to listen. She still has many challenges and requires an educational assistant at school but her family remains focused on her unique needs and the very next step.

During one of my last trips to work with this wonderful young girl, her mother invited me to join them for an early morning run. She wanted me to see how much her daughter had developed. I hadn't seen Julie for almost six months. She was now 11 years old and had grown lanky preteen legs, perfect for running. Her mother led our little pack, Julie ran behind her, and I followed. As she took her first strides, her strength, agility, and confidence were those of a trained runner. Her movements were coordinated and graceful. She kept her head up with her eyes focused on the path. I was amazed by her accomplishment, proud of her efforts, and excited for what possibilities lay ahead for her. The emotions hit me hard and I had to wipe a few happy tears out of my eyes to keep on course.

Once you adopt the belief that significant learning and change is possible in an older child with autism, the very next action to take is to look expectantly for any small evidence of positive new behaviour to reinforce.

• *Believe That Early Intervention Can Inform Lifelong Learning*
Educational strategies that work for children with autism at two years of age can be used at almost any age. Behaviour modification

principles, play-therapy techniques, language therapy, and socialization strategies can all be used with older children, adolescents, and adults, when the presentation and activity style is modified to be age-appropriate.

There's not much information on intervention and outcomes for older children, but research in special education tells us that best-practice, evidence-based teaching strategies can be good for all students. If a particular modification to a lesson or activity is effective, or simply helped one child learn better, then it is also likely helpful for many other children, including older students. There is a wealth of knowledge, expertise, and resources that have been developed for children in early intervention. We need to create bridges of communication and training to pass these resources up the education ladder for teachers and caregivers working at elementary and secondary school levels.

John Bruer, who wrote a book about early education and learning, summarized this best in an interview when he said: "Rather than emphasize early childhood, the bigger challenge is to say, 'For a citizen of any age that wants to learn something—how do we design learning experiences and environments that will facilitate those changes?' Children can benefit from that research; adolescents can benefit from that research. So can adults."

• Focus on Other Evidence-Based Factors for Success

Professionals and family counsellors should educate parents about several other factors, along with early intervention, that have been scientifically shown to improve outcomes for children with autism. The National Research Council's 2001 report *Educating Children with Autism* is widely considered one of the most comprehensive reviews of the research and treatment of autism. The 350-page report identifies factors that are not age-dependent that make a significant difference for children with autism, including the following:

- Interventions should be "intensive" for at least 20-25 hours per week.

- Interventions should include well-planned and structured learning opportunities that match each individual child's developmental deficits.

- Parental involvement in therapy and education concerns leads to better outcomes.

- Adult-led, one-to-one-style instruction is a common element among top-rated treatment programs.

So, while it is important to begin intervention before three years of age if possible, it is just as important to find treatments that satisfy these important keys to success, regardless of age. Oftentimes families can't access early intervention because of long waiting lists. or low income, or because they live in remote rural areas. They shouldn't give up hope. While early intervention is an age-restricted concept, the above key factors are not. A family with a six-year-old son just beginning therapy should not focus on what opportunities they've missed but instead on the strategies they can manage that will make a difference today.

• Believe That Time Is Not the Enemy

Becky Estepp and Moira Giammatteo of the organization Talk About Curing Autism (TACA), both mothers of older children with autism, wrote about the myth of the five-year window in their article "Does the 'Window' Ever Close?" After describing several stories of older children who continued to make significant gains past age five, they leave the reader with an important message: "Time is not our enemy and we haven't missed the window. . . . As tiring as this journey may be, there is no reason to give up hope."[8]

Time doesn't stop a person's learning. Time pressures are imposed by service-provider schedules, waiting lists, school calendars, and funding and education policies. Early intervention services are a limited-time offer: there's pressure to get them before they expire. School starts at age five: there's pressure to be ready before it begins. These are very real time limits and they are very real stressors.

However, the fight is not against time (the window doesn't close) but it should be against the restrictions that are placed by governments and their advisers on early-education services. I have heard too many stories about children developing very well in early-intervention programs only to have them stopped because the child's "X" birthday arrived. This doesn't make any sense at all. Why stop an education program that is making a positive difference? Limited funding and policy restraints are what stop learning, not time.

• Change How You Talk about Early Intervention

Yes, early intervention is extremely important but parents and educators need to be informed on the benefits of intensive education past age five as well. Public service guidelines in government brochures, websites, and Early Years Centres and Head Start literature could all include information on the benefits of continued intervention and lifelong learning.

The US Centers for Disease Control and Prevention website includes the following good advice in their "Learn the Signs. Act Early" campaign: "Research shows that early intervention services can greatly improve a child's development. In order to make sure your child reaches his or her full potential, it is very important to get help for an ASD as soon as possible." Without taking away from the strength of this message, I believe it could also help inform parents if they added, "Education and intensive intervention strategies have been shown to greatly improve a child's development from the early years through the primary grades and into the teens."

• *Promote Stories That Debunk the Myth*

One true story that turns the myth of the five-year window on its head was featured in news reports across North America. Carly Fleischmann of Toronto exhibited all of the classic symptoms of severe autism and was diagnosed at an early age. After years of intensive intervention she still could not talk and appeared limited by her unusual repetitive behaviours.

Then, one day during a therapy session at age 11, unable to communicate what she was feeling, she ran over to a computer and typed the words "HELP" and "HURT," and then went behind the couch to vomit. The therapists and her parents were stunned. She had communicated for the first time at age 11. Through more intensive training, Carly is now able to type and fully communicate on her own. She does not use the controversial facilitated communication technique in which a facilitator holds the writer's hand or arm, putting into question who is really doing the communicating. Unfortunately, however, even though videos and interviews show Carly typing entirely independently, some people doubt that her communication is real. But looking past the skepticism, the thoughts and ideas Carly types display an intelligent and mature mind. She keeps a blog and is partway through writing a book. When Carly appeared on television she was asked what she would say to therapists. She typed without assistance, "Never to give up on the children that they work with."[9]

CHAPTER SEVEN

THE MYTH OF IMAGINATION

"Children with Autism Lack Imagination and Creativity"

Their play is often repetitive and characterized by limited imagination (neatly arranging crayons instead of coloring with them).
Patrick J. Skerritt and Dr. Jane A. Leopold, *Newsweek*

Harriet was practically nonverbal and absorbed in her own world of tiny paper pieces and beads. She would sit for up to 20 minutes at times, holding tiny bits by her eyebrows, and ever so particularly sprinkle them in front of her eyes, like rain or snowflakes. Her eyes would widen, her gaze fixed, and you could hear the cringe-inducing sound of her teeth grinding from her intense concentration. She quickly scooped up the paper bits that collected in her lap and repeated the self-encapsulating ritual. This kind of repetitive and unchanging behaviour is used as proof that people with autism lack imagination. Harriet isn't pretending anything we recognize and it doesn't look creative.

Over the past three years I directed a treatment program for Harriet, diagnosed with autism, who, just two years earlier, was nonverbal. Last fall I was leaving the family's home when I happened to see a wonderful expression of creativity and imagination. As I walked outside, Harriet's mother brought my attention to the miniature pumpkins that decorated the front porch in time for Halloween. Each one was painted with a face but one stood out in particular: it was painted entirely red with the stem painted bright green. "That's Harriet's other one!" she pointed out proudly. "We each decorated one with a jack o' lantern face and Harriet wanted to do a second one, which was entirely her own unique thing. Then, unprompted, Harriet just held it up and said 'Apple!'" Her mother was so excited by this milestone. Harriet had imagined the little pumpkin was something different than it was. She demonstrated imagination, creativity, and a capacity to pretend.

But if Harriet hadn't learned to speak or if she wasn't able to organize her motor-planning well enough to use the paintbrush, like so many children with autism, we might not have discovered her imagination. It was through many hundreds of hours of therapy that Harriet developed to the point where she can express her creativity in ways others can see and understand. Is it possible that many or maybe even all people with autism have the capacity to imagine but may not be able to express or demonstrate it?

Maybe even all people with autism have the capacity to imagine.

Real-life stories of imagination in people with autism like Harriet exist juxtaposed to the limiting characterizations portrayed in popular media and books. The facts I read are challenged by the facts I observe. I *saw* Harriet's imagination, her ability to make-believe and even to initiate it. The media, the *Washington Post* in this example, reports that children with autism have an "apparent lack of imagination." In his book *A Mind Apart,* Dr. Peter Szatmari of McMaster University in Hamilton, Ontario, describes a young patient diagnosed with Asperger's syndrome who loved subway trains. Szatmari writes that "at age four, there was still no evidence of imaginative play." The boy, he explains, played in a routinized way with toy trains and didn't use the miniature characters in an animated way. Yet, Szatmari goes on to describe how the boy "would sometimes walk down the hallways at school backward, presumably imitating the sensation of riding in a subway car."[1] For the good doctor, this was evidence of more abnormal behaviour. Walking backwards is not usual, true. But it's also possibly important proof of the young boy's capacity for make-believe and imagination.

Over the years I've worked with hundreds of children diagnosed with autism who have shown me their great capacities for imaginative play and creativity, despite their repetitive and unusual behaviours.

Tina was short for a six-year-old. When I arrived at her home for the initial consultation, she stood in the doorway and swayed crookedly, negotiating balance on her flat feet, with hunched shoulders, staring at my briefcase. She looked at my shoes, then she slowly scanned up to my hand, then shoulder to face. Our eyes met briefly and she beamed the smile that, as it does for many people, melts my heart.

Her parents, hopeful I could help, explained Tina's condition of DiGeorge syndrome, a rare congenital genetic disease caused by the lack of chromosome 22q11. Tina is fed through a tube extending out from her stomach. The hole in her throat from having a tracheotomy was just healing over, and her deformed palate makes it incredibly difficult for her to produce intelligible sounds.

When I first met her, she also had a diagnosis of autism and spent many hours every day involved in repetitive and routinized play. I watched her sit while holding a clear plastic CD music case. She flipped the cover up and then down, up and down, hundreds of times in a row without ever looking up. She was often in her own world. She didn't seek out play with other children. Instead, she stared off into the space in front of her and turned away from anyone who interrupted her focus.

No one, not her parents, not the doctors, not my 20 years' experience could know what Tina was thinking while she flipped CD covers. If she was dreaming of a fanciful jungle with colourful animals, she couldn't tell us. Was she pretending the CD cover was a dragon flapping its wings in outer space, or was she really caught in a compulsive dysfunctional behaviour loop? Watching Tina for the first time,

I thought about these possibilities. I didn't draw any conclusions, though, and reminded myself that I simply didn't and couldn't know what she held in her mind. Until we had further proof, Tina was quite possibly a genius, or an artist planning her next canvas, or a world explorer plotting her next adventure. I wanted to start my relationship with her from a baseline full of hope and potential—"cup half-full until proven otherwise."

Tina is now eight years old and has thrived in the multi-treatment education program that I designed for her unique challenges. Recently, during a training session, I had the chance to observe a therapist engage her in practising writing letters. Tina sat focused and still in her little chair. She held the pencil correctly and even listened to the instructions. Through several thousand hours of therapy, Tina had come a long way in her ability to learn and to communicate. And communicate she does! On this day, each time the therapist used Tina's name, Tina corrected her. Poking her finger into her chest emphatically, Tina said, "I'm Mrs. Jackson!" The therapist was somewhat impatient because this wasn't Tina's family name. Tina is highly motivated by ballet and was pretending she was her ballet instructor named Mrs. Jackson, whom she adores. "Yes, Tina . . . okay, you're Mrs. Jackson. Now, let's keep writing . . ." But, in his determination to get through the exercise, the therapist had once again mistakenly invoked Tina's name and was not enjoying the pretend-play. "Mrs. Jackson," Tina corrected. "Yes, of course, okay Mrs. Jackson . . . please write the next letter D . . . you have three more to do . . . Mrs. Jackson." Happily, with a nod of approval and a big smile, Mrs. (Tina) Jackson put her head down and diligently drew three more beautiful letter Ds.

Children with autism have the ability to grow their imagination.

For me, this real-life example illustrates many important points that challenge the myth of lack of imagination in autism. Tina's role-play, pretending that she was her ballet instructor, is evidence that she has the capacity to imagine and pretend. Compared to her stereotypical routines two years prior, through combining play-therapy and structured learning, Tina showed us that, just like her normally developing peers, children with autism have the ability to grow their imagination.

Sadly, this isn't the perspective most professionals take. The norm is to believe that Tina's repetitious CD-cover flipping is a maladaptive behaviour and a symptom of a lack of imagination. The difference in perspectives is how we interpret the children's behaviour. One young boy with autism sits silently and stares at a toy block in his hand. His normally developing peer uses the same block to build a pretend house. But we will never know that perhaps the boy with autism, while sitting and apparently doing nothing with the toy block, was imagining a more fanciful house than his peer actually built or than any architect has ever designed. Without the capacity to communicate his thoughts well enough, we interpret his staring off as a sign that he's devoid of imagination. If you suspend the belief that these special children can't imagine, you open your eyes to new creative possibilities—theirs *and* your own.

WHY DOES IT EVEN MATTER?

Exploring and experimenting with objects is what kids do. An infant sitting in a high chair reaches for daddy's keys on the table but he doesn't use them to open a door. He shakes them to hear the musical clanging. Then he drops them crashing to the floor and learns about gravity. If dad picks up the keys and returns them to his son they might end up next in the child's mouth to explore how they taste and if they're edible. This is the course of learning and it's critical for healthy development.

Children with autism also explore their environments but in different ways. An autistic child might hold a set of keys up in front of his eyes and shake them, watching the reflective surfaces closely.

However, because of his diagnosis, the keys would likely be promptly taken away to stop the strange behaviour. When you believe a child with autism doesn't have imagination, you'll interpret their behaviour differently. Young children will often say silly and nonsensical things, rhyming words or even gibberish, just for fun to create, explore, and enjoy language. We hear this playful banter and think, "Oh, she's just being silly . . . listen to how creative she is." But when a child with autism repeats and enjoys a verbal sound or makes up nonsensical words and sentences, we tend to judge it as inappropriate.

Adriano (about whom I wrote in the previous chapter) was a highly energetic six-year-old diagnosed with autism who exhibited all of the classic behaviours and symptoms. His language development was delayed and he was aggressive at times. He was a fun kid but very much kept to himself. During therapy sessions he paced back and forth, didn't make any eye contact, and avoided interaction with others. Then, suddenly, he would stand still in front of the window and begin to talk to himself. He was deeply focused, drawing letters, words, and shapes in the air with his finger in front of his eyes. He was engaged in a thought process. Imagining, perhaps?

Adriano's behaviour was repetitive and routinized, which many interpreted as proof of an inability to play and a lack of imagination. Before my program with him, his family had been taught to interrupt his repetitive behaviours. Therapists told them these were unconstructive. One of the main behaviours Adriano was *creating* was deemed inappropriate and stopped.

During my training sessions, I stood as close as he allowed, faced the window too, and listened without interrupting. I coached the therapists to tune in to the most important sounds in the room— what I called "Adriano FM." I was determined to listen to all of his sounds for any words I could detect that would possibly help me understand his thoughts. Then I heard names of characters from children's television, like "Percy" and "Thomas" from *Thomas the Tank Engine,* and lines from shows like *The Wiggles* and *Veggie Tales.*

I realized then that Adriano had been using his finger to recreate scenes from videos he had seen. Standing at the window for up to 20 minutes at a time, he imagined dozens of scenes, his finger the actor, with dialogue, even. He was doing more than simply remembering the lines. It was clear that he was picturing the images in his mind as his finger danced in front of his eyes acting out the imagined scenes. There are two different views of Adriano's repetitious behaviour: one sees evidence for lack of imagination, the other sees evidence of a rich imagination. One leads to plans to stop the behaviour; the other could lead to better understanding of Adriano's interests, his motivations, and his capacities for learning.

Based on our observation of Adriano's intelligence to learn through TV, I implemented a video-lesson component to his multi-treatment therapy. There are many programs in the US that use videos during therapy, like John Sprecher's Special Kids video-modelling program, one of the pioneering approaches, or www.modelmekids. com. Each week, Adriano's therapists used three-minute video lessons that he watched as homework. These proved to be a valuable key to a lot of new learning. Our belief that Adriano had imagination made us listen more closely. Instead of stopping his creative behaviour, we learned from it and gained new insights into how to work with his strong visual memory.

Years ago I was invited to observe a young student with autism in a special-needs school in England. The class was highly structured with workstations where students sat on their own to complete various tasks. The design was loosely modelled on the TEACCH method developed by researchers at the University of North Carolina and required students to follow tasks in a specific routine represented by tiny pictures on schedule boards. The idea is to help with organization and to provide clear expectations with limited chance of distraction. As the students rotated through their schedules, I wondered where the opportunity was for free play. When could they explore, pretend play, and use their imaginations? I asked. The teacher explained that children with autism aren't able to do pretend play and instead need to rely on routine and structure to function.

Much of the curriculum designed for children with autism doesn't include the opportunity to express imagination. Instead, children are put through routines or repeated "trials" to learn life skills (sitting at a table, using a fork, or pointing to picture cards, for example). No imagination required. While most other three-year-olds are enjoying open-ended free play in kindergartens using sandboxes, play kitchens, and painting stations, their autistic counterparts are sitting at small tables across from an adult doing rote memory work and matching-and-sorting tasks. Most children get a blank piece of paper to draw whatever they imagine, while autistic kids get pre-drawn outlines of dinosaurs or trucks to colour . . . within the lines, of course. Again, no imagination required. When we impose very linear, set, and highly structured learning routines, we limit opportunities to explore and pretend so imagination can't mature. It's a self-fulfilling myth. The types of activities we provide can either encourage or limit imagination.

If we adopt a new belief that children with autism are indeed imaginative, we might hear their words and sounds in a different way. We might accept the wordplay and by delighting in it encourage more communication. The child might share new words more socially because they see others enjoying their sounds. A shift in belief can dramatically shift our behaviour and theirs.

Ironically, developmentally delayed children who might benefit the most from lots of exploration and creative play are the ones we typically regulate and control, and whose play we limit the most by imposing rote and routinized drills.

Ironically, developmentally delayed children who might benefit the most from lots of exploration and creative play are the ones we typically regulate and control, and whose play we limit the most.

HOW DID THE MYTH GET STARTED?

Tracing back not long ago, people didn't think of autism as lacking imagination. To the contrary, there are ample accounts linking them together. For example, in the very beginning, the term autism was first used in medicine by Dr. Eugen Bleuler back in 1911 to describe a type of creative and imaginative thinking process. In *The History of Autism*, author Adam Feinstein explains that Bleuler referred to autism as a mode of thinking that could be observed "in dreams, pretend play and reveries, and in the fantasies and delusions of the schizophrenic."[2] Later on in 1943, in what is considered one of the original descriptions of autism in children, Leo Kanner also saw imagination in autism. He described a five-year-old boy named Paul who "helped himself to a toy engine, ran around the room holding it up high and singing over and over again, 'The engine is flying.'"[3] Paul used his imagination to pretend.

Despite fantasies, pretend play, and flying toy trains, in 1979 imagination was unintentionally amputated from autism. In a game-changing journal article, Dr. Lorna Wing, one of the most respected early theorists and mother of a daughter with autism, connected autism to a deficit in imagination. When Wing and her colleague Judith Gould developed their own rating system to assess a group of children in England, they invented a category called "abnormalities of symbolic, imaginative activities."[4] This was their attempt to describe an autistic child's inability to pretend play with others. When playing with toy cars, for example, if the adult flips a car pretending to crash, an autistic child is less likely than other children to look over and come to the rescue, preferring instead to continue playing their own game. Lorna Wing and many other professionals believe the autistic child doesn't respond to the pretend crash scenario appropriately because he can't take the perspective of the other person, who may be hurt and feel sad.

"Autistic children *do* have an imagination, but it is not social."

In an interview with Adam Feinstein, Lorna Wing explained that she used the word "imagination" to mean empathizing with what others might be thinking and feeling. She believes that impaired imagination (i.e., the inability to "imagine" relationship dynamics) is the root of social problems in autism. She also believes that without understanding the social contexts in pretend play, autistic children engage in routinized stereotyped behaviours instead. For example, how could you pretend to feed a baby doll if you can't "imagine" that it might feel hungry? In her interview, Wing clarified that "autistic children *do* have an imagination, but it is not social."[5] Today, on the Lorna Wing Center for Autism website, the category is described more accurately as "difficulty with social imagination." Unfortunately, this extremely important nuance (social imagination versus imagination) wasn't made clear enough in her original 1979 research. She admitted that "she and Gould did not emphasize the social impairment in autism strongly enough at first."[6] As a result, I believe most people have misinterpreted "abnormalities of imaginative activities" to mean abnormal imagination in general. This is possibly how the myth was born.

WHY DOES THE MYTH PERSIST?

As recently as the 1980s, the criteria to diagnose autism didn't include a lack of imagination. But in 1984, Dr. Wing was invited to give her recommendations for a revised, third edition of the official *Diagnostic and Statistical Manual of Mental Disorders (DSM)*. So, by 1987, the official diagnosis included Wing's "impairment in imagination" category, but the authors elaborated it even further to "absence of imaginative activity, such as play-acting of adult roles, fantasy character or animals; lack of interest in stories about imaginary events." Imagination in the autistic population was being defined right out of existence.

To help interpret the criteria, a doctor might reference a guide like the *DSM-IV Training Guide for Diagnosis of Childhood Disorders*, which explains that "in most cases, play activity lacks imaginative content, [and] is devoid of symbolic or fanciful behavior with toys or others."[7]

Over 50 years, imagination in people with autism shifted from "pretend play and flying toy trains"[8] to "abnormalities in"[9] to "absence of"[10] to "devoid of."[11] Today, researchers like Simon Baron-Cohen, Uta Frith, and Francesca Happé propose various elaborate theories to explain the lack of imagination in autism.* In some way, because people still aren't clear that these researchers mean *social* imagination, the myth lingers on.

Simon Baron-Cohen uses imagination to mean that we make successful social decisions by "imagining" what others might be thinking and feeling based on their behaviour. His popular book *Mindblindness* argues that people with autism can't "imagine" these things. Uta Frith has been a remarkably prolific and influential writer on the topic too. She modified Baron-Cohen's theory slightly for her theory of central coherence. The hypothesis is that people with autism focus too much on discrete details (on just one part of a social interaction at a time, like a person's mouth). She uses imagination to mean that they don't synthesize or "imagine" the bigger picture of social information and therefore can't make appropriate social decisions. It's clear that both of these theorists are using extremely narrow and specific definitions of imagination. What about fantasy (imagine a dragon flying in outer

---

* One of the most articulate analyses of all of these different perspectives on imagination as related to autism is Bruce Mills's essay "Autism and the Imagination." Mills briefly yet insightfully traces the theory of human imagination through great philosphers like Coleridge and Emerson to Foucault. He then discusses two of the most prominent modern autism-related cognitive theories—the theory of central coherence by Uta Frith, and the theory of mind by Simon Baron-Cohen.

space made out of a CD cover), and what about innovation (imagine a mini-pumpkin painted to look like an apple), and what about memory (imagine a television show and replay it back in your mind while acting out the scenes with your fingers)?

What we really need is for Lorna Wing or one of these well-respected academics to send out a bulletin worldwide to the autism community that clarifies once and for all what is meant by the word "imagination" in autism.

Today, the current version of the *DSM (IV-TR)* no longer uses the word imagination, keeping the focus on make-believe play and social imitative play. Maybe there's been a turn for the better.

PEOPLE WITH AUTISM REALLY DO HAVE IMAGINATION

Most people think about imagination as the capacity to picture an image—real or pretend—in the mind, and to think about and manipulate it in relation to other things, maybe even generating something new. There are many examples of imagination in people with autism. In his seminal paper, Leo Kanner described how one of his patients named Donald visualized numbers: "Many of his replies were metaphorical or otherwise peculiar. When asked to subtract 4 from 10, he answered: 'I'll draw a hexagon.'"[12] This is creative associative thinking.

The incredible drawing abilities of Stephen Wiltshire, a young man with autism, are a remarkable example of a strong vision-based imagination. After seeing a cityscape just once, he can literally picture the entire scene in his mind and recreate it in a drawing perfectly to scale.

Wendy Lawson and Tito Rajarshi Mukhopadhyay are both autistic authors and poets who demonstrate a rich capacity to imagine. Tito was a mute non-communicative boy diagnosed with classic autism. His mother worked intensely with him, especially in the area of communication and writing. At the young age of eight, he began to share his deeply philosophical thoughts. He wrote several books by the time he was 11, full of the kind of wisdom rarely articulated by adults five times his age:

Beyond the world of what and why
Beyond the reasons and the concrete,
The "abstract" lies with a richer glory
Somewhere in imaginations deep! [13]

Donna Williams, an internationally known author diagnosed with autism, expresses her intensely sensory-based imagination through writing, painting, sculpting, and playwriting. She describes in detail how, as a child, she had the ability to hyper-focus her sight. She would focus on almost anything in her environment but people, including "the patterns on the wall paper or the carpet."[14] Instead of seeing the rest of the whole room, including the people in it, she zoomed in on just one part. Entirely absorbed in studying the fine details of the wallpaper in ways that most of us don't take time for and may not be visually able to do, she was happily inside her imagination. Interestingly, science tells us that one use of our imagination is to examine separate pieces of a whole, in order to solve problems, for example. Yet, if it's not used for socialization, this hyper-imagining ability is not recognized as a strength in people with autism.

THINKING IN PICTURES

Temple Grandin is arguably the most well-known person with autism. In her own words, Grandin "emerged" from being a mute and recluse child to an articulate and insightful yet still autistic adult. But it's her work in veterinary and livestock handling systems as professor of animal science at Colorado State University that has garnered worldwide attention. She seems to have the ability to imagine from an animals' perspective navigating through a farmyard, a slaughterhouse, or a routine veterinary checkup. She then designs safer and more humane systems for the animals. She calls this "thinking in pictures."

In the first chapter of Grandin's book *Thinking in Pictures* she explains:

> *I translate both spoken and written words into full-color movies, complete with sound, which run like a VCR tape in my head. . . . Visual thinking has enabled me to build entire systems in my imagination . . . I learned that my visualization skills far exceeded those of most other people.*[15]

Despite her social awkwardness and challenges with communication, Grandin's great imagination has benefited animals and farmers around the world. Temple goes on to describe the mental-visual imagination skills of other adults with autism she has met:

> *Discussions with other autistic people reveal similar visual styles of thinking about tasks that most people do sequentially. An autistic man who composes music told me that he makes "sound pictures" using small pieces of other music to create new compositions. A computer programmer with autism told me that he sees the general pattern of the program tree. After he visualizes the skeleton for the program, he simply writes the code for each branch. I use similar methods when I review scientific literature . . . I take specific findings or observations and combine them to find new basic principles and general concepts.*[16]

Interestingly, Temple Grandin's imagination seems to have developed along similar stages as her neurotypical peers. From imaginary characters to using metaphors to make sense of hard times, her imagination was prominent at an early age. In her self-penned book

Emergence: Labeled Autistic, Grandin describes her childhood struggles and sheds light on the autistic experience. At one point during elementary school she wrote several letters to the school principal demanding they purchase a fairground ride for the students to use. Pretending she was an imagined ghostwriter, she explains: "Reverting to my childhood fanciful character, Alfred Costello, I wrote frenzied communications supposedly from him to me."[17] To allay any suspicion of schizophrenia, she goes on to confirm that "I knew the Shadow, Alfred Costello, was a figment of my imagination. . . ."[18]

Temple Grandin's figments of imagination challenge the myth.

From thinking in pictures to pretend characters, Temple Grandin's figments of imagination challenge the myth. Yet, when she was younger her odd behaviours and poor social skills obscured her peers' and teachers' understanding of her creativity. Her mother, Eustacia Cutler, was the exception. Grandin quotes a letter her mother had written to a doctor explaining, "I think Temple is a child of enormous potential, [and] unusually imaginative, although some of her oddities may tend to make her a bit conspicuous."[19] In my own work, I find it's most often mothers who recognize their children's abilities even if professional tests and diagnoses don't. Maybe we should place a greater value on what parents know and tell us about their children. Maybe we could observe and listen to and place more value on what people with autism themselves tell us about their imaginations.

UNDERSTANDING AND NURTURING IMAGINATION IN AUTISM

There is a large body of research that has tried to understand imagination in autism. Most of it seems biased toward proving that people with autism lack imagination. To understand instructions and answer questions, tests of imagination usually require a certain level of communication that many children with autism simply don't have. If a child can't answer a test question, does this mean he lacks imagination?

One of the world's foremost experts on behavioural treatment for children with autism is the late Ivar Lovaas. He also recognized the language limitations in assessing and teaching imagination:

Obviously, since these [training] programs on pretending and imagining require a considerable amount of language, it is best to start these programs after the child has become proficient in his use of abstract language, after he can easily identify and describe events and behaviors around him, and after he has developed conversation skills.[20]

Perhaps surprising for some staunch applied behavioural analysis enthusiasts, even Lovaas recognized the pretend play and imagination abilities (when facilitated) of children with autism. In his seminal training manual *Teaching Developmentally Disabled Children: The ME Book,* Lovaas wrote: "Children with developmental retardation [including children with autism] are quite able to learn to pretend and to fantasize . . . and will show signs of enjoying this kind of activity as much as any average person."[21]

The key here is that Lovaas and others like Professor Pamela Wolfberg, author of the acclaimed book *Play and Imagination in Children with Autism,* don't deny imagination in children with autism but do highlight their need to learn and practise pretend play and imaginative play.

Imagination develops through different stages. Many theorists and philosophers, from Plato and Freud to Vygotsky and Einstein, have explored the structure of human imagination and how it develops in childhood. One of the first stages involves children pretending and re-enacting familiar routines—events, places, and activities they've observed others do and that they've already themselves experienced. A child who has watched his mother talk on the phone may re-enact this routine with a toy. In countries where children don't typically see this, they are not likely to pretend it.

At this early imitation stage, we can assume that children's capacity to pretend will depend on how many different experiences they have had. A young child who has actually sat in a boat and held a fishing rod will be more likely to pretend to fish than a child who has never experienced this activity. Children with autism, for many reasons, often have not had the same range of experiences in early life as their non-autistic peers. When they are included, they don't necessarily pay attention to the same kinds of social dynamics either. Lower attention spans, less eye contact, and more focus on objects than on social routines means they don't learn the social routines of daily life in the same way as their neurotypical peers. It follows then that a child with autism may not be able to re-enact fishing, but she may be able to describe the sparkle on the water or recite the make and brand name of the fishing rod because that's where her attention to detail was focused.

On a train ride, a typically developing child will observe the social aspects of the experience. Passengers get on and off the train and the conductor passes through the cabin collecting tickets. In contrast, a child with autism may fixate on the turning wheels of the train or the number and letter codes stamped on the side of the engines. Each child has learned different things about the train ride. Later, when the autistic child has a toy train, his capacity to pretend play is limited to his experience of the wheels and numbers that he studied while his neurotypical peer includes toy characters to represent the passengers and conductor.

Further in development, children will try to copy and re-enact routines and events they observed but have not necessarily experienced themselves. For example, a young child might play an imaginary game of shopping for groceries. While the child has never yet actually carried money or paid for groceries, she will pretend to reach into a pocket or toy purse for imaginary or play coins, all the while imitating adultlike behaviours she has seen when shopping for groceries with her parents. Again, I believe we can propose a similar assumption about the initial social and range-of-activity deficits a child with autism is starting with. Given that many people with autism may be focused on different objects and stimuli in their environments, due to a range of heightened sensations, they are not as likely as their neurotypical peers to observe as much of the routines of others or to re-enact them later. A young child with autism sitting in a shopping cart in a mall may be happily absorbed with the visual effect of the store's marble floor tiles and consequently miss the opportunity to observe and learn about his parent's daily shopping routine. Nonetheless, imagination and pre-tend play can mature and develop in children with autism.

Years ago, I worked with a family in Ohio whose autistic daughter drew thousands of pictures of the Disney character Minnie Mouse. This mute little girl sat for hours, without looking at anyone, with-out speaking a word, incredibly focused on drawing and re-drawing the same picture of the cartoon mouse. Her parents and therapists explained to me that if they tried to change the routine, to add a bow on Minnie's head, a pair of shoes, or a necklace, she would just scratch it out and start over on a fresh piece of paper. Yet, when I took a closer look through the pile of literally hundreds of the drawings her mother had saved, I saw an evolution. She had used different colours and added her own details over time. The earli-est drawings were simplistic and lacked detail. Then after her first hundred or so, there was a subtle yet noticeable evolution starting with more details in Minnie's face—eyebrows were added, and then lips and hair details. Each new detail was replicated dozens of times without change as it became part of the repetitious routine. Still later on in the immense pile, examples of different eye positions, clothing, and jewellery emerged. She hadn't accepted others' input into her play, but over time this little girl clearly demonstrated an evolving imagination, in her own way, in her own time.

Treatment programs focus so heavily on teaching so-called appropriate behaviour that any unique, different, or otherwise creative behaviour is quashed. Few treatment or education programs provide time for creativity and unstructured pretend play. To do my best with the children I work with, I set out to find their strengths, their interests, and their motivations. I spend time trying to learn as much as I can about them. For many children with no or little language, this often means observing their behaviours, without judgment, to try to understand more about how they perceive and think.

Not everyone believes the myth. The Rosehill School in Nottingham, England, is founded on the belief that people with autism have great imaginations. They offer many classes and workshops including digital photography, film, painting, pottery, and dance. As a result, the students have created artistic pieces that express their far-reaching imaginations. Papier mâché masks are painted, unique pottery is sculpted, poems are written, digital photography is shot, and dances are choreographed. I encourage you to view the documentary video about the school on YouTube.

> Imagination is alive and accessible
> in people with autism for anyone who chooses
> to see it and nurture it.

Another inspiring program was founded by the pioneering spirit. Dr. Nehama Baum. Named after her son, the MukiBaum centre in Toronto uses the tagline "Finding human treasures beyond disabilities." The centre offers services for people with dual diagnoses including autism. I was impressed when I toured the facility to see room after room of colour and materials that invite creativity and opportunities to express imagination. One of their main programs, expressive arts therapy, gives children with autism, among other disabilities, the chance to explore their emotions, thoughts, and imaginations with a variety of art materials. Students have even shown their works in galleries around Toronto to great acclaim. Imagination is alive and accessible in people with autism for anyone who chooses to see it and nurture it. The only limits to their imaginations are those that we shackle them with.

WHAT YOU CAN DO

• *Believe*

People with autism have imaginations. This statement opens up new possibilities in the way we perceive and treat what we call autistic behaviour. I met Adriano with the belief that he was intelligent and had an imagination. This perspective helped me hear and see the pretend play that he did using his finger to act out television episodes as purposeful.

When we believe a child has an imagination, we welcome new behaviours as learning to create and experiment rather than as inappropriate ones that need to be stopped. When we believe a child has an imagination, we model more play and creativity in our own actions and words with them. When we are too serious, we don't.

• *Look for Imagination beyond Speaking*

Core challenges for people with autism such as communicating, socializing, and repetitive behaviours can impede their expression of imagination. Just because a child is nonverbal doesn't mean he lacks imagination. In the absence of recognizable words and actions, however, we should assume that thoughts, feelings, and dreams still flourish. It's in moments of quiet meditation that we are able to concentrate best on our internal dialogue and imagination.

• *Provide a Safe Space for Imagination*

Sharing your thoughts, feelings, hopes, and fears is an intimate process. Will your ideas be judged or accepted? Even young children learn to censor which ideas they share and with whom. Children make up nonsense rhymes and experiment with moving their bodies in unusual ways, dancing down the sidewalk, for example, as they explore the full range of what they can do with their minds and bodies. At the same time, they get social feedback like "That's silly," or "That's amazing," or "Don't ever let me see you do that again!" By our reactions, we encourage their creativity to keep exploring and trying new things, or we limit, regulate, and shut it down. Children with autism can exhibit even more unusual sounds and behaviours than their peers. It's important to provide an accepting space in which they can express their feelings, thoughts, and imagination.

• Include Time for Imagination

Understandably, parents and teachers are eager to teach an autistic child to behave "appropriately" so they can be included in public activities with their peers and family. Unfortunately, monitoring "appropriate" behaviour means that taking the time to explore creative imagination is neglected. Therefore, children with autism may not have the same opportunities or encouragement to expand their imaginations.

Schools, education programs, and treatment centres could reconsider their curriculum and programming for students with autism. Are age-appropriate amounts of time and opportunity to imagine, pretend play, and be creative provided? Oftentimes, intensive behaviour interventions are heavily focused on super-structured rote learning tasks with little time for exploration and creativity. The most successful programs I have assessed include ample time for adult- and peer-facilitated play through semistructured games with materials that inspire creativity. When a child is allowed to play on his or her own for five minutes, this doesn't mean "break time." The idea is to surround the autistic child with people who will react in positive ways to creative exploration, to spontaneous expressions, and to novel communications. Ironically, many treatment programs provide positive reinforcement almost exclusively for structured, rote, and adult-directed tasks—the opposite of self-initiated creative imagination. School and treatment programs could include learning objectives to discover and enhance the imagination of every child with autism, starting with the belief that it is there.

• Give Imagination a Chance to Grow

For all children, neurotypical and autistic alike, imagination and the ability to pretend develop over time. Artists, composers, and writers can take decades to nurture their imaginations and express them creatively. Be the supportive, patient coach.

Choose toys and materials that invite exploration, communication, and imagination. Is a toy an open-ended one inviting interaction or does it have only one function? An electronic toy car that makes its own engine sound takes the place of the child trying to create their own sound effects like "vrrrooom" for go, "eeerrt" for stop, and "bee beep" for move please. I typically encourage parents to remove most battery-operated toys and replace them with human-animated toys like hand puppets, dress-up clothes for role play, and various real-life props like a backpack, a snorkel and mask set, a toy frying pan, a map, and anything else you might find around your house to pretend play and create imaginary adventures with. This aspect of programming is all very much along the lines of play-therapy, and isn't play the best time to exercise imagination?

• Discover the Autistic Imagination

Research could explore a whole new frontier of what could be called the *autistic imagination*. It may or may not be any different from what we already know imagination to be. Countless papers could be published and facts discussed about the incredible diversity of thinking and imagination we might discover. Books and theories of human imagination might be revised and updated to incorporate the extended range of imagination that *is* there.

One way to discover the imagination of a person with autism

is to take the role of student. Step away from being the parent or therapist or caregiver for ten minutes and adopt the perspective of being a student of your autistic "teacher," with the belief that there is something you can learn from them. Pay attention to them instead of trying to get them to pay attention to you. Follow their lead instead of expecting them to follow you. Be eager to learn something new that you didn't know before instead of anticipating the same old routines you've already learned. A child whose senses are overstimulated might be compelled to cover his ears and rock himself to calm his nerves. His behaviours look repetitive and unimaginative. He may not even be in control of them. Despite this, he may still have a fertile and active imagination. In order to discover something new, we have to put aside our habits and assumptions and put energy into finding what we've never seen before.

· *Talk about an Austistic Person as Imaginative*
When you meet with your autistic child's teacher, ask for some examples of creativity and imagination they've noticed in your child. When you talk to others about a person with autism whom you know, include a positive story of his or her unique imagination. Textbooks that educate future teachers and clinicians could reflect the more accurate and hopeful characterization too. This in turn would lead to more reports of imagination in autism in popular media like newspapers, magazines, and websites until the myth is transformed and we accept as fact: people with autism have imagination.

EPILOGUE

In the summer of 2008, I had only just sketched out the autism myths I would one day write about when a storm of outrage suddenly swept the autism community. Radio talk show host Michael Savage offended a nation when he broadcast,

> *"I'll tell you what autism is. In 99 percent of the cases, it's a brat who hasn't been told to cut the act out. That's what autism is....They don't have a father around to tell them, 'Don't act like a moron. You'll get nowhere in life. Stop acting like a putz. Straighten up. Act like a man. Don't sit there crying and screaming, idiot.'"* *

Like thousands of parents, I too was angry. I knew that the myths of autism had to be challenged as publicly as Michael's savage rant had been. I wanted my book to be a resource that empowered parents with well researched information that they could use to engage their friends, neighbours, teachers, and politicians. I hoped the book would do more than simply present new ideas and that parents and therapists would commit to the action steps in the "What You Can Do" sections and join in an international manifesto for the positive welfare of people with autism.

---

* Michael Savage speaking on Talk Radio Network's syndicated show, *The Savage Nation*, on July 16, 2008.

As I sat down to write and began to dive deeply into the origins of the myths, I came face to face with how pervasive they really were. At the same time I kept my practice going, working with families each week, being happily reminded of alternative views. I saw evidence that challenged the myths and witnessed the positive outcomes that are possible when we adopt new perspectives, new strategies, and new hope. It took a certain amount of focus to navigate as I teeter-tottered between writing about the myths in the morning and applying practical solutions to them in the afternoon.

While I wrote, news reports and autism newsletters frequently reminded me why it is necessary now more than ever to discuss, debate, and take action to change how we think about and treat people with autism. Just last week I read a disturbing account in the newspaper of a young boy diagnosed with Asperger's disorder. Early one morning nineteen-year-old Reginald Latson sat on the front lawn of the local library in Stafford County, Virginia, waiting for it to open. Some school kids apparently reported a suspicious black male, possibly with a gun, sitting by the library, and soon enough Latson was approached by a police officer. When the officer asked him his name he didn't respond. The officer searched the young man and didn't find a weapon but continued to press him until a struggled ensued. Latson was ultimately arrested, held in isolation without bail for eleven days, and sentenced to ten and a half years in prison for assaulting an officer. News reports suggested it was a potential case of racial profiling but what is painfully clear is that the judge didn't care or understand enough to take into account Latson's Asperger's diagnosis.

We need to educate ourselves and others about autism. We need to pursue greater acceptance and care toward this special population.

People who set policy need to challenge the myths they hold about autism too. Canadian immigration officials sparked outrage recently when they threatened to deport a South Korean family from their home and family business in New Brunswick. The hard-working family had been in Canada for almost a decade, contributing positively to the local community, when they received notice from Citizenship and Immigration that they were no longer welcome because their fourteen-year-old son with autism and epilepsy was "inadmissible" because he would be an excessive drain on health and social services Thankfully, public outrage pressured the government to grant a reprieve. Meanwhile, just two weeks later, yet another family received a similar letter. Thomas Reynolds, a professor at the University of Toronto who had moved to Canada from the United States, was notified by Citizenship and Immigration that his twenty-year-old son, who had been diagnosed with Asperger's, would diminish the family's chances for residency in this country. Mr. Reynolds summed up his disappointments by saying "The end verdict is a judgment of worthlessness."*

These are examples of how the myths of autism cloud our understanding, limit our compassion, and lead to bad decisions and grave consequences. The importance of challenging the myths of autism could not be clearer.

People with autism can have creative imaginations. They can show affection and love. They can have above-average intelligence. And most importantly, like every human being, they deserve respect, acceptance, love, and care. I've witnessed children with autism make the most remarkable changes and have had the honour to work with their loving and dedicated parents. It is their anecdotes in this book that challenge the myths. I simply gave the evidence a more public voice.

Looking back at the first college course in which I learned about autism, I can't help but imagine the positive impact of having psychology and autism therapy courses that teach this new paradigm and challenge the myths of autism. Imagine an entire generation of teachers, therapists, doctors, researchers, and policy makers offering

---

* Nicholas Keung, "Family ripped apart, immigration says son with Asperger's 'inadmissible,'" *Toronto Star*, June 14, 2011.

parents hope by highlighting the strengths and unique talents of people with autism.

The truth is that change is already afoot. I know I'm not alone in challenging the myths of autism. There are many truly inspired and talented therapists who capture the attention and affection of their autistic students. There are parents who will read the words in this book and think "That's exactly what I believe." This book was written for you. It is my attempt to reach out to connect with like-minded parents and professionals—to join hands in common support and with a common vision. I look forward to hearing from you.

JOIN THE CONVERSATION

You can help rewrite these myths into positive statements of ability and possibility.

Be an active and empowered force of change, debunking these and other myths of autism by joining like-minded parents and professionals who are leading an international movement promoting a new empowered understanding of autism.

If you have an example or a story about a child with autism that dispels any of the myths covered in this book, I'd love to hear from you. You're invited to join the conversation on the website I've created, *www.challengethemyths.com.*

ABOUT THE AUTHOR

Jonathan Alderson completed his Masters of Education at Harvard University. He has a private educational consulting practice in South-western Ontario, working primarily as an autism treatment specialist training families with special needs children. He was the Curriculum Specialist Coordinator with Teach for America in Houston, Texas, and undertook an internship with the Harvard Family Research Project. Jonathan's diverse experience provides the inspiration for his innovation in the field of autism treatment.

Jonathan developed an early interest in education and childhood development while working with children with cancer as well as working in a remedial reading program for children from disadvantaged homes. After completing an undergraduate degree in developmental and educational psychology at the University of Western Ontario and a year at the Sorbonne University in Paris, he published his honours thesis in the *Journal of the Society for Accelerative Learning and Teaching*.

Jonathan completed a three-year intensive certification training at the Autism Treatment Center of America, which included over 1,500 hours of one-to-one floor time with autistic children. This training strongly influenced his current focus on a humanistic approach to autism treatment. He worked in the center's Son-Rise Program as Administrator and as a senior family trainer for eight years. This was followed by a year in London, England, providing support to families in the United Kingdom, Ireland, Holland and

Spain. He has instructed more than 3,000 families and special needs children around the world.

Jonathan has worked internationally, delivering seminars and training workshops in Europe, the Middle East and Australia. He has been a speaker at the Royal College of Pediatricians (University of Nottingham) and the Canadian Psychiatric Research Foundation. He currently serves as Chair of the Board of Drum Artz Canada, and is also a member of the Phi Delta Kappa professional educators association.

Jonathan specializes in merging educational and biomedical treatments of autism through the integrated model he developed called Intensive Multi-Treatment Intervention. He lives in Toronto. Visit him at *www.jalderson.com*.

ACKNOWLEDGEMENTS

First and foremost I share my deepest gratitude with the parents and children who are the heart and soul of this book. Your real-life stories invite others to challenge the myths. Becki Gordon and Laura Geiberson, your dedication to these special families and to the IMTI program has positively touched the lives of many. You're all shining lights.

To Minelle Mahtani, I bow in humble gratitude and love. You offered endless patience, abiding love, a keen intelligence, and home-cooked meals. Most importantly, you were a deep source of encouragement, believing in the project and in me. Thank you.

Gratitude to my editor, Brad Wilson, for handling my thousand questions with graciousness and for guiding me through the process with a steady calm. I was honoured to work alongside the HarperCollins Canada team: David Kent, Cory Beatty, Lindsey Love, Allegra Robinson, and Rob Firing—all top-notch professionals. I am especially indebted to Shelley Tangney for championing the book concept in the very beginning and for opening the door for me. Thank you.

To my first mentor and trainer, Bryn Hogan, who modelled teaching through love and acceptance that touched me profoundly. Gregory MacKenzie, my dearest friend, cheered loudly and provided a voice of moderation for me to use diplomacy while challenging the status quo.

Andreas Hagelstam offered on-tap writing expertise while gently facilitating my own voice and direction. Thank you, friend.

Acknowledgements

As a gifted autism therapist, Andrew Shahan discussed invaluable insights into the complex field of autism that helped shape some of the nuances in this book. Hilary Alderson and Burton Moon made themselves available to read and re-read countless drafts. My stellar research assistants, Mel Hergott and Robyn Shylitt, went above and beyond and made my work lighter. Thank you.

Professionals including Barry Neil Kaufman, Barry Prizant, Brooke Ingersoll, Pamela Wolfberg, Simon Baron-Cohen, Leo Buscaglia, and Thomas Hehir have all influenced my own practice and thinking. To those whose work I've cited, discussed, and critiqued, hopefully with respect and collegiality, I ask for your forgiveness in advance if, in my enthusiasm to debunk the myths, I have been overly critical. My aim is to trigger change for the better, recognizing we are all doing the best we can to help families and children.

For friendship and support that fuelled me, I thank Andrea Pearson, Patrick and Elizabeth Gladney, Vic and Nazmin Gupta, Michael Burns, Susan MacKenzie and the Scarrow family, Trevor French and Theresa Rozario, Farideh Afshar and Ray Mahtani, Andrea Lekushoff, Mano Watsa, Veronica Martini, Nicolette Felix and William Oldacre, Martin Troughton, Jeremy Sikkema, Donna Masters, and David Patchell-Evans. And thanks to Douglas Cottrell for pushing me to write. Play breaks with Spencer and Scotty, Savannah, and Noodle kept me smiling. You are all a part of the fabric of these pages.

END NOTES

CHAPTER 1

1. E. M. Itard, *An Historical Account of the Discovery and Education of a Savage Man: Or the First Developments, Physical and Moral, of the Young Savage* (Whitefish, MT: Kessinger Publishing LLC, 2007), 17.
2. Leo Kanner, "Autistic Disturbances of Affective Contact," *Nerv Child*, 2 (1943), 249–50.
3. Bruno Bettelheim, *The Empty Fortress: Infantile Autism and the Birth of the Self* (New York: Free Press, 1972), 125.
4. Leo Kanner, "Follow-up Study of Eleven Autistic Children Originally Reported in 1943," *Journal of Autism and Childhood Schizophrenia*, 1971, 1 (2), 119–145.
5. Adam Feinstein, *A History of Autism: Conversations with the Pioneers* (Hoboken, NJ: Wiley-Blackwell, 2010), 147.
6. O. Ivar Lovaas, *Teaching Developmentally Disabled Children: The ME Book* (Austin, TX: University Park Press, 1981), 87.
7. O. Ivar Lovaas, B. Schaeffer, and J. Q. Simmons, "Building Social Behavior in Autistic Children by Use of Electric Shock," *Journal of Experimental Research in Personality*, 1 (1965), 99–109.
8. Carol Stock Kranowitz, *The Out-of-Sync Child: Recognizing and Coping with Sensory Processing Disorder* (New York: Perigee, 2005), 57.
9. Temple Grandin and Margaret M. Scariano, *Emergence: Labeled Autistic* (New York: Warner Books, 1986), 87.
10. Ibid., p. 22.
11. Judith Bluestone, *The Fabric of Autism: Weaving the Threads into a Cogent Theory* (Southlake, TX: Sapphire Enterprises LLC, 2005), 75.
12. Oliver Sacks, *An Anthropologist on Mars: Seven Paradoxical Tales* (New York: Vintage, 1996), 85.

CHAPTER 2

1. Donna Williams, *Nobody Nowhere: The Extraordinary Autobiography of an Autistic* (New York: Times Books, 1992), 3.
2. Wendy Lawson, *Concepts of Normality: The Autistic and Typical Spectrum* (London: Jessica Kingsley Publishers, 2008), 33.

3. Leo Kanner, "Autistic Disturbances of Affective Contact," *Nerv Child*, 2 (1943), 245.
4. Ibid.
5. O. Ivar Lovaas, *Teaching Developmentally Disabled Children: The ME Book* (Austin, TX: University Park Press, 1981), 32.
6. Judith Bluestone, *The Fabric of Autism: Weaving the Threads into a Cogent Theory* (Southlake, TX: Sapphire Enterprises LLC, 2005), xiv.
7. James W. Bodfish, Frank J. Symons, Dawn E. Parker, and Mark H. Lewis, "Varieties of Repetitive Behavior in Autism: Comparisons to Mental Retardation," *Journal of Autism and Developmental Disorders*, 30, no. 3 (2000), 237.
8. S. H. Lee, S. L. Odom, and R. Loftin, "Social Engagement with Peers and Stereotypic Behavior of Children with Autism," *Journal of Positive Behavior Interventions*, 9, no. 2 (April 2007), 67–79.
9. Stanley Greenspan and Serena Wieder, *Engaging Autism: Using the Floortime Approach to Help Children Relate, Communicate, and Think* (Cambridge, MA: Da Capo Press, 2006), 312.
10. Ibid., p. 313.
11. Howard Buten, *Through the Glass Wall: Journeys into the Closed-Off Worlds of the Autistic* (New York: Bantam Books, 2004), 99.
12. Ibid., p. 165
13. M. J. Baker, "Incorporating the Thematic Ritualistic Behaviors of Children with Autism into Games: Increasing Social Play Interactions with Siblings," *Journal of Positive Behavior Interventions*, 2, no. 2 (April 2000), 70.
14. Ibid.

CHAPTER 3

1. J. Harrower and G. Dunlap, "Including Children with Autism in General Education Classrooms: A Review of Effective Strategies," *Behavior Modification*, 25, no.5 (October 2001), 762.
2. P. Strain, "Generalization of Autistic Children's Social Behavior Change: Effects of Developmentally Integrated and Segregated Settings," *Analysis and Intervention in Developmental Disabilities*, 3, no. 1 (1983), 34.
3. Pamela Wolfberg, *Play and Imagination in Children with Autism*, 2nd ed (New York: Teachers College Press, 2009), 149.
4. Laura Schreibman, *The Science and Fiction of Autism* (Cambridge, MA: Harvard University Press, 2007), 260.
5. R. L. Simpson, S. R. de Boer-Ott, and B. Smith-Myles, "Inclusion of Learners with Autism Spectrum Disorders in General Education Settings," *Topics in Language Disorders*, 23, no. 2 (April–June 2003), 119.
6. US National Research Council, Catherine Lord and James P. McGee, editors, *Educating Children with Autism*, Committee on Educational Interventions for Children with Autism, Division of Behavioral and Social Sciences and Education (Washington, D.C. 2001: National Academy Press, 2001), 118.
7. Simpson et al., 116–33.
8. Yude Henteleff, "The Fully Inclusive Classroom is Only One of the Right Ways to Meet the Best Interests of the Special Needs Child," Paper presented at the National Summit on Inclusive Education, Ottawa, Ontario, November 2004, 6.

9. US National Research Council, 13.
10. T. Kennedy, G. Regehr, J. Rosenfield, S. W. Roberts, and L. Lingard, "Exploring the Gap between Knowledge and Behavior: A Qualitative Study of Clinician Action Following an Educational Intervention," *Academic Medicine,* 79, no. 5 (May 2004), 386–93.
11. B. Chamberlain, C. Kasari, and E. Rotheram-Fuller, "Involvement or Isolation? The Social Networks of Children with Autism in Regular Classrooms," *Journal of Autism and Developmental Disorders,* 37, no. 2 (July 2006), 230.
12. D. Tantum, "Psychological Disorder in Adolescents and Adults with Asperger Syndrome," *Autism,* 4, no. 1 (2000), 47–62.
13. Strain, 23–24.
14. T. Yang, P. J. Wolfberg, S. Wu, and P. Hwu, "Supporting Children on the Autism Spectrum in Peer Play at Home and School: Piloting the Integrated Play Groups Model in Taiwan," *Autism: The International Journal of Research and Practice,* 7, no. 4 (December 2003), 439.
15. "Education and Autism Spectrum Disorders in Australia: The Provision of Appropriate Educational Services for School-Age Students with Autism Spectrum Disorders in Australia," Position paper, Australian Advisory Board on Autism Spectrum Disorders, 2010, 5.
16. R. L. Simpson and B. Smith-Myles, *Educating Children and Youth with Autism: Strategies for Effective Practice,* 2nd ed (Austin, TX: PRO-ED, Inc., 1998).

CHAPTER 4
1. Bernard Rimland, "The ABA Controversy," *Autism Research Review International,* 13, no. 3 (1999), 3.
2. Barry Prizant, "Is ABA the Only Way?" *Autism Spectrum Quarterly* (Spring, 2009), 1.
3. New York State Department of Health, Early Intervention Program, *Clinical Practice Guideline: Report of the Recommendations—Autism/ Pervasive Developmental Disorders: Assessment and Intervention for Young Children (Age 0–3 Years)* (Albany, NY: New York State Department of Health, 1999).
4. US Department of Health and Human Services, Substance Abuse and Mental Health Services Administration, *Mental Health: A Report of the Surgeon General, 1999.*
5. Maine Department of Health and Human Services and Maine Department of Education (MASDEC), *Interventions for Autism Spectrum Disorders: State of the Evidence, Report of the Children's Services Evidence-Based Practice Advisory Committee, October 2009.*
6. National Autism Center, *National Standards Report—Addressing the Need for Evidence-Based Practice Guidelines for Autism Spectrum Disorders* (Randolph, MA: National Autism Center, 2009), 43.
7. Ibid., 93.
8. C. Aldred, J. Green, and C. Adams, "A New Social Communication Intervention for Children with ASD: Pilot Randomized Control Treatment Study Suggesting Effectiveness," *Journal of Child Psychology and Psychiatry,* 45 (2004) 1420–1430.
9. G. Dawson, S. Rogers, J. Munson, M. Smith, J. Winter, J. Greenson, A. Donaldson, and J. Varley, "Randomized, Controlled Trial of an Intervention for

Toddlers with Autism: The Early Start Denver Model," *Pediatrics* (2010) 125: e17-e23.

10. L. Christensen, T. Hutman, A. Rozga, G. S. Young, S. Ozonoff, and S. J. Rogers, "Play and Developmental Outcomes in Infant Siblings of Children with Autism," *Journal of Autism and Developmental Disorders,* 40, 946–957.

11. Bernard Rimland, "The ABA Controversy," *Autism Research Review International,* 13, no. 3 (1999), 3.

12. O. Ivar Lovaas, *Teaching Developmentally Disabled Children: The ME Book* (Austin, TX: University Park Press, 1981), 3.

13. Ibid.

14. Adrienne Perry and Rosemary Condillac, *Evidence-Based Practices for Children and Adolescents with Autism Spectrum Disorders: Review of the Literature and Practice Guide, Children's Mental Health,* Ontario, 2003.

15. B. Ingersoll, "Teaching Social Communication: A Comparison of Naturalistic Behavioral and Development, Social Pragmatic Approaches for Children with Autism Spectrum Disorders," *Journal of Positive Behavior Interventions,* 12, no. 1 (2010), 38.

16. Stars Children's Clinic, Singapore. Taken from http://www.vapc.sg/naturalistic-aba.html

17. Ingersoll.

CHAPTER 5

1. Laura Schreibman, *The Science and Fiction of Autism* (Cambridge, MA: Harvard University Press, 2007).

2. US National Research Council, *Educating Children with Autism* (Washington, DC: National Academy Press, 2001), 86.

3. Leo Kanner, "Autistic Disturbances of Affective Contact," *Nerv Child,* 2 (1943), 247.

4. Ibid.

5. M. Goldberg Edelson, "Are the Majority of Children with Autism Mentally Retarded? A Systematic Evaluation of the Data," *Focus on Autism and Other Developmental Disabilities,* 21, no. 2 (Summer 2006), 66.

6. Gregory L. Wallace, Mike Anderson, and Francesca Happé, "Brief Report: Information Processing Speed is Intact in Autism but Not Correlated with Measured Intelligence," *Journal of Autism and Developmental Disorders,* 39, no. 5 (May 2009), 813.

7. Michael Guillen, *Five Equations That Changed the World: The Power and Poetry of Mathematics* (London: Abacus, 1995), 222.

8. Ibid., p. 224.

9. Stephen Jay Gould, *The Mismeasure of Man* (New York: W. W. Norton & Company, 1981), 151.

10. Stuart Murray, *Representing Autism: Culture, Narrative, Fascination* (Liverpool: Liverpool University Press, 2008), 67.

11. Anne Martin, "Screening, Early Intervention, and Remediation: Obscuring Children's Potential," *Special Education at the Century's End: Evolution of Theory and Practice Since 1970,* edited by T. Hehir and T. Latus (Cambridge, MA: Harvard Educational Review Reprint Series, vol. 23, 1992), 408.

12. Thomas Hehir, "Some Assessments Treat Learning-Disabled Students Unfairly," *The Digital Classroom: How Technology is Changing the Way We Teach and Learn,* edited by David T. Gordon (Cambridge, MA: Harvard Education Publishing Group, 2000), 9–50.

CHAPTER 6

1. Autism-PDD.net Forum , post April 10 2010 (http://www.autismpdd.net/forum/forum_posts.asp?TID=35681&PN=2&TPN=1)
2. Pattey L. Fong, "Cognitive Appraisals in High- and Low-Stress Mothers of Adolescents with Autism," *Journal of Consulting and Clinical Psychology,* vol. 59, no. 3 (1991), 471–474.
3. S. Eikeseth, T. Smith, and E. Jahr, "Outcome for Children with Autism who Began Intensive Behavioral Treatment between Ages 4 and 7: A Comparison Controlled Study," *Behavior Modification,* volume 31, no. 3 (2007) 264–278.
4. E. A. Laugeson, F. Frankel, C. Mogil, and A. R. Dillon, "Parent-Assisted Social Skills Training to Improve Friendships in Teens with Autism Spectrum Disorders," *Journal of Autism Developmental Disorders,* 39(4), (April 2009), 596–606.
5. Edward C. Fenske, Stanley Zalenski, Patricia J. Krantz, and E. Lynn, "Age at Intervention and Treatment Outcome for Autistic Children in a Comprehensive Intervention Program," *Analysis and Intervention in Developmental Disabilities,* volume 5, issues 1–2 (1985), 49–58.
6. E. Pickett, O. Pullara, J. O'Grady, and B. Gordon, "Speech Acquisition in Older Nonverbal Individuals with Autism: A Review of Features, Methods and Prognosis," *Cognitive Behavior Neurology* (2009), 221.
7. Patricia Howlin speaking at *Falling Through the Cracks: Why is the Outcome so Poor for Adults with Autism?* A national conference presented by Research Autism, held on July 16, 2009.
8. Becky Estepp and Moira Giammatteo, "Does the 'Window' Ever Close?" April 2008, http://www.talkaboutcuringautism.org/support/does-the-window-ever-close.htm
9. John McKenzie, "Autism Breakthrough: Girl's Writings Explain Her Behavior and Feelings," February 19, 2008, from http://abcnews.go.com/Health/story?id=4311223&page=2 on April 6, 2011.

CHAPTER 7

1. Peter Szatmari, *A Mind Apart: Understanding Children with Autism and Asperger Syndrome* (New York: Guilford Press, 2004), 82.
2. Adam Feinstein, *A History of Autism: Conversations with the Pioneers* (Hoboken, NJ: Wiley-Blackwell, 2010), 6.
3. Leo Kanner, "Autistic Disturbances of Affective Contact," *Nerv Child,* 2 (1943), 227.
4. L. Wing and J. Gould, "Severe Impairments of Social Interaction and Associated Abnormalities in Children: Epidemiology and Classification," *Journal of Autism and Childhood Schizophrenia,* 9 (1979), 16.
5. Ibid.
6. Ibid.
7. J. Rapoport, D. Ismond, *DSM-IV Training Guide for Diagnosis of Childhood*

Disorders, 4th ed. (New York: Routledge, 1996).

8. Kanner.
9. Wing.
10. American Psychiatric Association, *Diagnostic and Statistical Manual of Mental Disorders: DSM-III-R.* 3rd ed. (Washington, DC: American Psychiatric Association, 1987).
11. Rapoport.
12. Kanner.
13. Tito Mukhopadhyay, *The Mind Tree: A Miraculous Child Breaks the Silence of Autism* (New York: Arcade Publishing, 2003), 77.
14. Donna Williams, *Nobody Nowhere: The Extraordinary Autobiography of an Autistic* (New York: Times Books, 1992), 4.
15. Temple Grandin, *Thinking in Pictures: And Other Reports from My Life with Autism* (New York: Vintage, 1996), 19–20.
16. Ibid.
17. Temple Grandin and Margaret M. Scariano, *Emergence: Labeled Autistic* (New York: Warner Books, 1986), 87.
18. Ibid.
19. Ibid.
20. Ovar Lovaas, *Teaching Developmentally Disabled Children: The ME Book* (Austin, TX: University Park Press, 1981), 33.
21. Ibid.

SOURCES

BOOKS

American Psychiatric Association. *Diagnostic and Statistical Manual of Mental Disorders: DSM-IV-TR.* 4th ed. Washington, DC: American Psychiatric Association, 2000.

Aquilla, Paula, Ellen Yack, and Shirley Sutton. *Building Bridges through Sensory Integration.* 2nd ed. Arlington, TX: Future Horizons, 2002.

Baron-Cohen, Simon. *The Essential Difference: Male and Female Brains and the Truth about Autism.* New York: Basic Books, 2004.

———. "The Extreme-Male-Brain Theory of Autism." In *Neurodevelopmental Disorders,* edited by H. Tager-Flusberg. Cambridge, MA: MIT Press, 1999.

———. *Mindblindness: An Essay on Autism and Theory of the Mind.* Cambridge, MA: Bradford Books/MIT Press, 1997.

Baron-Cohen, Simon, Svetlana Lutchmaya, and Rebecca Knickmeyer. *Prenatal Testosterone in Mind: Studies of Amniotic Fluid.* Cambridge, MA: Bradford Books/MIT Press, 2006.

Bettelheim, Bruno. *The Empty Fortress: Infantile Autism and the Birth of the Self.* New York: Free Press, 1972.

Bleuler, E. "Dementia praecox oder die Guppe der Schizophrenien." In *Handbuch der Psychiatrie,* edited by G. Hrsg. Aschaffenburg. Leipzig: Deuticke, 1911.

Bluestone, Judith. *The Fabric of Autism: Weaving the Threads into a Cogent Theory.* Southlake, TX: Sapphire Enterprises LLC, 2005.

Bruer, John T. *The Myth of the First Three Years: A New Understanding of Early Brain Development and Lifelong Learning.* New York: Free Press, 2002.

Buten, Howard. *Through the Glass Wall: Journeys into the Closed-Off World of the Autistic.* New York: Bantam Books, 2004.

Sources

Davis, Ronald. *The Gift of Dyslexia*. New York: Perigee,1997.

Feinstein, Adam. *A History of Autism: Conversations with the Pioneers*. Hoboken, NJ: Wiley-Blackwell, 2010.

Fitzgerald, Michael, and Brendon O'Brian. *Genius Genes: How Asperger Talents Changed the World*. Overland Park, KS: Autism Asperger Publishing Company, 2007.

Gardner, Howard. *Multiple Intelligences: New Horizons in Theory and Practice*. New York: Basic Books, 1993.

Gould, Stephen Jay. *The Mismeasure of Man*. New York: W. W. Norton & Company, 1981.

Grandin, Temple. *Thinking in Pictures: And Other Reports from My Life with Autism*. New York: Vintage, 1996.

Grandin, Temple, and Margaret M. Scariano. *Emergence: Labeled Autistic*. New York: Warner Books,1986.

Greenspan, Stanley, and Serena Wieder. *Engaging Autism: Using the Floortime Approach to Help Children Relate, Communicate, and Think*. Cambridge, MA: Da Capo Press, 2009.

Michael Guillen. *Five Equations That Changed the World: The Power and Poetry of Mathematics*. London: Abacus, 1995.

Hehir, Thomas. "Some Assessments Treat Learning-Disabled Students Unfairly." In *The Digital Classroom: How Technology Is Changing the Way We Teach and Learn*, edited by David T. Gordon, 9–50. Cambridge, MA: Harvard Education Publishing Group, 2000.

Itard, E. M. *An Historical Account of the Discovery and Education of a Savage Man: Or the First Developments, Physical and Moral, of the Young Savage*. Whitefish, MT: Kessinger Publishing LLC, 2007.

Janzen, Janice E. *Understanding the Nature of Autism: A Guide to the Autism Spectrum Disorders*. 2nd ed. San Antonio: Pearson, 2003.

Kaufman, Barry Neil. *Son-Rise*. New York: Harper & Row Publishers, 1976.

Kranowitz, Carol Stock. *The Out-of-Sync Child: Recognizing and Coping with Sensory Processing Disorder*. New York: Perigee, 2005.

Lawson, Wendy. *Concepts of Normality: The Autistic and Typical Spectrum*. London: Jessica Kingsley Publishers, 2008.

Lord, Catherine, and James P. McGee, eds. *Educating Children with Autism*. Washington, DC: National Academy Press, 2001.

Sources

Lovaas, O. Ivar. *Teaching Developmentally Disabled Children: The ME Book*. Austin, TX: University Park Press, 1981.

Lovaas, O. Ivar, and T. Smith. "Intensive Behavioral Treatment for Young Autistic Children." In *Advances in Clinical Child Psychology*, 11, edited by B.B. Lahey and A.E. Kazdin, 285–324. New York: Plenum Publishing Corporation, 1988.

Maine Administrators of Services for Children with Disabilities (MADSEC). *MADSEC Autism Task Force Report*. Manchester, ME: MADSEC, 1999.

Martin, Anne. "Screening, Early Intervention, and Remediation: Obscuring Children's Potential." In *Special Education at the Century's End: Evolution of Theory and Practice Since 1970*, edited by T. Hehir and T. Latus. Cambridge, MA: Harvard Educational Review Reprint Series, vol. 23, 1992.

Mills, Bruce. "Autism and the Imagination." In *Autism and Representation*, edited by Mark Osteen, 117–32. New York: Routledge, 2007.

Mukhopadhyay, Tito. *The Mind Tree: A Miraculous Child Breaks the Silence of Autism*. New York: Arcade Publishing, 2003.

Murray, Stuart. *Representing Autism: Culture, Narrative, Fascination*. Liverpool: Liverpool University Press, 2008.

National Autism Center. *National Standards Report: Addressing the Need for Evidence-Based Practice Guidelines for Autism Spectrum Disorders*. Randolph, MA: National Autism Center, 2009.

New York State Department of Health, Early Intervention Program. *Clinical Practice Guideline: Report of the Recommendations: Autism/Pervasive Developmental Disorders: Assessment and Intervention for Young Children (Age 0–3 Years)*. Albany, NY: New York State Department of Health, 1999.

Perry, Adrienne, and Rosemary Condillac. *Evidence-Based Practices for Children and Adolescents with Autism Spectrum Disorder: Review of the Literature and Practice Guide*. Toronto: Children's Mental Health Ontario, 2003.

Pollak, Richard. *The Creation of Dr. B.: A Biography of Bruno Bettelheim*. New York: Simon & Schuster, 1997.

Rapoport, J., and D. Ismond. *DSM-IV Training Guide for Diagnosis of Childhood Disorders*. 4th ed. New York: Routledge, 1996.

Rimland, Dr. Bernard. *Infantile Autism: The Syndrome and Its Implication for a Neural Theory of Behavior*. New York: Appleton-Century-Crofts, Inc., 1964.

Sacks, Oliver. *An Anthropologist on Mars: Seven Paradoxical Tales*. New York: Vintage, 1996.

————. *Migraine: Understanding a Common Disorder*. Berkeley: University of California Press, 1986.

Schreibman, Laura. *The Science and Fiction of Autism*. Cambridge, MA: Harvard University Press, 2007.

Schwartz, Jeffrey M., and Sharon Begley. *The Mind and the Brain: Neuroplasticity and the Power of Mental Force*. New York: HarperCollins, 2002.

Shumaker, Laura. *A Regular Guy: Growing Up with Autism: A Family's Story of Love and Acceptance*. Ithaca, NY: Landscape Press, 2008.

Simpson, Richard L., and Brenda Smith Myles, eds. *Educating Children and Youth with Autism: Strategies for Effective Practice*. 2nd ed. Austin, TX: PRO-ED, Inc., 1998.

Szatmari, Peter. *A Mind Apart: Understanding Children with Autism and Asperger Syndrome*. New York: Guilford Press, 2004.

Timimi, Sami, Neil Gardner, and Brian McCabe. *The Myth of Autism: Medicalising Men's and Boys' Social and Emotional Competence*. New York: Palgrave Macmillan, 2010.

Tinbergen, Niko, and Elizabeth A. Tinbergen. *Autistic Children: New Hope for a Cure*. New York: Routledge, 1986.

Tweed, Lindsey, Nancy Connolly, and Amy Beaulieu. *Interventions for Autism Spectrum Disorder. State of the Evidence: Report of the Children's Services Evidence-Based Practice Advisory Committee*. Manchester, ME: Maine Department of Health & Human Services and the Maine Department of Education, 2009.

Welch, Dr. Martha G. *Holding Time: How to Eliminate Conflict, Temper Tantrums, and Sibling Rivalry and Raise Happy, Loving, Successful Children*. New York: Simon & Schuster, 1988.

Williams, Donna. *Nobody Nowhere: The Extraordinary Autobiography of an Autistic*. New York: Times Books, 1992.

Wolfberg, Pamela. *Play and Imagination in Children with Autism*. 2nd ed. New York: Teachers College Press, 2009.

ARTICLES

Adolphs, Ralph, Lonnie Sears, and Joseph Piven. "Abnormal Processing of Social Information from Faces in Autism." *Journal of Cognitive Neuroscience*, 13, no. 2 (February 2001): 232–40.

Sources

Aldred, C., J. Green, and C. Adams. "A New Social Communication Intervention for Children with ASD: Pilot Randomized Control Treatment Study Suggesting Effectiveness." *Journal of Child Psychology and Psychiatry*, 45, no. 8 (November 2004): 1420–30.

"Autistic patients labeled 'mentally retarded' in state." *Indian Express*, April 2010.

Baker, M. J. "Incorporating the Thematic Ritualistic Behaviors of Children with Autism into Games: Increasing Social Play Interactions with Siblings." *Journal of Positive Behavior Interventions*, 2, no. 2 (April 2000): 66–84.

Baron-Cohen, S., and S. Wheelwright. "Obsessions in Children with Autism or Asperger Syndrome: A Content Analysis in Terms of Core Domains of Cognition." *British Journal of Psychiatry*, 175 (1999): 484–90.

Baron-Cohen, S., S. Wheelwright, J. Hill, Y. Raste, and I. Plumb. "The 'Reading the Mind in the Eyes' Test, Revised Version: A Study with Normal Adults and Adults with Asperger Syndrome or High-Functioning Autism." *Journal of Child Psychology and Psychiatry*, 42, no. 2 (February 2001): 241–51.

Begley, Sharon. "The Puzzle of Hidden Ability." *Newsweek*, August 2007.

Bodfish, J. W., F. J. Symons, D. E. Parker, and M. H. Lewis. "Varieties of Repetitive Behavior in Autism: Comparisons to Mental Retardation." *Journal of Autism and Developmental Disorders*, 30, no. 3 (June 2000): 237–43.

Bourreau, Y., S. Roux, M. Gomot, F. Bonnet-Brilhault, and C. Barthelemy. "Validation of the Repetitive and Restricted Behaviour Scale in Autism Spectrum Disorders." *European Child and Adolescent Psychiatry*, 18, no. 11 (November 2009): 675–82.

Campbell, J. M. "Efficacy of Behavioral Interventions for Reducing Problem Behavior in Persons with Autism: A Quantitative Synthesis of Single-Subject Research." *Research in Developmental Disabilities*, 24, no. 2 (March–April 2003): 120–38.

Chamberlain, B., C. Kasari, and E. Rotheram-Fuller. "Involvement or Isolation? The Social Networks of Children with Autism in Regular Classrooms." *Journal of Autism and Developmental Disorders*, 37, no. 2 (July 2006): 230–42.

Creak, M. "Schizophrenic Syndrome in Childhood: Further Progress Report of a Working Party (April, 1964)." *Developmental Medicine and Child Neurology*, 6, no. 5 (October 1964): 530–35.

Christensen, L., T. Hutman, A. Rozga, G. S. Young, S. Ozonoff, S. J. Rogers, B. Baker, and M. Sigman. "Play and Developmental Outcomes in Infant Siblings of Children with Autism." *Journal of Autism and Developmental Disorders*, 40, no. 8 (August 2010): 946–57.

Sources

Dawson, M., I. Soulières, M. A. Gernsbacher, and L. Mottron. "The Level and Nature of Autistic Intelligence." *Psychological Science*, 18, no. 8 (August 2007): 657–62.

Dawson, G., and L. Galpert. "Mothers' Use of Imitative Play for Facilitating Social Responsiveness and Toy Play in Young Autistic Children." *Development and Psychopathology*, 2 (1990): 151–62.

Dawson, G., S. Roger, J. Munson, M. Smith, J. Winter, J. Greenson, A. Donaldson, and J. Varley. "Randomized, Controlled Trial of an Intervention for Toddlers with Autism: The Early Start Denver Model." *Pediatrics*,125, no. 1(January 2010): e17–23.

Edelson, M. Goldberg. "Are the Majority of Children with Autism Mentally Retarded? A Systematic Evaluation of the Data." *Focus on Autism and Other Developmental Disabilities*, 21, no. 2 (Summer 2006): 66–83.

Edelson, M. Goldberg, D. T. Schubert, and S. M. Edelson. "Factors Predicting Intelligence Scores on the TONI for Individuals with Autism." *Focus on Autism and Other Developmental Disabilities*, 13, no. 1 (Spring 1998): 17–26.

"Education and Autism Spectrum Disorders in Australia: The Provision of Appropriate Educational Services for School-Age Students with Autism Spectrum Disorders in Australia." Position paper, Australian Advisory Board on Autism Spectrum Disorders, 2010.

Eikeseth, S., T. Smith, and E. Jahr. "Outcome for Children with Autism Who Began Intensive Behavioral Treatment between Ages 4 and 7: A Comparison Controlled Study." *Behavior Modification*, 31, no. 3 (May 2007): 264–78.

Elliott, R. O., A. R. Dobbin, G. D. Rose, and H. V. Soper. "Vigorous, Aerobic Exercise Versus General Motor Training Activities: Effects on Maladaptive and Stereotypic Behaviors of Adults with Both Autism and Mental Retardation." *Journal of Autism and Developmental Disorders*, 24, no. 5 (October 1994): 565–76.

Fenske, Edward C., Stanley Zalenski, Patricia J. Krantz, and Lynn E. McClannahan. "Age at Intervention and Treatment Outcome for Autistic Children in a Comprehensive Intervention Program." *Analysis and Intervention in Developmental Disabilities*, 5, nos. 1–2 (1985): 49–58.

Field, Tiffany, Tory Field, Chris Sanders, and Jacqueline Nadel. "Children with Autism Display More Social Behaviors after Repeated Imitation Sessions." *Autism*, 5, no. 3 (September 2001): 317–23.

Fong, Pattey L. "Cognitive Appraisals in High- and Low-Stress Mothers of Adolescents with Autism." *Journal of Consulting and Clinical Psychology*, 59, no. 3 (1991): 471–74.

Grant, Alan. "Screams, Slaps, and Love: A Surprising, Shocking Treatment Helps Far-Gone Mental Cripples." *Life*, 1965.

Sources

Green, J., T. Charman, H. McConachie, C. Aldred, V. Slonims, P. Howlin, A. Le Couteur et al. "Parent-Mediated Communication-Focused Treatment in Children with Autism (PACT): A Randomised Controlled Trial." *Lancet*, 375, no. 9732 (June 2010): 2152–60.

Greenspan, Stanley I., Robert J. Shaffer, Robert F. Tuchman, Paul J. Stemmer, and Lee E. Jacokes. "Effect of Interactive Metronome Rhythmicity Training on Children with ADHD." *American Journal of Occupational Therapy*, 55, no. 2 (2001): 155–62.

Harrower, J., and G. Dunlap. "Including Children with Autism in General Education Classrooms: A Review of Effective Strategies." *Behavior Modification*, 25, no.5 (October 2001): 762–84.

Herera, Sue. "Autism Research Focuses on Early Intervention: Genetic Clues Sought in Fight against Disorder." *CNBC TV*, February 2005. http://www.msnbc.msn.com/id/7013251/.

Hollander, E., A. T. Wang, A. Braun, and L. Marsh. "Neurological Considerations: Autism and Parkinson's Disease." *Psychiatry Research*, 170, no. 1 (November 2009): 43–51.

Ingersoll, B. "Teaching Social Communication: A Comparison of Naturalistic Behavioral and Development, Social Pragmatic Approaches for Children with Autism Spectrum Disorders. *Journal of Positive Behavior Interventions*, 12, no. 1 (2010): 33–43.

Ingersoll, B., and K. Lalonde. "The Impact of Object and Gesture Imitation Training on Language Use in Children With Autism Spectrum Disorder." *Journal of Speech, Language, and Hearing Research*, 53, no. 4 (August 2010): 1040–51.

Ingersoll, B., and L. Schreibman. "Teaching Reciprocal Imitation Skills to Young Children with Autism Using a Naturalistic Behavioral Approach: Effects on Language, Pretend Play, and Joint Attention." *Journal of Autism and Developmental Disorders*, 36, no. 4 (May 2006): 487–505.

Jacobson, John W., James A. Mulick, and Allen A. Schwartz. "A History of Facilitated Communication: Science, Pseudoscience, and Antiscience." *American Psychologist*, 50, no. 9 (September1995): 750–65.

Kanner, Leo. "Autistic Disturbances of Affective Contact." *Nerv Child*, 2 (1943): 217–50.

———. "Follow-Up Study of Eleven Autistic Children Originally Reported in 1943." *Journal of Autism and Childhood Schizophrenia*, 1, no. 2 (1971): 119–45.

———. "Reprint." *Acta Paedopsychiatrica*, 35, no. 4 (1968): 100–36.

Laugeson E. A., F. Frankel, C. Mogil, and A. R. Dillon. "Parent-Assisted Social Skills

Training to Improve Friendships in Teens with Autism Spectrum Disorders. *Journal of Autism and Developmental Disorders*, 39, no. 4 (April 2009): 596–606.

Lee, S. H., S. L. Odom, and R. Loftin. "Social Engagement with Peers and Stereotypic Behavior of Children with Autism." *Journal of Positive Behavior Interventions*, 9, no. 2 (April 2007): 67–79.

Lewis, M., and J. Bodfish. "Repetitive Behavior Disorders in Autism." *Mental Retardation and Developmental Disabilities Research Reviews*, 4 (1998): 80–89.

Lovaas, O. Ivar, B. Schaeffer, and J. Q. Simmons. "Building Social Behavior in Autistic Children by Use of Electric Shock." *Journal of Experimental Research in Personality*, 1 (1965): 99–105.

Lundqvist, L. O., G. Andersson, and J. Viding. "Effects of Vibroacoustic Music on Challenging Behaviors in Individuals with Autism and Developmental Disabilities." *Research in Autism Spectrum Disorders*, 3, no. 2 (2009): 390–400.

MacFabe, D. F., N. E. Cain, F. Boon, K. P. Ossenkopp, and D. P. Cain. "Effects of the Enteric Bacterial Metabolic Product Propionic Acid on Object-Directed Behavior, Social Behavior, Cognition, and Neuroinflammation in Adolescent Rats: Relevance to Autism Spectrum Disorder." *Behavioral Brain Research*, 217, no. 1 (February 2011): 47–54.

Martin, Douglas. "About New York: Illness That Can Steal a Child's Sparkle." *The New York Times*, January 1989.

Mayes, S. D., and S. L. Calhoun. "Analysis of WISC-III, Stanford-Binet:IV, and Academic Achievement Test Scores in Children with Autism." *Journal of Autism and Developmental Disorders*, 33, no. 3 (June 2003): 329–41.

Mayes, S. D., S. L. Calhoun, M. J. Murray, J. D. Morrow, K. K. Yurich, F. Mahr, S. Cothren et al. "Comparison of Scores on the Checklist for Autism Spectrum Disorder, Childhood Autism Rating Scale, and Gilliam Asperger's Disorder Scale for Children with Low Functioning Autism, High Functioning Autism or Asperger's Disorder, ADHD, and Typical Development." *Journal of Autism and Developmental Disorders*, 39, no. 12 (December 2009): 1682–93.

McConachie, H.,V. Randle, D. Hammal, and A. Le Couteur. "A Controlled Trial of a Training Course for Parents of Children with Suspected Autism Spectrum Disorder." *The Journal of Pediatrics*, 147, no. 3 (September 2005): 335–40.

McKenzie, John. "Autism Breakthrough: Girl's Writings Explain Her Behavior and Feelings." *ABC News/Health*, February 2008. http://abcnews.go.com/Health/story?id=4311223&page=2.

Mundy, Peter, Marian Sigman, Judy Ungerer, and Tracy Sherman. "Defining the Social

Sources

Deficits of Autism: The Contribution of Non-Verbal Communication Measures."
Journal of Child Psychology and Psychiatry, 27, no. 5 (September 1986): 657–69.

O'Connor, Anahad. "In Autism, New Goal Is Finding It Soon Enough to Fight It." *The New York Times*, December 2004.

O'Connor, Anne. "Parenting Rollercoaster: What is Autism?" *Sunday Business Post*, April 2010.

Pollack, M. "Brain Damage, Mental Retardation, and Childhood Schizophrenia." *The American Journal of Psychiatry*, 115, no. 5 (November 1958): 422–28.

Pickett, E., O. Pullara, and B. Gordon. "Speech Acquisition in Older Nonverbal Individuals with Autism: A Review of Features, Methods and Prognosis." *Cognitive Behavior Neurology*, 22 (2009): 1–21.

Prizant, Barry. "Is ABA the Only Way?" *Autism Spectrum Quarterly* (Spring, 2009): 28–32.

Rimland, Bernard. "The ABA Controversy." *Autism Research Review International*, 13, no. 3 (1999): 3.

Scheuffgen K., F. Happé, M. Anderson, and U. Frith. "High Intelligence, Low IQ? Speed of Processing and Measured IQ in Children with Autism." *Development and Psychopathology*, 12, no. 1 (Winter 2000): 83–90.

Sears, L. L., C. Vest, S. Mohamed, J. Bailey, B. J. Ranson, and J. Piven. "An MRI Study of the Basal Ganglia in Autism." *Progress in Neuro-Psychopharmacology and Biological Psychiatry*, 23, no. 4 (May 1999): 613–24.

Shao, Y., M. L. Cuccaro, E. R. Hauser, K. L. Raiford, M. M. Menold, C. M. Wolpert, S. A. Ravan et al. "Fine Mapping of Autistic Disorder to Chromosome 15q11-q13 by Use of Phenotypic Subtypes." *American Journal of Human Genetics*, 72, no. 3 (March 2003): 539–48.

Simpson, Richard. L., S. R. de Boer-Ott, and B. Smith-Myles. "Inclusion of Learners with Autism Spectrum Disorders in General Education Settings." *Topics in Language Disorders*, 23, no. 2 (April–June 2003): 116–33.

Skerrett, Patrick J., Jane A. Leopold, Kerim Menir, Suzanne Coulter Rose, John H. Growdon, and Ann MacDonald. "Detecting Autism—How to Solve Three Puzzles." Newsweek, January 2008.

Spake, Amanda. "It's Like Wishing I Could Be Normal." *Washington Post*, May 1992.

Strain, Phillip. "Generalization of Autistic Children's Social Behavior Change: Effects of Developmentally Integrated and Segregated Settings." *Analysis and Intervention in Developmental Disabilities*, 3, no. 1 (1983): 23–34.

Sources

Tantum, Digby. "Psychological Disorder in Adolescents and Adults with Asperger Syndrome." Autism, 4, no. 1 (2000): 47–62.

Tarkan, Laurie. "Autism Therapy Is Called Effective, but Rare." *The New York Times*, October 2002.

Wallace, Gregory L., Mike Anderson, and Francesca Happé, "Brief Report: Information Processing Speed is Intact in Autism but Not Correlated with Measured Intelligence." *Journal of Autism and Developmental Disorders*, 39, no. 5 (May 2009): 809–14.

Wing, L., and J. Gould. "Severe Impairments of Social Interaction and Associated Abnormalities in Children: Epidemiology and Classification." *Journal of Autism and Childhood Schizophrenia*, 9 (1979): 11–29.

Wolman, David. "The Truth about Autism: Scientists Reconsider What They *Think* They Know." *Wired*, 16, no. 3 (February 2008). http://www.wired.com/medtech/health/magazine/16-03/ff_autism?currentPage=all.

World Heath Organization. "Atypical Autism." *International Classification of Diseases (ICD-10)*, F-84 (1992).

Yang, T., P. J. Wolfberg, S. Wu, and P. Hwu. "Supporting Children on the Autism Spectrum in Peer Play at Home and School: Piloting the Integrated Play Groups Model in Taiwan." *Autism: The International Journal of Research and Practice*, 7, no. 4 (December 2003): 437–53.

Zazzo, René. "Alfred Binet (1857–1911)." *Prospects: Tne Quarterly Review of Comparative Education*, 23, no. 1/2 (1993): 101–12.

LECTURES, PRESENTATIONS AND HEARINGS

Gould, Dr. Judith. "The Triad of Impairments Past, Present and Future." PowerPoint presentation, June 2010. http://www.docstoc.com/docs/33120174/The-Triad-of-Impairments-Past_-Present-and-Future

Henteleff, Yude. "The Fully Inclusive Classroom is Only One of the Right Ways to Meet the Best Interests of the Special Needs Child." Paper presented at the National Summit on Inclusive Education, Ottawa, Ontario, November 2004.

Howlin, Patricia. "Falling Through the Cracks: Why is the Outcome so Poor for Adults with Autism?" Presented at the National Research Autism Conference, Westminster, UK, July 2009.

Sources

Schreibman, Dr. Laura. "Grey Matters: The Science and Fiction of Autism." Paper presented at the University of California, San Diego. Posted January 2008. http://www.youtube.com/watch?v=sbt6HYGeJrc&feature=related.

Sim, Miranda. "Intensive Behaviour Intervention (IBI) for Children with Autism." Workshop presented at the Toronto Public Library (Eglinton Square branch), September 2010.

Standing Committee on Social Affairs, Science and Technology. *Jason Oldfield Testifies before the Canadian Senate Committee Studying Autism Funding in Canada.* New Brunswick: December 6, 2006. http://autismrealitynb.wordpress.com/2007/01/23/jason-oldford-testifies-before-the-canadian-senate-committee-studying-autism-funding-in-canada/

WEBSITES

Autism-PDD Message Boards: Parents of Children Living with Autism. Item posted April 10, 2010. http://www.autism-pdd.net/forum/forum_posts.asp?TID=35681&PN=2&TPN=1.

Autism Rocks. http://www.autism-rocks.blogspot.com.

Estepp, Becky, and Moira Giammatteo. "Does the 'Window' Ever Close?" (April 2008). Talk about Curing Autism. Last modified July 11, 2010. http://www.talkaboutcuringautism.org/support/does-the-window-ever-close.htm.

"General Behavioural/Educational Suggestions for Autistic Children." Autism Treatment Services of Canada/ Society for the Treatment of Autism. http://autism.ca/educsugg.htm.

"How Does Intensive Interaction Work—What Do You Do?" Intensive Interaction. http://www.intensiveinteraction.co.uk/about/how-does-intensive-interaction-work/.

MDJunction Message Boards: Autism Support Group. Item posted January 1, 2009. http://www.mdjunction.com/forums/autism-discussions/general-support/296327-anyone-with-an-affectionate-autistic-child.

Shumaker, Laura. "It's Never Too Late to Learn as We Grow." Easter Seals FaceBook page, accessed on March 5, 2010.

INDEX